AF897922

Inner Ward.

A White tower.
B Wardrobe tower.
C Cold Harbour.
D St. Peter's Church.
E Block on Tower Green.
F Officer's house.
G Lieutenant's house.
H The Garden.
I Queen's apartments.
K Queen's garden.
L Gunners' quarters.

On the Wall.

a Beauchamp tower.
b Prisoners' walk.
c Belfry.
d Raleigh's walk.
e Bloody tower.
f Lantern.
g Salt tower.
h Broad Arrow tower.
i Constable tower.
k Martin tower.
l Northumberland's walk.
m Brick tower.
n Bowyer tower.
o Flint tower.
p Develin tower.

Outer Ward.

1 Postern.
2 Middle tower.
3 Byeward tower.
4 Gateway under Bloody tower.
5 Hall tower.
6 Great hall.
7 Queen's stairs.
8 Traitor's gate.
9 St. Thomas' tower.
10 Cradle tower.
11 Well tower.
12 Galleyman tower.
13 Iron gate.
14 Brass mount.
15 Legge mount.
16 Soldiers' quarters.

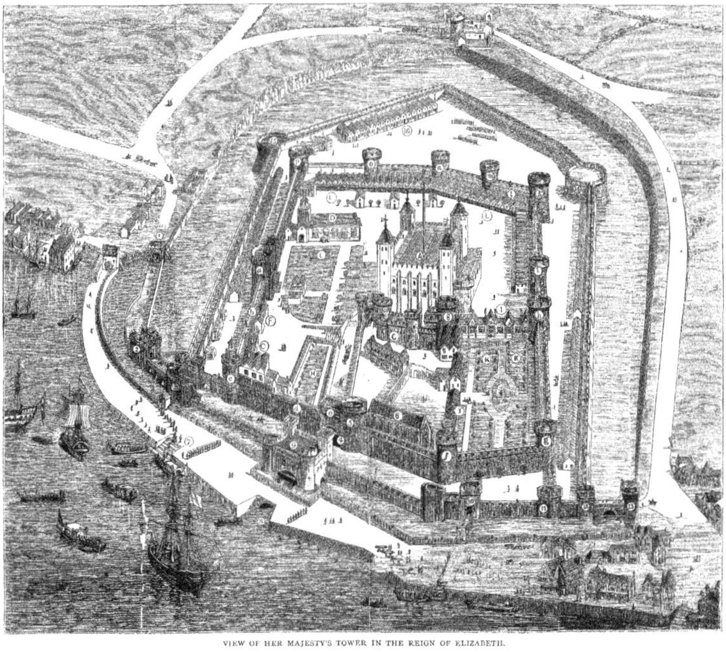

VIEW OF HER MAJESTY'S TOWER IN THE REIGN OF ELIZABETH.

Her Majesty's Tower.

BY

WILLIAM HEPWORTH DIXON.

NEW YORK:
HARPER & BROTHERS, PUBLISHERS,
FRANKLIN SQUARE.
1869.

TO

QUEEN VICTORIA,

THESE STUDIES IN

HER MAJESTY'S TOWER

ARE

DEDICATED

BY

EXPRESS PERMISSION.

PREFACE.

TWENTY years ago I wrote some chapters on the Tower—especially on the human interests which cling around it; and since that time I have noted, with care, such passages in either the State Papers or printed books as threw light into the cells once occupied by the heroes and heroines of English story. This volume—a book of identifications—is the fruit of this long-continued search.

In the labour of reading and deciphering the State Papers, for the purposes of this work, I stand indebted to Her Majesty's Deputy-keeper of the Records, Mr. T. Duffus Hardy, to an extent which no words of mine can adequately express.

6 St. James's Terrace,
New Year's Day, 1869.

CONTENTS.

HER MAJESTY'S TOWER.

CHAPTER I.

THE PILE.

HALF a mile below London Bridge, on ground which was once a bluff, commanding the Thames from St. Saviour's Creek to St. Olave's Wharf, stands the Tower; a mass of ramparts, walls, and gates, the most ancient and most poetic pile in Europe.

Seen from the hill outside, the Tower appears to be white with age and wrinkled by remorse. The home of our stoutest kings, the grave of our noblest knights, the scene of our gayest revels, the field of our darkest crimes, that edifice speaks at once to the eye and to the soul. Grey keep, green tree, black gate, and frowning battlement, stand out, apart from all objects far and near them, menacing, picturesque, enchaining; working on the senses like a spell; and calling us away from our daily mood into a world of romance, like that which we find painted in light and shadow on Shakspeare's page.

Looking at the Tower as either a prison, a palace, or a court, picture, poetry, and drama crowd upon the mind; and if the fancy dwells most frequently on the state prison, this is because the soul is more readily kindled by a human interest than fired by an archaic and official fact. For one man who would care to see the room in which a council met or a court was held, a hundred men would like to see the chamber in which Lady Jane Grey was lodged, the cell in which Sir Walter Raleigh wrote, the tower from which

Sir John Oldcastle escaped. Who would not like to stand for a moment by those steps on which Ann Boleyn knelt; pause by that slit in the wall through which Arthur De la Pole gazed; and linger, if he could, in that room in which Cranmer, Latimer, and Ridley searched the New Testament together?

The Tower has an attraction for us akin to that of the house in which we were born, the school in which we were trained. Go where we may, that grim old edifice on the Pool goes with us; a part of all we know, and of all we are. Put seas between us and the Thames, this Tower will cling to us, like a thing of life. It colours Shakspeare's page. It casts a momentary gloom over Bacon's story. Many of our books were written in its vaults; the Duke of Orleans' 'Poesies,' Raleigh's 'Historie of the World,' Eliot's 'Monarchy of Man,' and Penn's 'No Cross, no Crown.'

Even as to length of days, the Tower has no rival among palaces and prisons; its origin, like that of the Iliad, that of the Sphinx, that of the Newton Stone, being lost in the nebulous ages, long before our definite history took shape. Old writers date it from the days of Cæsar; a legend taken up by Shakspeare and the poets, in favour of which the name of Cæsar's tower remains in popular use to this very day. A Roman wall can even yet be traced near some parts of the ditch. The Tower is mentioned in the Saxon Chronicle, in a way not incompatible with the fact of a Saxon stronghold having stood upon this spot. The buildings as we have them now in block and plan were commenced by William the Conqueror; and the series of apartments in Cæsar's tower—hall, gallery, council-chamber, chapel—were built in the early Norman reigns, and used as a royal residence by all our Norman kings. What can Europe show to compare against such a tale?

Set against the Tower of London—with its eight hundred years of historic life, its nineteen hundred years of traditional fame—all other palaces and prisons appear like things of an hour. The oldest bit of palace in Europe, that of the west front of the Burg in Vienna, is of the time of Henry the Third. The Kremlin in Moscow, the Doge's Palazzo in Venice, are of the fourteenth century. The Seraglio in Stamboul was built by Mohammed the Second. The oldest part of the Vatican was commenced by Borgia, whose name it bears. The old Louvre was commenced in the reign of Henry the Eighth; the Tuileries in that of Elizabeth. In the time of our Civil War Versailles was yet a swamp. Sans Souci and the Escorial belong to the eighteenth century. The Serail of Jerusalem is a Turkish edifice. The palaces of Athens, of Cairo, of Tehran, are all of modern date.

Neither can the prisons which remain in fact as well as in history and drama—with the one exception of St. Angelo in Rome—compare against the Tower. The Bastile is gone; the Bargello has become a museum; the Piombi are removed from the Doge's roof. Vincennes, Spandau, Spilberg, Magdeburg, are all modern in comparison with a jail from which Ralph Flambard escaped so long ago as the year 1100, the date of the First Crusade.

Standing on Tower Hill, looking down on the dark lines of wall—picking out keep and turret, bastion and ballium, chapel and belfry—the jewel-house, the armoury, the mounts, the casemates, the open leads—the Bye-ward gate, the Belfry, the Bloody tower—the whole edifice seems alive with story; the story of a nation's highest splendour, its deepest misery, and its darkest shame. The soil beneath your feet is richer in blood than many a great battle-field; for out upon this sod has been poured, from generation to generation, a stream of the noblest life in our land.

Should you have come to this spot alone, in the early day, when the Tower is noisy with martial doings, you may haply catch, in the hum which rises from the ditch and issues from the wall below you—broken by roll of drum, by blast of bugle, by tramp of soldiers—some echoes, as it were, of a far-off time; some hints of a May-day revel; of a state execution; of a royal entry. You may catch some sound which recalls the thrum of a queen's virginal, the cry of a victim on the rack, the laughter of a bridal feast. For all these sights and sounds—the dance of love and the dance of death—are part of that gay and tragic memory which clings around the Tower.

From the reign of Stephen down to that of Henry of Richmond, Cæsar's tower (the great Norman keep, now called the White tower) was a main part of the royal palace; and for that large interval of time, the story of the White tower is in some sort that of our English society as well as of our English kings. Here were kept the royal wardrobe and the royal jewels; and hither came with their goodly wares, the tiremen, the goldsmiths, the chasers and embroiderers, from Flanders, Italy, and Almaigne. Close by were the Mint, the lions' dens, the old archery-grounds, the Court of King's Bench, the Court of Common Pleas, the Queen's gardens, the royal banqueting-hall; so that art and trade, science and manners, literature and law, sport and politics, find themselves equally at home.

Two great architects designed the main parts of the Tower: Gundulf the Weeper and Henry the Builder; one a poor Norman monk, the other a great English king.

Gundulf, a Benedictine friar, had, for that age, seen a great deal of the world; for he had not only lived in Rouen and Caen, but had travelled in the East. Familiar with the glories of Saracenic art, no less than with the Norman simplicities of Bec, St. Ouen, and St. Etienne; a pupil of

Lanfranc, a friend of Anselm; he had been employed in the monastery of Bec to marshal, with the eye of an artist, all the pictorial ceremonies of his church. But he was chiefly known in that convent as a weeper. No monk at Bec could cry so often and so much as Gundulf. He could weep with those who wept; nay, he could weep with those who sported; for his tears welled forth from what seemed to be an unfailing source.

As the price of his exile from Bec, Gundulf received the crozier of Rochester, in which city he rebuilt the cathedral, and perhaps designed the castle, since the great keep on the Medway has a sister's likeness to the great keep on the Thames. His works in London were—the White tower, the first St. Peter's church, and the old barbican, afterwards known as the Hall tower, and now used as the Jewel house.

The cost of these works was great; the discontent caused by them was sore. Ralph, Bishop of Durham, the able and rapacious minister who had to raise the money, was hated and reviled by the Commons with peculiar bitterness of heart and phrase. He was called Flambard, or Firebrand. He was represented as a devouring lion. Still the great edifice grew up; and Gundulf, who lived to the age of fourscore, saw his great keep completed from basement to battlement.

Henry the Third, a prince of epical fancies, as Corffe, Conway, Beaumaris, and many other fine poems in stone attest, not only spent much of his time in the Tower, but much of his money in adding to its beauty and strength. Adam de Lamburn was his master mason; but Henry was his own chief clerk of the works. The Water gate, the embanked wharf, the Cradle tower, the Lantern, which he made his bedroom and private closet, the Galleyman tower, and the first wall, appear to have been his gifts. But the prince who did so much for Westminster Abbey, not content with giving stone and piles to the home in which he dwelt, enriched the chambers with frescoes and sculpture, the chapels with carving and glass; making St. John's chapel in the White tower splendid with saints, St. Peter's church on the Tower Green musical with bells. In the Hall tower, from which a passage led through the Great hall into the King's bedroom in the Lantern, he built a tiny chapel for his private use—a chapel which served for the devotion of his successors until Henry the Sixth was stabbed to death before the cross. Sparing neither skill nor gold to make the great fortress worthy of his art, he sent to Purbeck for marble, and to Caen for stone. The dabs of lime, the spawls of flint, the layers of brick, which deface the walls and towers in too many places, are of either earlier or later times. The marble shafts, the noble groins, the delicate traceries, are Henry's work. Traitor's gate, one of the noblest arches in the world, was built by him; in short, nearly all that is purest in art is traceable to his reign.

Edward the First may be added, at a distance, to the list of builders. In his reign the original church of St. Peter fell into ruin; the wrecks were carted away, and the present edifice was built. The bill of costs for clearing the ground is still extant in Fetter Lane. Twelve men, who were paid twopence a-day wages, were employed on the work for twenty days. The cost of pulling down the old chapel was forty-six shillings and eight pence; that of digging foundations for the new chapel forty shillings. That chapel has suffered from wardens and lieutenants; yet the shell is of very fine Norman work.

From the days of Henry the Builder down to those of Henry of Richmond, the Tower, as the strongest place in the south of England, was by turns the magnificent home and the miserable jail of all our princes. Here Richard the Second held his court, and gave up his crown. Here Henry the Sixth was murdered. Here the Duke of Clarence was drowned in wine. Here King Edward and the Duke of York were slain by command of Richard. Here Margaret of Salisbury suffered her tragic fate.

Henry of Richmond kept his royal state in the Tower, receiving his ambassadors, counting his angels, making presents to his bride, Elizabeth of York. Among other gifts to that lady on her nuptial day was a Royal Book of verse, composed by a prisoner in the keep.

CHAPTER II.

INNER WARD AND OUTER WARD.

The Tower was divided into two main parts—an Inner Ward and an Outer Ward; the first part being bounded by the old wall, crowned by twelve mural towers; the second part being bounded by the soil which fringed the slopes leading down into the ditch. A man who would read aright the many curious passages in our history of which the State Prison is the scene, must bear this fact of the two wards constantly in his mind.

The Inner Ward, planned and partly built by the Monk of Bec, was the original fortress, of which the defending ditch lay under the ballium wall. It contained the keep, the royal galleries and rooms, the Mint, the Jewel house, the Wardrobe, the Queen's garden, St. Peter's Church, the open green, the Constable's tower, the Brick tower, in which the Master of the Ordnance lived, the Great hall, quarters for the archers and bowmen, and, in later days, the Lieutenant's house. This ward was flanked and covered by twelve strong works, built on the wall, and forming part of it; the Beauchamp tower, the Belfry, the Garden tower (now famous as the Bloody tower), the Hall tower, the Lantern, the Salt tower, the Broad Arrow tower, the Constable tower, the Martin tower, the Brick tower, the Flint tower, the Bowyer tower, and the Develin tower; all of which may be considered, more or less, as defensive works; even the Lantern, which had a vault for prisoners on the ground, a royal bed-chamber on the main floor, a guard-room for archers and balisters in the upper story, and a round turret over these for the burning lights. Only one gateway pierced the wall; a narrow and embattled outlet near the Water gate, passing under the strong block house, now the Bloody tower, into Water Lane. The road springs upward by the main guard—a rise of one in ten—so as to give the men inside a vast advantage in a push of pikes.

This Inner Ward was the royal quarter.

The Outer Ward, which owed its plan and most of its execution to Henry the Third, lay between the ballium and the outer scarp of the ditch, with a protected passage into the Thames. It contained some lanes and streets below the wall, and works which overlooked the wharf. In this ward stood the Middle tower, the Bye-ward tower, the Water gate, the Cradle tower, the Well tower, the Galleyman tower, the Iron Gate tower, Brass Mount, Legge Mount, and the covered ways. Into it opened the Hall tower, afterwards called the Record tower, now known as the Jewel house. Close by the Hall tower stood the Great Hall, the doors of which opened into this outer court. Spanning the ditch, towards the Thames, stood the Water gate, a fine structure, built by Henry the Builder, which folk called St. Thomas's tower, after our Saxon saint. Under this building sprang the wide arch, through which the tides flowed in and out from the river and the ditch; the water-way known as Traitor's gate.

This Outer Ward was the folk's quarter.

To the Inner Ward, common folk had no right of access, and they were rarely allowed to enjoy as a privilege that which they could not claim as a right. This Inner Ward was the King's castle, his palace, his garrison, his wardrobe, his treasury. Here, under charge of a trusty officer, he kept the royal jewels, secreted from every eye, except on a coronation day. Here rose his keep, with the dungeons in which he could chain his foes. Here stood his private chapel, and not far from it his private block. No man ever dreamt of contesting the King's right to do what he pleased in this quarter; and thus, an execution within these lines was regarded by the world outside as little better than a private murder.

Into the Outer Ward, the Commons had always claimed a right of entry, and something more than a right of entry; that is to say, free access, guarded by possession of the outer gates and towers.

This right of entry was enforced on stated occasions with an observance which is highly comic. Baron and citizen—that is to say, alderman and commoner—met in Barking Church, on Tower Hill, whence they sent six sage men of their body into the Tower to ask leave for a deputation of citizens to see the king, and free access for all people to the courts of law. These six sage persons were to beg that the king, according to custom, would forbid his guards either to close the gates or to keep watch over them, while the citizens were coming and going; it being wrong in itself and against their freedom, they alleged, for any one to keep guard over the gates and doors of the Tower, save such of their own people as they should appoint to that duty. On this request being granted by the king, the six messengers would return to their fellows in Barking Church, report what they had done, and send the citizen guard to their posts. Then would the Commons elect from their body three men of mature age, moderate opinions, and cautious speech, to act as presenters. The rules by which they acted were rather strict. The sheriffs and beadles were to be decently clothed and shod, since it was laid down that no man should come before the king either in dirty rags or without his shoes. Their followers were to be trim and spruce; their capes and cloaks laid aside; their coats and overcoats put on. No man was to go with them into the presence who had sore eyes; no man was to join them who had weak legs. Mayor, alderman, sheriff, cryer, every one going into the Tower on public duty, was to have his hair cut short and his face newly shaved.

The object of these rules was to guard the right of access to the courts of justice; the Court of King's Bench, and the Court of Common Pleas.

Where were these courts of justice held?

No writer on the Tower has sought to find the true localities of these great tribunals. Yet the sites are clearly enough described in our ancient writs, hundreds of which may be found in Fetter Lane. One court stood in the royal quarter, another court stood in the folk's quarter. The King's Bench was held in a room which the writs describe as the Lesser Hall, lying under the east turret of the keep. The Common Pleas were held in a place which the writs describe as the Great hall by the river; a hall now gone, but of which the identification is quite as sure. It stood by the Hall tower, to which it lent a name, and into which it led.

A view of the Tower in the Royal Book of verse, shows that this Great Hall was a Gothic edifice, in the style of Henry the Third.

Many a dark scene in the history of our public liberties

and our private manners grows suddenly luminous when we bear these facts in mind; that the Tower consisted of two parts—an inner court and an outer court; that the Court of King's Bench was held in the royal quarter, the Court of Common Pleas in the folk's quarter; that the people had free access to the outer court, and only to the outer court.

The Hall tower, in which Henry the Third had built a chapel for his private use, being an outer work, with doors and windows opening on the rampart and Water Lane, could not be used as a prison for men of a dangerous class. A feeble prince, like Henry the Sixth, who shrank from state and power, may have enjoyed a mild detention in the hall now sparkling with the crown jewels; for he was softly kept; and this tower was in his day a part of the royal palace. Old traditions make this room his cage; the scene of his pious meditations; and of his deliberate murder by the Duke of Gloucester. After Henry's death, if not before, this tower was used as a paper office; for which purpose, as a hall adjoining the Court of Common Pleas, and opening into the folk's quarter, it was well adapted. Hence it came to be known as the Record tower.

On the wall above Water Lane, stood the two signal towers, the Belfry and the Lantern; each surmounted by a turret; of use to vessels coming up the Thames. On the first swung a bell; on the second burned a light.

CHAPTER III.

THE WHARF.

Turning through a sally-port in the Bye-ward gate, you cross the south area of the ditch, and come out on the Wharf; a strip of sand in front of the fortress, won from the river, and kept in its place by masonry and piles. This wharf, the work of Henry the Builder, is one of the wonders of his reign; for the whole strip of earth had to be seized from the Thames, and covered from the daily ravage of its tides. Piles had to be driven into the mud and silt; rubble had to be thrown in between these piles; and then the whole mass united with fronts and bars of stone. All Adam de Lamburn's skill was taxed to resist the weight of water, yet keep the sluices open by which he fed the ditch. Most of all was this the case when the King began to build a new barbican athwart the sluice. This work, of which the proper name was for many ages the Water gate, commands the only outlet from the Tower into the Thames; spanning the ditch and sweeping the wharf, both to the left and right. So soon as the wharf was taken from the river-bed, this work became essential to the defensive line.

London folk felt none of the King's pride in the construction of this great wharf and barbican. In fact, these works were in the last degree unpopular, and on news of any mishap occurring to them the Commons went almost mad with joy. Once they sent to the King a formal complaint against these works. Henry assured his people that the wharf and Water gate would not harm their city. Still the citizens felt sore. Then, on St. George's night (1240), while the people were at prayer, the Water gate and wall fell down, no man knew why. No doubt the tides were high that spring, and the soft silt of the river gave way beneath the wash. Anyhow they fell.

Henry, too great a builder to despair, began again; this time with a better plan; yet on the self-same night of the ensuing year his barbican crashed down into the river, one mass of stones. A monk of St. Alban's, who tells the tale, asserts that a priest who was passing near the fortress saw the spirit of an archbishop, dressed in his robes, holding a cross, and attended by the spirit of a clerk, gazing sternly on these new works. As the priest came up, the figure spake to the masons, 'Why build ye these?' As he spake, he struck the walls sharply with the holy cross, on which they reeled and sank into the river, leaving a wreath of smoke behind. The priest was too much scared to accost the more potent spirit; but he turned to the humble clerk, and asked him the Archbishop's name. 'St. Thomas the Martyr,' said the shade. The priest, growing bolder, asked him why the Martyr had done this deed? 'St. Thomas,' said the spirit, 'by birth a citizen, mislikes these works, because they are raised in scorn, and against the public right. For this cause he has thrown them down beyond the tyrant's power to restore them.'

But the shade was not strong enough to scare the King. Twelve thousand marks had been spent on that heap of ruins; yet the barbican being necessary to his wharf, the builder, on the morrow of his second mishap, was again at work, clearing away the rubbish, driving in the piles, and laying in a deeper bed the foundation stones. This time his work was done so well that the walls of his gateway have never shrunk, and are as firm to-day as the earth on which they stand.

The ghost informed the priest that the two most popular saints in our calendar, the Confessor and the Martyr, had undertaken to make war upon these walls. 'Had they been built,' said the shade, 'for the defence of London, and in order to find food for masons and joiners, they might have been borne; but they are built against the poor citizens; and if St. Thomas had not destroyed them, the Confessor would have swept them away.'

The names of these popular saints still cling to the Water gate. One of the rooms, fitted up as an oratory, and having a piscina still perfect, is called the Confessor's Chapel; and the barbican itself, instead of bearing its official name of Water gate, is only known as St. Thomas's tower.

The whole wharf, twelve hundred feet in length, lay open to the Thames, except a patch of ground at the lower end, near the Iron gate, leading towards the hospital of St. Catharine the Virgin, where a few sheds and magazines were built at an early date. Except these sheds, the wharf was clear. When cannon came into use, they were laid along the ground, as well as trained on the walls and the mural towers.

Three accents marked, as it were, the river front—the Queen's stair, the Water way, and the Galleyman stair. The Queen's stair, the landing-place of royal princes, and of such great persons as came to the Tower on state affairs, lay beneath the Bye-ward gate and the Belfry, having a passage into the fortress by a bridge and postern, through the Bye-ward tower into Water Lane. The Water way was that cutting through the bank which passed under St. Thomas's tower to the flight of steps in Water Lane; the entrance popularly known as Traitor's gate. The Galleyman stair lay under the Cradle tower, by which there was a private entrance into the royal quarter. This stair was not much used, except when the services of Traitor's gate were out of order. Then prisoners who could not enter by the approach of honour were landed at the Galleyman stair.

Lying open to the river and to the streets, the wharf was a promenade, a place of traffic and of recreation, to which folk resorted on high days and fair days. Men who loved sights were pretty sure to find something worth seeing at either the Queen's stair or Traitor's gate. All personages coming to the Tower in honour were landed at the Queen's stair; all personages coming in disgrace were pushed through the Traitor's gate. Now, a royal barge, with a queen on board, was going forth in her bravery of gold and pennons; now a Lieutenant's boat, returning with a culprit in the stern, a headsman standing at his side, holding in his hand the fatal axe.

Standing on the bank, now busy with a new life, these pictures of an old time start into being like a mystic writing on the wall. Two of these scenes come back with warm rich colouring to the inner eye.

Now:—it is London in the reign of that Henry the Builder, who loved to adorn the fortress in which he dwelt. Whose barge is moored at yon stair, with the royal arms? What men are those with tabard and clarion? Who is that proud and beautiful woman, her fair face fired with rage, who steps into her galley, but whose foot appears to scorn the plank on which it treads? She is the Queen; wife of the great builder; Elinor of Provence, called by her minstrels Elinor la Belle. A poetess, a friend of singers, a lover of music, she is said to have brought song and art into the English court from her native land. The first of our laureates came in her train. She has flushed the palace with jest and joust, with tinkle of citherns, with clang of horns. But the Queen has faults, for which her gracious talent and her peerless beauty fail to atone. Her greed is high, her anger ruthless. Her court is filled with an outcry of merchants who have been mulcted of queen-geld, a wrangle of friars who have been robbed by her kith and kin, a roar of tiremen and jewellers clamorous for their debts, a murmur of knights and barons protesting against her loans, a clatter of poor Jews objecting to be spoiled. Despite her gifts of birth and wit, Elinor la Belle is the most unpopular princess in the world. She has been living at the Tower, which her husband loves; but she feels that her palace is a kind of jail; she wishes to get away, and she has sent for her barge and watermen, hoping to escape from her people and to breathe the free air of her Windsor home.

Will the Commons let her go? Proudly her barge puts off. The tabards bend and the clarions blare. But the Commons, who wait her coming on London Bridge, dispute her passage and drive her back with curses, crying, 'Drown the witch! Drown the witch!' Unable to pass the bridge, Elinor has to turn her keel, and, with passionate rage in her heart, to find her way back.

Her son, the young and fiery Edward, never forgets this insult to his mother; by-and-bye he will seek revenge for it on Lewes field; and by mad pursuit of his revenge, he will lose the great fight and imperil his father's crown.

Again:—it is London in the reign of Bluff King Hal—the husband of two fair wives. The river is alive with boats; the air is white with smoke; the sun overhead is burning with golden May. Thousands on thousands of spectators dot the banks; for to-day a bride is coming home to the King, the beauty of whose face sets old men's fancies and young men's eyes agog. On the wharf, near the Queen's stair, stands a burly figure; tall beyond common men; broad in chest and strong in limb; dressed in a doublet of gold and crimson, a cap and plume, shoes with rosettes and diamonds, a hanger by his side, a George upon his breast. It is the King, surrounded by dukes and earls, awaiting the arrival of a barge, in the midst of blaring trumpets and exploding sakers. A procession sweeps along; stealing up from Greenwich, with plashing oars and merry strains; fifty great boats, with a host of wherries on their flanks; a vessel firing guns in front, and a long arrear of craft behind.

From the first barge lands the Lord Mayor; from the second trips the bride; from the rest stream out the picturesque City Companies. Cannons roar, and bells fling out, a welcome to the Queen; for this is not simply a great day in the story of one lovely woman; but a great day in the story of English life. Now is the morning time of a new era; for on this bright May—

'The gospel light first shines from Boleyn's eyes,'

and men go mad with hope of things which are yet to come.

The King catches that fair young bride in his arms, kisses her soft cheek, and bears her in, through the Byeward Tower.

The picture fades from view, and presently reappears. Is it the same? The Queen—the stair—the barge—the crowd of men—all these are here. Yet the picture is not the same. No burly Henry stands by the stair; no guns disturb the sky; no blast of trumpets greets the royal barge; no train of aldermen and masters waits upon the Queen. The lovely face looks older by a dozen years; yet scarcely three have passed since that fair form was clasped in the King's arms, kissed, and carried by the bridge. This time she is a prisoner, charged with having done such things as pen cannot write; things which would be treason, not to her lord only, but to her womanhood, and to the King of kings.

When she alights on the Queen's stair, she turns to Sir William Kingston, Constable of the Tower, and asks, 'Must I go into a dungeon?' 'No, madam,' says the Constable; 'you will lie in the same room which you occupied before.' She falls on her knees. 'It is too good for me,' she cries; and then weeps for a long time, lying on the cold stones, with all the people standing by in tears. She begs to have the sacrament in her own room, that she may pray with a pure heart; saying, she is free from sin, and that she is, and has always been, the King's true wedded wife.

'Shall I die without justice?' she inquires. 'Madam,' says Kingston, 'the poorest subject would have justice.' The lady only laughs a feeble laugh.

Other, and not less tragic, scenes drew crowds to the Water-way from the Thames.

Beneath this arch has moved a long procession of our proudest peers, our fairest women, our bravest soldiers, our wittiest poets—Buckingham and Strafford; Lady Jane Grey, the Princess Elizabeth; William Wallace, David Bruce; Surrey, Raleigh—names in which the splendour, poetry, and sentiment of our national story are embalmed. Most of them left it, high in rank and rich in life, to return, by the same dark passage, in a few brief hours, poorer than the beggars who stood shivering on the bank; in the eyes of the law, and in the words of their fellows, already *dead.*

From this gateway went the barge of that Duke of Buckingham, the rival of Wolsey, the last permanent High Constable of England. Buckingham had not dreamed that an offence so slight as his could bring into the dust so proud a head; for his offence was nothing; some silly words which he had bandied lightly in the Rose, a City tavern, about the young king's journey into France. He could not see that his head was struck because it moved so high; nay, his proud boast that if his enemies sent him to the Tower, ten thousand friends would storm the walls to set him free, was perhaps the occasion of his fall. When sentence of death was given, he marched back to his barge, where Sir Thomas Lovel, then Constable, stood ready to hand him to the seat of honour. 'Nay,' said the Duke to Lovel, 'not so now. When I came to Westminster I was Lord High Constable and Duke of Buckingham; now I am but poor Edward Stafford.

Landed at the Temple stair, he was marched along Fleet street, through St. Paul's Churchyard, and by way of Cheap to the Tower; the axe borne before him all the way; Sir William Sandys holding him by the right arm, Sir Nicholas Vaux by the left. A band of Augustine friars stood praying round the block; and when his head had fallen into the dust they bore his remains to St. Austin's Church.

On these steps, too, beneath this Water-gate, Elizabeth, then a young fair girl, with gentle, feminine face and golden hair, was landed by her jealous sister's servants. The day was Sunday—Palm Sunday—with a cold March rain coming down, and splashing the stones with mud. She could not land without soiling her feet and clothes, and for a moment she refused to leave her barge. Sir John Gage, the Constable, and his guards, stood by to receive her. 'Are all these harnessed men for me?' she asked. 'No, madam,' said Sir John. 'Yea,' she replied, 'I know it is so.' Then she stood up in her boat and leaped on shore. As she set foot on the stone steps, she exclaimed, in a spirit prouder than her looks—for in her youth she had none of that leonine beauty of her later years—'Here landeth as true a subject, being a prisoner, as ever landed at these stairs; and before Thee, O God, I speak it.' Perhaps she was thinking of her mother, who had landed on the neighbouring wharf. Anne had fallen on her knees on these cold stones, and here had called on God to help her, as she was not guilty of the things of which she stood accused. In those two attitudes of appeal one reads the nature of these two proud and gentle women, each calling Heaven to witness her innocence of crime—Elizabeth defiant, erect; Anne suppliant, on her knees.

CHAPTER IV.

RIVER RIGHTS.

THE wharf has story of another kind.

Under our Plantagenet kings, the English folk—then called in derision the 'Englishry,' just as under our Tudor kings the Irish kernes were called in derision the 'Irishry'—claimed the right of going into the Tower, when they wished, to make complaint either to the king or to his judges, of any wrong from which they suffered. One of the king's officers, the Tower warden, was a man with extensive powers, and a hundred archers at his back. A subject always in dispute between this officer and the city folk was a claim put forth by him, to catch fish in what the Commons called an unfair way. The warden claimed a right to put kidels in the water, not only in front of the wharf, but in any other part of the stream. Now a kidel was a weir, filled up with nets, which caught all fish coming down with the tide, both the small fry and the old flappers. What free angler could stand this claim? Through five or six reigns our fathers fought against this abuse; and the question of a warden's right to put kidels in the Thames was a topic which roused the water-side folk into fiercer passion than reports of fighting in Picardy and pilgrimage in the Holy Land.

A kidel in front of the wharf was an outrage as well as an injury. Our fathers loved the rod and line. Hundreds of years before Izaac quaffed the village ale and listened to the milkmaid's song, his foregoers had been wont to cast their lines into the Lea, the Wandle, and the Thames. Nor was the gentle craft pursued by them in sport alone. Fish was an article of food; the fisheries on the Thames being large enough to employ, and rich enough to feed, a tenth of the population on its banks; and to all these pleasures and profits, the right of a Tower warden to net the stream with kidels was a serious bar. The water-side taverns were up in arms, when these water-side taverns were the meeting-houses of all our turbulent and daring spirits. They had, indeed, good reason for their wrath; since the king's warden, not content with setting his own kidels in the Thames, rented to others his privilege of interfering with honest sport and decent trade. For a small sum of money any rascal on the river could buy his license, and set up kidels in the Lea and in the Medway as well as in the Thames. The effect of netting these rivers was to destroy the salmon and shad, as well as to capture the flounder and the trout.

Now and then, a prince in his distress consented to forego this river right; but his warden took scant notice of a pledge which he thought injurious to his pocket and derogatory to his prince.

Lion Heart strove to bring this quarrel to an end; and, in the eighth year of his reign, in the press of a sharp war, he made what he said was a high sacrifice in giving up kidels, and putting his warden of the Tower on a level with humbler and fairer folk. For this surrender Lion Heart expected to be paid, not only in earthly coin, but in heavenly grace. In the grant, by which he gave the public their own, he declared that—for the salvation of his soul, for the salvation of his father's soul, and for the salvation of the souls of all his ancestors, as well as for the benefit of his people and the peace of his realm—no more kidels should be set up in the Thames.

But Lion heart failed to keep his pledge. The warden was always nigh; the king was often far away; and the kidel question helped to keep alive the long resistance to King John.

In the Great Charter there was a special clause on kidels; King John consenting, among other things, that, under pain of excommunication, all kidels should be removed from the Thames and from his other streams. Yet the warden, paying scant attention to a parchment which he probably could not read, laid down his weirs and nets as before, only desisting for a time when the Sheriff of London, backed by an armed band, dropped down the river and seized his nets.

One fight was made by the London folk in the reign of Henry the Third, in behalf of sport and trade, which became famous in City story, and got a niche in every old chronicle and in many a popular song.

Complaints were laid before Andrew Buckrell, Mayor, Henry de Cotham, Sheriff, and other magistrates, that many new kidels had been laid in the Thames and the Medway, by authority of the Tower warden, contrary to the City franchise, and to the great injury of the common people. More than elsewhere this wrong was being done to them in the neighbourhood of Yantlet Creek. This was a ticklish thing; for although the Thames lay under the jurisdiction of London for many purposes, it was not clear that the Mayor and a City band had any right to pursue offenders up the Medway, and to seize them under the walls of Rochester Castle. They put their right to the test. Jordan de Coventry, second sheriff, with a body of men, well armed and resolute, started, on the 6th of January, 1236–7, for Yantlet Creek, where they fell suddenly and stoutly on the master fishermen and their servants. They found no less than thirty kidels beyond that creek towards the sea. With little ado they tore up the nets and seized the masters; Joscelyn and four good men of Rochester; seven good men of Strood; three good men of Cliff, all master-mariners, with nine others, their helpers and abettors in the wrong.

Jordan brought these captured nets and culprits up to London, where he gave the nets to the first sheriff, and lodged the master-mariners in Newgate.

When the news of this raid reached Rochester, Strood, and Cliff, much din arose, and men from these towns rode up to London to see what could be done for Joscelyn and his fellows. They applied to the King for help, on the ground that no man had power to seize the King's subjects by force, and cast them into jail, without his license. Henry inclined to take this view; but the mayor and sheriffs maintained their right to arrest offenders against the King's laws and the City franchises. Being then absent from London, Henry sent a writ to the mayor commanding him to accept bail for the appearance of his prisoners, until such time as the King could hold a court to try the case.

This court was called in the Palace of Kennington; when Buckrell and the citizens, Joscelyn and the master-mariners, appeared before the Archbishop of York, the Lord Chancellor, and other great personages, among whom the most eminent was William de Raleigh, the famous justiciar, a collateral ancestor of Sir Walter.

William de Raleigh, who held a brief, as it were, for the Crown, put Buckrell and his men on their mettle. 'How,' he asked them, 'had they, with such rash daring, seized the king's liegemen in their boats, and cast them into a common jail?' Buckrell answered him: 'that he had seized Joscelyn and the rest for just reasons: because, being taken in the act of using kidels, they were infringing the rights of the City, lessening the dignity of the Crown, and incurring the ban of excommunication, in accordance with an express clause in the Great Charter.' He asked, in conclusion, that the judges should enforce the law, and punish the master-mariners by a heavy fine.

William de Raleigh took this view of the kidel business, and his verdict gave immense delight at Guildhall. He sentenced Joscelyn and the other masters to pay a fine of ten pounds each—the fines to be rendered to the chief men in the City.

A great fire was lighted in Westcheape, and the captured nets from Yantlet Creek were burned in presence of a joyful crowd.

CHAPTER V.

THE WHITE TOWER.

The shell of the White tower, ninety feet high, from twelve to fifteen feet thick, is in four tiers, without reckoning the leads and turrets: (1) the vaults; (2) the main floor; (3) the banqueting floor; (4) the state floor. Each tier contains three rooms; not to count the stairs, corridors, and chambers which are sunk into the solid wall; a west room, extending from north to south, the whole length of the tower; an east room, lying parallel to the first; and a cross chamber, occupying the south-west corner of the pile. These rooms are parted from each other by walls, not less than ten feet thick, which rise from the foundation to the roof. On each angle of the tower stands a turret, one of which is round. The parapet is pierced for defending fire.

(1.) The vaults lie underground, with no stairs and doors of their own. Some piercings in the shell let in a little air and still less light. These vaults were the old dungeons of the keep—the home of pirates, rebels, and persecuted Jews. One of these rooms, the cross chamber, is darker and damper than the other two. It was called Little Ease, and is, in fact, a crypt beneath a crypt. When the Tower was full of prisoners, these vaults were used as prison lodgings, even in the Tudor and Stuart times. A few inscriptions can still be traced in the stone; one of which is that of Fisher, a Jesuit Father who was concerned in the Powder Plot.

SACRIS VESTIBUS INDUTUS
DUM SACRA MYSTERIA
SERVANS, CAPTUS ET IN
HOC ANGUSTO CARCERE
INCLUSUS. I. FISHER.

There is some ground for believing that Little Ease was the lodging of Guy Fawkes.

Out of the north-east vault a door opens into a secret hole, built for some purpose in the dividing wall—a cell in which there is neither breath of air nor ray of light. By a rule of the Tower which assigns every mysterious room to Raleigh, this vault is called Walter Raleigh's cell.

(2.) The main floor consists of two large rooms, and the crypt. This tier was the garrison stage; held by the King's guards, who fought with halberds and pikes. The crypt, a lofty and noble room, was occasionally used as a prison. Two niches have been scooped from the solid wall; one of them larger than the other; and this niche is also called Raleigh's cell. Of course, he was never in it. May it not have been that 'secret jewel-room in the White tower' of which we read so often in the royal books? On the jambs of this room a man may read these words and dates:

HE THAT INDURETH TO THE ENDE
SHALL BE SAVID.
M. 10.
R. RUDSTON.
DAR. KENT. AN°. 1553.

This is the work of Robert Rudston, of Dartford. Another writing on the wall runs thus:

BE FAITHFUL UNTO THE DETH AND I WILL
GIVE THEE A CROWNE OF LIFE.
T. FANE. 1554.

Below the second inscription comes the name—
T. CULPEPPER OF DARFORD.

These three prisoners were taken, with their Captain, Sir Thomas Wyat, in the Rising of the Men of Kent.

(3.) The banqueting floor was a part of the royal palace, though not of the personal and domestic part. The long room was the banqueting-hall, and is noticeable as being the only room in the Keep provided with a fire-place. The cross chamber was the chapel of St. John the Evangelist, which occupied two tiers of the Keep. Most of our royal and princely captives lived in these apartments—men like Ralph Flambard, Bishop of Durham; Griffin, Prince of Wales; John de Baliol, King of Scots; Prince Charles of France, the famous troubadour.

(4.) The state floor contained the great council-chamber; a smaller room called the Lesser hall, in which the justiciars sat; and the galleries of St. John's chapel, from which there was a passage into the royal apartments.

The roof was flat, with oaken supports and bands of

enormous strength. The council-chamber beneath it is one of the marvels of early English construction; being strong enough to bear not only the balisters and bowmen for whom it was built, but the sakers and carronades which came into use in a later reign. One of the four turrets, round, and larger than the rest, was added as a watch-tower. In early times this round turret was the prison of Maud the Fair; in later times it was an observatory, from which Flamsteed outwatched the stars.

The most surprising feature in Gundulf's keep is the scanty means of access. He seems to have given it only one door, and that so narrow, that a man marching through the corridor filled it up. The vaults had no entrance from without; and no means of communication with the upper tiers except by one well-stair. The main-floor had no way either up or down except by the same well-stair, which could only be approached through a passage built in the wall. The upper tiers had other stairs, so that people could pass from the banqueting-hall to the council-chamber and the parapets with comparative ease; but the communications of those lower tiers could be stopped by the halberds of three or four resolute men.

Yet Gundulf's castle on the Thames was not a safe prison for daring and ingenious men. The first offender ever lodged within its walls contrived to escape from his guards, to let himself down from a window, and to slip through the postern to his boat. This bold offender was that Ralph of Durham, called the Firebrand and the Lion, who for many years had been treasurer and justiciar to the Norman kings. On the death of Rufus he was seized by the Commons until the new king's pleasure should be known about him; and Henry the Scholar, who had good deeds rather than good rights to befriend him in his contest with Robert for the crown, sent the unpopular prelate to the Tower.

Henry was not inclined to harshness; and Ralph, though lodged in the keep which he had helped to build, was treated like a guest. He lived in the upper rooms, on the tier now known as the banqueting-floor; his rooms having plenty of space and light, a good fire-place, a private closet, and free access to St. John's chapel. William de Mandeville, Constable of the Tower, was appointed his keeper, and two shillings a-day were paid from the King's exchequer for his diet. He was suffered to have his own servants and chaplains in his rooms, and to send out for such wines and meats as his stomach craved and his purse could buy. One of the richest men in England, he could buy a good deal; one of the cleverest men in England, he could scheme a long way. But before resorting to his money and his wits in self-defence, Ralph tried how far he could reckon on the virtues of his pastoral staff. A bishop was not only a baron of the realm, but a prince of the universal Church. No doubt he had exercised lay functions; acting as a financier, sitting as a judge; but still he was a priest, on whom secular laws were held to have no binding force. On this ground he appealed to Anselm, then Lord Primate, as to his brother and his chief. Anselm, who had just come back from that exile into which he had been driven by Ralph and his master, was in no saintly humour. 'Out on this caitiff,' cried the Lord Primate, 'I know him not, neither as brother nor as priest.' Anselm took the part of Henry, whom his flock was beginning to call Gaffer Goodrich, and to love with exceeding warmth on account of Goody Maud, the young Saxon princess whom he had taken from a convent to make his wife.

Failing in this appeal, Ralph took counsel with his wits. The stout Norman knights who kept guard in his chamber were jolly fellows, fond of good cheer and lusty at a song. On this weakness he began to play. Sending for good wine, and giving orders to his cook, he invited to his table a belt of boisterous knights. When folks looked up at the keep, in which their enemy was caged, they saw lights in the windows rather late, and haply went to bed in the pious hope that their bad bishop was going quickly to his doom. At length his scheme was ripe. Asking the knights to supper, he sent out for jars of wine; a potent liquor which, in due time, laid those warriors asleep on bench and floor. The time was winter (the date February, 1101), and night came down quickly on the Tower. When the guards were all drunk, the sober bishop rose from his table, drew a long coil of rope from one of the jars, passed into the South room, tied his cord to the window shaft, and taking his crozier with him, let himself down. He was a fat, heavy man; the cord was rather short, and he fell some feet to the ground. But trusty servants who were in waiting, picked him up, and hurried him away into a boat, by which he escaped, with his staff and his money to France.

The window from which he escaped is sixty-five feet from the ground.

In the reign of King John, the White tower received one of the first and fairest of a long line of female victims, in that Maud Fitzwalter, who was known to the singers of her time as Maud the Fair. The father of this beautiful girl was Robert, Lord Fitzwalter, of Castle Baynard on the Thames, one of John's greatest barons; yet the King, during a fit of violence with his Queen, Isabella of Angouleme, fell madly into love with this young girl. As neither the lady herself nor her powerful sire would listen to his disgraceful suit, the King is said to have seized her at Dunmow by force, and brought her to the Tower. Fitzwalter raised an outcry, on which the King sent troops into Castle Baynard and his other houses; and when the baron protested against these wrongs, his master banished him from the realm. Fitzwalter fled to France, with his wife and his other children, leaving his daughter Maud in the Tower, where she suffered a daily insult in the King's unlawful suit. On her proud and scornful answer to his passion being heard, John carried her up to the roof, and locked her in the round turret, standing on the north-east angle of the keep. Maud's cage was the highest, chilliest den in the Tower; but neither cold, nor solitude, nor hunger, could break her strength. In the rage of his disappointed love, the King sent one of his minions to her room with a poisoned egg, of which the brave girl ate, and died.

Her father now returned to England; put himself in front of the great revolt of prelates and nobles; took command of the insurgent forces, who hailed him proudly as Marshal of the army of God and Holy Church. Fitzwalter fought against John, until the tyrant, bending before his outraged people, signed the Great Charter of our liberties at Runnymede.

Maud was buried in the abbey of Dunmow. Her father took possession of the Tower as a pledge; at a later time he went forth as a Crusader; and died at Damietta, fighting for the Tomb of Christ.

At a distance of fifty years, the Banqueting hall received two royal tenants in John de Baliol and David Bruce.

After the hot encounter at Dunbar, Baliol yielded his crown and kingdom to Edward the First, who returned to London, bringing with him, not only his royal captive, but Prince Edward of Scotland, a host of noble chiefs, the Scottish crown and sceptre, and that stone of destiny which lies in Westminster Abbey, the seat of our English kings. David, son of the famous Robert Bruce, was taken prisoner by Queen Philippa at the battle of Neville's Cross.

Among old papers in the Record Office is a book of account, kept by Ralph de Sandwich, Constable of the Tower, during the confinement of John de Baliol, from which we get some glimpses into his household life in the White tower. Payments are made to Dominus William his chaplain; to Master Adam his tailor; to Richard his pantler, and to Henry his butler; to Chyware and Gautrier his two chamberlains; to Peter his barber; to Henry his clerk of the chapel. The household was large; including a stall of horses and a pack of dogs; and the expense was fixed by King Edward's council at seventeen shillings a day. After a while, one esquire, one huntsman, one page, one barber, two greyhounds, ten beagles, and one horse were sent away; reducing the daily cost to the country by half-a-crown. The Scottish King had still one chaplain, two esquires, two grooms of the chamber, three pages, one barber, one tailor, one laundress, one butler, and one pantler. Baliol remained in the White tower for 189 days, after which he was given up to John de Pontissera, Papal Nuncio and Bishop of Winchester, on the understanding that he would in future reside abroad.

Griffin, Prince of Wales, a man who had been yielded into Henry the Builder's power by his own brother, Prince David, was lodged in the upper room from which Flambard was known to have escaped. Griffin, who was a fat man, like Flambard, thought a soldier should be able to do what a priest had done. Tearing his bed-clothes into shreds, he twisted them into a rope, by means of which he hoped to lower himself to the ground; but the clothes would not bear his weight; the coil snapped as he was slipping down; he broke his neck in the fall, and was killed on the spot. He seems to have found no means of getting from Flambard's window, and to have tried his chance of dropping some ninety feet from the leads. In the margin of Matthew Paris' beautiful copy of his own *Historia Anglorum*, there is a drawing of Griffin's fall. The coil of bed-linen is fastened to the parapet on the roof. Matthew, who was living at the time, and often in London, must have known how the Welsh prince came by his death. Griffin's son, then a mere child, was left a prisoner in the Tower. A few years later the young prince got away, when he returned to Wales, regained his principality, and fought with desperate valour against his English foes. Slain in the reign of Edward Longshanks, his head was brought to London, and fixed upon the turret, from which his father had fallen into his grave.

Edward the Second and his Queen, Isabella the Fair, kept a splendid, riotous court in the Tower, enlivened by love and war, by political quarrels, by religious festivals, and criminal intrigues. Here the princess known in story as Joanna de la Tour was born. The royal apartments in which the mother lay were so worn and rent, that the rain came rattling through the rafters into her bed; and John de Cromwell, then Constable, was dismissed from office for this neglect, and for other offences against his lord and lady. When Edward went away from London, on his wars and other follies, the fair Isabella ruffled her indolent mood by receiving visits in her chamber from Roger Mortimer, the handsome and reckless Border chief, who was then a prisoner in the keep. Mortimer got into the kitchen, crept up the kitchen chimney, and came out on the roof, from which he escaped to the river, and so away into France. It is an old story: you can easily break prison when you have fallen in love with the jailor's wife. Queen Isabella and Mortimer were not long apart. Every one is familiar with the tale of their guilty passion, their stormy career, their tragic end; the most singular episode in the history of our royal race.

CHAPTER VI.

CHARLES OF ORLEANS.

Of the captives who have helped to make this Banqueting hall a place of poetic memories, the most engaging is Prince Charles of Orleans, the unhappy troubadour. This young French prince, grandson of Charles the Fifth, father of Louis the Twelfth,—a soldier, a poet, a politician,—one of the chief commanders of the French chivalry, fell, together with a host of princes and nobles, into the hands of Harry of Monmouth, on the field of Agincourt.

Charles's life is an epic of love and war, of glory and defeat, of suffering and resignation. Nature and events conspired to throw the conquering Harry and the captive Charles into opposite lists. Not only were they enemies in the field, but rivals in love. The Prince's father, Louis of Orleans, and the King's father, Henry of Lancaster, had each affected to consider himself heir to the crown of France; a splendid claim, which came down, in time, to their sons. Louis of Orleans, making himself the champion of a royal and unhappy lady, Isabella of Valois, Queen of England, widow of Richard the Second, had sent a challenge to Henry of Lancaster, as he contemptuously called the King of England, which Henry had declined with a cold and proud disdain. Louis called Henry a coward; Henry called Louis a fool. The young princes had both been in love with the 'fair woman,' as Shakspeare calls her,—the widowed English queen, a daughter of Charles the Sixth—and Charles had carried away the prize. Harry was then our madcap Prince of Wales, the friend of

Poins, the companion of Sir John. Charles was a poet, a musician, a courtier; and although Hal was of higher rank and riper age, Isabella had chosen the softer, more accomplished prince for her future mate. Rivals in ambition and in love, every turn in their fortunes helped to make English Henry dislike the young French prince.

The married life of Charles and Queen Isabella had been brief and clouded, though they had loved each other with a perfect heart. His father, Duke Louis, was a reprobate; her father, the King of France, was mad. Her mother, Isabeau the Wicked, was suspected of carrying on a guilty intrigue with Louis. Suspected is an ugly world, not lightly to be raised against a woman; but conjugal infidelity was not the lightest of Queen Isabeau's crimes. Duke Louis, her lover, was murdered in the streets at midnight, just as he was leaving her palace gates; murdered by command of John the Fearless, Duke of Burgundy, who openly avowed and justified his act. Violante, Charles's mother, and Isabella, his betrothed wife, went about the streets of Paris, clad in the deepest mourning, crying for revenge against the shedder of blood; but no redress could be obtained from the crazy king against Fearless John. Violante died of a broken heart. Isabella, the beautiful English queen, was given to Charles; who lost her in a year—lost her in childbirth—when the young prince, only nineteen years of age when she died, whom grief had made a poet, bewailed her loss in verses which have made him famous, and are still recited as a consolation by many a widowed lip.

Reasons of state induced him to marry a second wife; Bona, daughter of Bernard, Count of Armagnac, the soul of his party in the court; and this Duchess Bona became a tender mother to the infant princess left to his care by the dying Queen.

When madcap Harry, casting off Poins and Jack, broke into Normandy, putting his claims on the crown of France to the rude arbitrament of war, the young poet, like all the princes of his house, Bourbon, d'Albret, Bar, Brabant, Alençon, flew to arms, to defend his uncle's crown and his own eventual rights. After capturing Harfleur, the English king, Henry, was marching by the coast-line into Picardy; but a vast, in their own belief an unconquerable, array of spears blocked up his way to Calais. In the tent scene on the night before Agincourt, Shakspeare has caught with subtle art, though merely in a few light words, the characters of the French princes then encamped by the Somme. Orleans, who talks of sonnets, and swears by the white hand of his lady, girds at the English king, his living rival in ambition and in love. Yet no braver soldier fell among the wounded on that fatal field than Charles, the poet-prince, who was found by his conqueror bleeding and speechless on a heap of slain. At first the Prince refused to eat food; but his royal captor, who carried him to his tent, persuaded him to live, brought him into England, clapped him into the White tower, and fixed a ransom of 300,000 crowns upon his head.

At that time Charles was twenty-four years old. His infant daughter by Queen Isabella, afterwards Duchess of Alençon, and his second wife, the Duchess Bona, were left behind in France. The latter he was not to see again; for how in a broken and defeated France could such a sum as 300,000 crowns be raised?

Henry, in fact, preferred his prisoner to his money; for, after his march on Paris, and his marriage to Princess Catharine of Valois, Isabella's sister, it became of vast importance to him that Charles should die without having a son. After the Dauphin's death, Henry was promised the crown of France; a promise which could never be made good, unless Charles of Orleans should die without male issue. So long, therefore, as the ransom was unpaid, and Henry had a pretext for detaining Charles in London, the poet was likely to remain a prisoner. He remained a prisoner five-and-twenty years!

This time was spent in writing verses in French and English, both of which languages he spoke and wrote with ease; lyrics on his lost love and on his absent wife. The dead Queen was his muse, and the most beautiful and tender of his verses were addressed to her.

In the Royal Book of verse, now in the British Museum, an exquisite volume, highly illuminated, which appears to have been given as a bridal present from Henry of Richmond to Elizabeth of York, there is an excellent picture of Prince Charles's life in the keep. One drawing in this book is of peculiar interest; in the first place, as being the oldest view of the Tower extant; in the second place, as fixing the chamber in which the poet lived; in the third place, as showing, in a series of pictures, the life which he led. First, we see the Prince in the Banqueting hall, seated at his desk, composing his poems, with gentlemen in attendance, and guards on duty. Next, we observe him leaning on a window-sill, gazing outwards into space. Then we have him at the foot of the White tower, embracing the messenger who brings the ransom. Again, we see him mounting his horse. Then we have him, and his friendly messenger, riding away. Lastly, he is seated in a barge, which lusty rowers are pulling down the stream, for the boat that is to carry him back to France.

Henry of Agincourt had been dead many years, and the French had recovered nearly the whole of France (thanks to Jeanne Darc, and to the poet's natural brother, the famous Bastard of Orleans) before Charles's day of liberation came. Every year his life had become more precious to France, as the sons of Charles the Sixth dropped, one by one, leaving no heirs to his crown. At length the Duke of Burgundy, as an act of expiation for the past, of reconciliation for the future, paid the enormous ransom fixed upon his head, and set the poet free.

When Charles arrived in Paris, he found the Duchess Bona dead, and his daughter, whom he had left a baby of five, a woman of thirty years. Reasons of state compelling him to begin life again, he married, for his third wife, Mary of Cleves, by whom he had a son, called Louis in remembrance of his father; and this child of the ransomed poet lived to mount the throne of France; the politic and successful prince so well known in history as Louis the Twelfth.

CHAPTER VII.

UNCLE GLOUCESTER.

> 'If I may counsel you, some day or two
> Your Highness shall repose you at the Tower.
> ——I do not like the Tower.'

Thanks to the great poet, no name is stamped so darkly on the Tower as that of Gloucester. Richard seems to haunt the pile. If the word Tower crops up in talk, nine persons out of ten will throw his figure into the front. They see, in their mind's eye, Gloucester with his knife at King Henry's throat; Gloucester denouncing Hastings at the board; Gloucester in rusty armour on the wall. Men picture him as drowning his brother Clarence in the butt of wine; as murdering his nephews, King Edward and the Duke of York. The localities of his crimes, and of the crimes imputed to him, are shown. He stabbed King Henry in the Hall tower, now the Jewel house. He accused Lord Hastings in the Council chamber, and struck off his head on the terrace below the keep. He drowned his brother in the Bowyer tower. He addressed the citizens from the terrace now known as Raleigh's walk. Brackenbury was kneeling in St. John's chapel, when he received the King's order to kill the princes. The boys were lodged by him in the rooms over the entrance gate, then known as the Garden tower. They were interred in the passage, at the foot of a private stair. The bones of these royal youths were afterwards dug out from behind a stair in the keep.

That the princes were murdered in the Tower there ought to be no doubt. Two of the greatest men in English story vouch it; not in the general feature only, but in the minor details of the crime. Sir Thomas More (the true author, as I think, of the book which bears his name) wrote at the time—about the year 1513—while he was acting as judge of the sheriffs' court, and while two of the four actors in the business were still alive. Lord Bacon, who knew the place and the story well; who probably heard the Tower authorities, when they read a welcome to King James, describe the Bloody tower as the scene of that royal murder; seems to have felt no doubt on the point. What More and Bacon wrote, received clinching proof in the discovery which was afterwards made of the children's bones.

Yet the story of this murder has been doubted; not in detail only, but in block. In the first place, political passion led to reports that the princes were not dead; and when these political reports fell away with time, they left behind them a bodiless spirit in the shape of historic doubt.

Partisans of Lambert Symnell and Perkin Warbeck were bound to say the two princes had not been killed by Tyrrell in the manner commonly supposed, and that one of them had not been killed at all. Duchess Marguerite (King Edward's sister) received young Warbeck as her nephew; the Irish nobles owned him for their prince; while a powerful English party, hating the victor of Bosworth field, were secretly disposed to push his claim. To all these partisans of the House of York, that story of a midnight murder was a fatal bar.

From that day to our own some ghost of a doubt has always fluttered round the tale. Bayley denies that if the crime were done at all it could have been done in the Gate house. But his reasons for rejecting a tradition which certainly goes back to the time of the alleged murder are very weak. He thinks it unlikely that Gloucester would confine the royal youths in so obscure a place. He thinks it absurd to call a room *bloody* because two boys had been *smothered* in it. He finds, in a survey made in the reign of Henry the Eighth, that this pile was called the Garden tower, not the Bloody tower, as he thinks it ought to have been styled if the legend of the crime had then been considered true. On what slight grounds historic doubt may rest!

Richard's scruples about putting his nephews into a dull lodging, after he had resolved to kill them, may be dismissed with a smile. Yet, fact being fact, it must be added that the rooms over the gate were a part of the royal palace, communicating with the King's bedroom in the Lantern, through the private chapel and the Great hall. Nothing about the Gate house then suggested dismal thoughts. It was the Garden tower, called from a garden into which it opened. It was lighted on both sides, so that the windows commanded views of the inner and outer wards, as well as of the wharf, the river, and the bridge. It had a separate entrance to the pleasant promenade on the wall. King Henry the Sixth had lived in the adjoining room. As to the fact of calling a place *bloody* on account of two boys having been smothered in it, a word may be said. Old writers do not say that *both* the boys were smothered; indeed, the very first narrative of this murder (that of John Rastall, brother-in-law of More) states that the ruffians smothered one of the boys with a pillow and cut the other boy's throat with a knife. As to the change of name, the answer is brief. Garden tower was an official name; the survey made by Henry the Eighth was an official work. It is only after many ages that in a public document you can expect to see an official name replaced by a popular name. The Bloody tower is not the only one which has changed its name in deference to public whim. The official name of the new Jewel house was once the Hall tower, that of the Lantern was once the New tower. Beauchamp tower is known as Cobham tower, Martin tower as Jewel tower, Brick tower as Burbage tower, and Water gate as St. Thomas' tower.

Edward the Fifth and his brother, Richard, Duke of York, one twelve years old, the other eight, were living in the palace, under charge of Sir John Brackenbury, then Lieutenant of the Tower; the young king having been deprived of his royal power without being deposed from his royal rank. Gloucester ruled the kingdom as Protector. The queen-mother, Elizabeth Woodville, who had seen her second boy torn from her arms, with wild foreboding of his fate, lived in sanctuary with the Abbot of Westminster; occupying the Jerusalem chamber and that adjoining room which is now used by the Westminster boys as a dining-room. The fair Saxon lady, whose pink and white flesh and shower of golden hair had won for her the wandering heart of Edward the Fourth, could hear the mallets of joiners in the abbey, could see the waggons of vintners and cooks bringing wine and meat to the great hall, by command of Gloucester, for the coronation of her eldest son. But the royal widow knew in her heart that the festival day would never dawn.

Her brother, who should have held the Tower for Edward, forsook his post to join her in sanctuary under the Abbot's roof, where he felt that, come what might, his head would be safe. Gloucester took charge of the fortress in his nephew's name. Working in the dark, with shrugs and hints, he began to sound the great earls and barons as to how far they would go with him; and to throw out bruits of a secret marriage having taken place between his brother, the late king, and Elinor Talbot; by which reports the legitimacy of his nephews would be brought into doubt before Holy Church. Robert Stillington, bishop of Bath, and Lord High Chancellor, is said to have helped the Duke, by saying that *he* had married the King to Elinor; a fact which he had concealed during Edward's reign, because his royal master had afterwards made the still more fascinating Elizabeth Woodville the public partner of his throne. Some earls and knights took up the prelate's tale; a few from fear of the Duke, others because they may have thought it true. Edward the Fourth, though light of love, had not been manly in protecting the frail ones whom his passions had brought to shame. Shore's wife was not the only woman whom he had loved and ruined. He was said to have left many a son in Cheapside. Men who rejected the tale of Perkin Warbeck being the actual Duke of York, could not help thinking, from his face and figure, that he must have been King Edward's natural son. Such would seem to have been Bacon's view. A mock marriage was not, indeed, beyond Edward's flight; and the Bishop of Bath and Wells may have aided him in some such frolic. That Edward had been guilty of entering into a clandestine marriage, and of keeping it secret, to the peril of his crown, is a story not to be received.

But men who could not see with Gloucester's eyes, soon found that the Duke had a swift and ugly way of freeing himself from lukewarm friends. Lord Hastings felt it first. Pushing forward the young king's coronation, Richard called a council, in which some of the men who knew his soul had seats. They met in the Council Chamber, where Lord Hastings, instead of playing into the Duke's hands, spoke up stoutly for the King; on which Gloucester, who had been listening in a passage, rushed into the Council room, tore up his sleeve, showed a withered arm, which he accused Hastings of having caused by impious arts, and asked his councillors what should be done. Words were useless. At a sign from Gloucester, bands of soldiers rushed from the corridor, tore Hastings from the table, dragged him downstairs, and, finding the block on the green out of order, threw him across a beam of wood and hacked off his head.

Then came, stroke on stroke, the crowning of Richard and the murder of his inconvenient kin.

Richard left London for the north while the crime was being done. His instruments had been chosen and his orders given. But the course of murder never quite runs smooth. Brackenbury was at his prayers, when the King's meaning was made known to him in a few sharp words. Finding him on his knees, the royal message was not likely to find him in the mood. He refused his task. The King had ridden so far as Warwick Castle when he heard that Sir John declined his office; and though it was midnight when the rider came in, he slipt from his couch, passed into the guard-room, where Sir James Tyrrell, his master of the horse, lay sleeping on a pallet-bed, and gave a few sure words of instruction to that trusty knight. Tyrrell rode back to London, bearing a royal order that Brackenbury should, for one night only, give up his command, with the keys and passwords. The month was August; the days were hot; and Tyrrell was much oppressed in soul; for murder is not an easy thing at best, and the errand on which he was riding to the Tower was one of the foulest ever known. But he feared the new king even more than he feared the devil and all his fires. Two trusty knaves were at his side—John Dighton and Miles Forrest; fellows on whose strong arms and callous hearts he could count for any deed which the King might bid them do. These men he took down to the Gate house, where the princes lay; and after getting the keys and passes from Brackenbury, he closed the Tower gates, and sent the two ruffians up into the princes' room.

In a few seconds the deed was done. Stealing downstairs, the murderers called their master, who stood watching near the gate, to come up and see that the boys were dead. Tyrrell crept up, by the private door; and, after giving a few orders to his agents, and calling the Tower priest to their help, he rode away from the scene and from London; bearing the dread news to his master, who was still going north towards York.

The two murderers, helped, as it would seem, by the priest, got the bodies downstairs into the gateway; dug a hole near the wall, and threw in the dead, and covered them over with earth and stones. But the new king, whose crimes made him superstitious, sent orders that the priest should bestow his nephews in some more decent place. The priest obeyed; but no one knew (unless it were the King) where he now laid them; and as he died soon after, the secret of their sepulchre passed from the knowledge of living men.

After the battle of Bosworth and the fall of Richard, the

new king had no reason to conceal that grave, and after the rising of Perkin Warbeck it became a pressing duty for him to find it and make it known. He could not. Forrest was dead; the priest was dead. Tyrrell and Dighton, though living, and eager to confess their crime, covering themselves with a royal pardon, could not help King Henry to prove, by the very best evidence—their bones—that the princes were not alive. Richard had sent orders for the priest to remove them; that was all they knew; and every apprentice boy in London knew as much. The fact of a first burial, and then a second burial, is stated in the writings ascribed to More, and is mentioned in Shakspeare's play:—

> 'The chaplain of the Tower hath buried them,
> But where, to say the truth, I do not know.'

As the priest would be likely to inter the princes in consecrated ground, search was made, not only in the open graveyard near St. Peter's, but within the church. To find these relics would have been to render a signal service to King Henry. No effort was spared; but fate was against the search; and as the bodies could not be found, the most cunning princes of Europe affected to believe that Perkin Warbeck the Pretender was King Edward's son.

Two hundred years after the deed was done, the mystery was cleared. In the reign of Charles the Second, when the keep (no longer used as a royal palace) was being filled with state papers, some workmen, in making a new staircase into the royal chapel, found under the old stone steps, hidden close away, and covered with earth, the bones of two boys, which answered in every way to those which had been sought so long. Deep public wonder was excited; full inquiry into all the facts was made; and a report being sent to Charles that these bones were those of the murdered princes, the King gave orders for their removal to a royal sepulchre in Westminster Abbey. The bones thus found now lie in the great chapel built by Henry the Seventh, side by side with some of the most eminent of English kings.

CHAPTER VIII.

PRISON RULES.

'Let the sorrowful sighing of the prisoners come before Thee.'

WHAT, in those days, were the rule and order of our first state prison?

The rule was simple, the order strict. In ancient times the government lay with the Constable, who had his official residence on the eastern wall, in Constable tower. This officer was paid in fees: twenty pounds on the committal of a duke, twenty marks on that of an earl, ten pounds on that of a baron, five pounds on that of a knight. A poor man had no right in the Tower at all; the officers sometimes complain that such and such a fellow could not afford to be a prisoner, and ought to be sent away. When a man was committed, the council seized his goods for the king's use, and the Treasury had to pay the Constable for his board and fire. So early as the reign of Richard the Second, the fees were fixed—for a duke at five marks a-week, for an earl at forty shillings, for a baron at twenty shillings, for a knight at ten shillings. A duke's chaplains were allowed six shillings and eight-pence a week; his gentlemen the same; his yeomen three shillings and four-pence. All other servants were allowed three shillings and four-pence; all other yeomen one shilling and eight-pence. These fees were raised as gold declined in value. In the reign of Edward the Sixth, the Duchess of Somerset, with two gentlewomen and three male servants, cost the Treasury eight pounds a-week. In Mary's reign, Lady Jane Grey was allowed eighty shillings a-week for diet, with thirteen shillings and four-pence for wood, coal, and candle. Her two gentlewomen cost twenty shillings a-week, and her three male servants the same sum. A bishop was treated like a baron. Nicholas Ridley, bishop of London, was allowed fifty-three shillings a-week for food, with six shillings and eight-pence for fire and light. Two servants waited on him, who cost the country ten shillings a-week.

The prisoners were cheated by their keepers, most of all in the comforts of fire and candle.

The Constable, always a man of high rank, appointed a Lieutenant, to whom he allowed a stipend of twenty pounds a-year, with such small savings as could be made in furniture and food. In the reign of Henry the Eighth, the Lieutenant, who had now become the actual prison warder, had built a new house for his accommodation, in a courtly quarter of the prison, under the belfry; which house was afterwards known as the Lieutenant's lodgings. Close by his house, on either side, stood two smaller houses for his officers; that to the east, in the garden, became famous in after times as the prison of Latimer and Raleigh; that to the north, on the green, became famous as the prison of Lady Jane Gray.

In time, the Lieutenant and his officers came to look on the state allowance for a prisoner's maintenance as a perquisite. They expected an offender to pay heavy fees, and to find himself in furniture and diet. Raleigh paid for his food 208*l.* a-year; equal to a thousand pounds in the present time. Bare walls, an oaken floor, a grated window, an iron-bound door, were all provided by his country. Chairs, arras, tables, books, plate, fire and victuals, he had to buy for himself, at his own cost, through porters, serving-men, and cheats who lived upon his purse. When he had bought these articles, they were not his. own, except for their immediate use. The rule was, that as a man brought nothing in, he could take nothing out. Whether he died in prison, or left it with a pardon, his goods of every kind were seized for his keeper's use.

How a prisoner fared in his cell may be seen by two examples taken from a heap of records.

The case of Sir Henry Wyat, of Allington Castle, Kent, father of the wit and poet, takes us back to the latter days of the Red and White Roses. Wyat, a Lancastrian in politics, spent not a little of his time under watch and ward. The Wyat papers say—'He was imprisoned often; once in a cold and narrow tower, where he had neither bed to lie on, nor clothes sufficient to warm him, nor meat for his mouth. He had starved there had not God, who sent a crow to feed his prophet, sent this his and his country's martyr a cat both to feed and warm him. It was his own relation unto them from whom I had it. A cat came one day down into the dungeon unto him, and, as it were, offered herself unto him. He was glad of her, laid her in his bosom to warm him, and, by making much of her, won her love. After this she would come every day unto him divers times, and, when she could get one, bring him a pigeon. He complained to his keeper of his cold and short fare. The answer was, 'He durst not better it.' 'But,' said Sir Henry, 'if I can provide any, will you promise to dress it for me?' 'I may well enough,' said he, the keeper; 'you are safe for that matter;' and being urged again, promised him, and kept his promise, and dressed for him, from time to time, such pigeons as his accator the cat provided for him. Sir Henry Wyat in his prosperity for this would ever make much of cats, as other men will of their spaniels or hounds; and perhaps you shall not find his picture anywhere but, like Sir Christopher Hatton with his dog, with a cat beside him.'

One picture of the old knight, with his faithful cat, pigeon in paw, was seen in the South Kensington gallery of portraits. Wyat was put to the torture, a thing unknown to our law, but well known to our judges. Racks, boots, barnacles, thumbscrews, were occasionally used. The barnacles was an instrument fastened to the upper lips of horses to keep them still while they were being bled; and Richard the Third was fond of putting this curb on his enemies. One day, after putting it on Wyat, the King exclaimed in a fit of admiration, 'Wyat, why art thou such a fool? Thou servest for moonshine in water. Thy master,' meaning Henry of Richmond, 'is a beggarly fugitive; forsake him and become mine. Cannot I reward thee? And I swear unto thee I will.' To all this the prisoner replied: 'If I had first chosen you for my master, thus faithful would I have been to you, if you should have needed it. But the Earl, poor and unhappy though he be, is my master, and no discouragement, no allurement, shall ever drive me from him, by God's grace.'

When the wars of the Roses came to an end, Sir Henry found that he had served for something better than moonshine in water; being made a Gentleman of the Privy Chamber, a knight banneret, Master of the Jewel house, Treasurer of the King's chamber, and a Privy Councillor; rich enough to buy Allington Castle, one of the noblest piles in Kent; where Lady Wyat, his wife, put the Abbot of Bexley in the stocks for taking liberties with one of her maids; where Sir Henry lived to see his son, Sir Thomas, renowned as a wit, a poet, and a servant of the Queen.

The case of Thomas Howard, third Duke of Norfolk, gives us glimpses of the prison seventy years later, in the reign of Edward the Sixth.

Norfolk was not only the first of English nobles, but the uncle of two queens, and nearly related to the King in blood. He had served his country in the council chamber and at foreign courts; in the fleet and on the field of battle; nay, he had so far won King Henry's confidence as to be named one of his executors during the minority of his son. He was an early reformer, and in the wild rising called the Pilgrimage of Grace he had smitten the Catholics hip and thigh. Yet, when Henry was on his deathbed, rivals and enemies whispered in his ear that Norfolk's eldest son, Lord Surrey, the poet of whose genius we are all so proud, was looking for the hand of Mary, and quartering the arms of Edward the Confessor on his shield. The dying man was alarmed for the public peace. Father and son, seized in the King's name, were lodged, unknown to each other, in the Tower. Surrey, not being a peer of the realm, was tried at Guildhall by a common jury, before whom he pleaded his right to wear the Confessor's arms; a right of usage which he said was sanctioned by the heralds; but the court pronounced this assumption of the king's arms treason, and the brilliant young noble laid his head upon the block. The Peers passed a bill of attainder against the old warrior; a warrant for his execution was signed; but in the night, while the headsmen were sharpening their axe and setting up the block, the King expired. Somerset, the Duke's rival, feared to carry out the warrant; yet Norfolk was kept in prison until King Edward died; and in this interval of quiet endurance there is one letter from him extant, in which he humbly begs to have some books sent to him from a house in Lambeth, saying, very pathetically, that unless he has a book to engage his mind, he cannot keep himself awake, but is always dozing, and yet never able to sleep, nor has he ever done so for a dozen years! Only one servant was allowed to wait upon him; a rare restriction in the case of men of his exalted rank. The Duchess of Somerset had two ladies and three male servants to attend her. Sir Edward Warner, the Lieutenant, made the usual charges for a duke, 22*l.* 18*s.* 8*d.* a month; charges which should have covered diet, light and fire. Yet Norfolk has to beg his good masters for leave to walk by day in the outer chamber of his cell, for the sake of his health, which suffers very much from his close confinement. They can still, he says, lock him up in his narrow cage at night. He craves to be allowed some sheets, to keep him warm in bed.

Such were the comforts of a prison, to the first peer in the realm, at a period when the laws did not pretend to be equal for the great and the obscure. A man of quality had one great advantage; he could not be stretched on the rack and hung by the cord. Cases occur of a baron in one cell urging his follower in another never to confess, but to stand out like a man; and the poor commoner replying that it is easy for a lord to stand out, since he is only examined by word of mouth; not so easy for a poor wretch, who, unprotected by his quality, has to answer with his thumb under a screw and his limbs on the wheel.

CHAPTER IX.

BEAUCHAMP TOWER.

Before the days of Henry of Agincourt, the keep had ceased to be a common prison, and that function had been transferred to the large and central work on the western wall. This work became known by the names of Beauchamp tower and Cobham tower; names which take us back to Thomas de Beauchamp, Earl of Warwick, and to Sir John Oldcastle, the Good Lord Cobham.

This tower consists of three floors; mainly of three large rooms, and a winding stair; a room on the green, which was used by keepers and servants; a middle room, used as a prison, for what may be called the second class of great offenders; an uppermost room for the servants of great lords and for prisoners of inferior rank.

The tenant to whom these chambers owe their first renown and lasting name, was a popular idol, Thomas de Beauchamp, son of that Earl of Warwick who had swept through the lines of Crecy and Poictiers. Beauchamp was of milder tastes and more popular manners than his sire; a friend of the good Duke of Gloucester, Thomas of Woodstock; a builder, a gardener, a student; a man who found more happiness in his park and his oratory than in courts and camps. When the House of Commons met to appoint a governor to the young king, Richard of Bordeaux, they fixed on Beauchamp as the man best gifted for so great a charge. It was a thankless office. Richard proved to be a boy, at once proud and base; fond of pomp and show; attached to low persons and degrading pleasures. For the King's own good, Gloucester and Beauchamp put their strength together, and, being joined by Arundel, Mortimer, and other great barons, marched on London, seized the rapacious Simon Burley, and, after an open trial, put this unpopular minion of the King to death. All honest men rejoiced in Burley's fall; but Richard was roused to anger; and for many years he nursed a bitter heart, masked by a smiling face, against the men who had done him this true service. In fact, the arrest of Burley was not their sole offence. They wished to keep him in the open path of law; while he and his flatterers were bent on ruling in a fashion of their own. Hence they acquired the name of 'sound advisers' to the court.

For some years, Richard had to wait and grow; but

when he came of age, he took the reins into his hands, dismissing his wise governor from his council, and banishing him into the midland shires.

Beauchamp repaired to Warwick Castle, where he found sweet employment for his genius in building towers, in strengthening walls, in planting trees. Some of his noble work remains in evidence of his taste and skill; among other things, Guy's tower, on the north-east corner of the castle, and the nave of St. Mary's Church in the town.

But even in the country, men so popular as the Duke of Gloucester and the Earl of Warwick were not to be endured by a prince who dreamt of seizing all the powers of the realm into his puny hands. At length his occasion came, and he struck his blow. Arundel was the first to fall; Beauchamp followed next; but they only fell when the liberties of England were destroyed, when parliaments were swept away, and the King, with the advice of eight lords and three commoners only, assumed the power of making all future laws for the government of his realm. It was a vast usurpation, and the men who became its victims were regarded as martyrs in a sacred cause.

The barons seized by the King were taken by perfidious arts. Lord Arundel was carried by his brother, the Lord Primate, to the King's closet, whence he was hurried to the Isle of Wight. Beauchamp was caught as he was leaving the royal table. The weak prince, who piqued himself on his guile, invited the great and popular Earl to dine with him, and on his arrival treated him with distinguished favor, sitting at the same board, and calling him his very good lord. A stranger who stood by would have supposed Beauchamp higher in grace than ever; but the King's servants knew their master; and were not surprised, on quitting the banquet, to find him a prisoner in the marshal's hands. In a few days, Beauchamp was given in charge to Ralph Lord Nevill, of Raby, Constable of the Tower, by whom he was lodged in the apartment to which he has bequeathed his name.

Thomas of Woodstock, known as the Good Duke of Gloucester, was taken next, at his castle of Plasley, near Dunmow, by an ingenious wile. Richard set out from London, dressed as for a royal hunt; rode on to Havering Park, where dinner had been prepared for him; and, after eating a hearty meal, got on his horse, and went on to Plasley, the Duke's residence, with a few gentlemen only in his train. It was five o'clock of a summer afternoon when they clattered into the open court; the Duke, who had just supped, led down the Duchess and his children to the court-yard to give his nephew welcome. Richard went into the house, and sat at table; but after a few minutes, he cried, 'Fair uncle, cause you some five or six horses to be brought, and let us away to London, where we need your counsels.' Uncle and nephew descended into the yard, leapt to their horses, and rode away; the King keeping in front, at a sharp trot, until they came upon an ambush of armed men, who seized the Duke's bridle and held him fast. Gloucester shouted to his nephew to come back; but the King rode forward, taking no heed of the Duke's cries, until he reached the Tower and threw himself on his couch. The Duke, brought up to London by his guards, was thrust on board a ship, carried over to Calais, and lodged in the castle of that town, from which he was never to escape with life.

Arundel was tried, condemned, and executed. Mortimer escaped from his pursuers into the wilds of Ulster, where he dwelt in safety with the Irish kernes.

From his cell on the west wall, Beauchamp was carried by Lord Nevill and his javelin men to the House of Peers, where John of Gaunt informed him that he stood accused by Edward Plantagenet, Earl of Rutland, of having, in times long past, committed divers crimes and offences against his lord the king. Beauchamp replied, that for these alleged offences he had received a pardon under the Great Seal. Of course this plea was final. But Sir John Clopton, Chief Justice of the King's Bench, declared that this pardon under the Great Seal would not serve his turn, since the King, for good and wise reasons, had, on the prayer of his faithful Parliament, repealed that instrument as void and of no effect. Seeing that the ancient law and franchise of the realm were set at naught, the Earl could do nothing else than put his cause in the hands of God and his Peers.

Rutland made the charge against him in two main parts. In the first part, he accused Beauchamp of high treason in having raised an armed force against the King's authority and crown; in the second part, in having arrested, tried, and executed Sir Simon Burley, without the King's consent, to the great scandal of his royal justice. Beauchamp knew they would condemn him; though he may have doubted whether they would dare to defy the City by sending him to the block. He pleaded guilty to the charge. In a version of his trial, which was published by the court, he is said to have confessed his faults with many tears; urging that he felt the wickedness of what he had done, and that his only hope was in the King's grace and mercy. Gaunt pronounced the same sentence as on Arundel; that he should be hanged, drawn, and quartered; that his name should be erased from the roll of Peers; that all his castles, manors, and estates, should revert to the Crown. With the weight of this sentence on his head, he was taken back to the Tower, where Lord Nevill replaced him in his cell until his majesty's pleasure should be further known.

Richard, covered with the odium of his uncle's murder,

could not bring his pen to sign the warrant for Beauchamp's death. The Earl had a great following, and his prison was a centre of public emotion, like that of Raleigh in a later reign. To get rid of these sympathies, he was sent away to the Isle of Man, a prisoner for life; but that small islet in the Irish Sea was found to be no safe jail for so great a man; and before the year ran out he was brought back to London and lodged once more under Nevill's eye. Here he remained for two years longer; when the star of Henry of Bolingbroke rising in the west, he was set at liberty, purged in honour, and restored to his rank and fortune.

His ashes lie at Warwick, in the noble church which he had built in the days of his happy exile from the court.

CHAPTER X.

THE GOOD LORD COBHAM.

'Oldcastle died a martyr.'

So runs the epilogue to Shakspeare's Second Part of King Henry the Fourth. 'Oldcastle died a martyr, and this is not the man!'

In the first draft of Shakspeare's play the mighty piece of flesh, now known to all men as Sir John Falstaff, was presented to a Blackfriars' audience under the name of Sir John Oldcastle. Why was such a name adopted for our great buffoon? Why, after having been adopted, was it changed? Why, above all, is Oldcastle first presented by the poet as a buffoon, and afterwards proclaimed a martyr?

These questions hang on a story which unfolds itself in the Beauchamp tower.

Sir John Oldcastle lived when his young friend, Harry of Monmouth, was a roguish lad, at Couling Castle, close by Gad's Hill, on the great Kent road. Besides being a good soldier, a sage councillor, and a courteous gentleman, Oldcastle was a pupil of Wycliffe, a receiver of the new light, a protector of poor Lollards, a contemner of monks and friars, a man who read the Bible on his knees, and took the word which he found there to be good for his soul. He was not only a friend of the reigning king, but of the graceless prince. He had fought with equal credit in the French wars and in the Welsh wars; but his fame was not confined to the court and camp. Rumour linked his name with some of the pranks of madcap Hal. We know, that he lived near Gad's Hill, that he built a new bridge at Rochester, and founded in that city a house for the maintenance of three poor clerks. We know nothing about him that suggests the pranks on Gad's Hill, and the orgies in Eastcheap. A high, swift sort of man; full of fight, keen of tongue, kind to the poor, impatient with the proud; such was the brave young knight who wedded Joan, last heiress of the grand old line of Cobham, in whose right he held Couling Castle; sitting in the House of Peers as Lord Cobham; a name by which he was not less widely known and dearly loved than by his own. Poor and pious people everywhere called him the 'Good Lord Cobham.'

Between this popular layman and his neighbour, Thomas Arundel, Archbishop of Canterbury, bad feeling had grown up. Oldcastle hated monks; and Arundel was a patron of monks. Oldcastle stood out for free inquiry; Arundel was the chief author of our atrocious act for burning heretics. The two men were opposed like day and night; no grace and favour could make them friends; and once in conflict, the tug of war was sure to be long and fierce.

Arundel, being bent on crushing the Lollard preachers, found his neighbour of Couling Castle in the way; for Sir John not only went to hear these Lollards preach, but lodged them in his house, and defended them by his power. Nay, Sir John set his face against the new policy introduced by Arundel, from Spain, of burning men alive. This burning of men alive was a new thing in the land; and although it had then been made law, it was known to be a foreign, and held to be a devilish device, not to be justified from the Word of God. Sir John, a man of quick temper and shrewd of tongue, let those prelates and friars who had got the law passed know what he thought of them.

Arundel drew up a charge against Sir John, on the score of his opposition to Holy Church, which, backed by some priests and monks, he laid before the King. Henry, who did not want to quarrel with his friend, replied that he would himself speak with Sir John, and show him the error of his way. Nothing came of this pause. Henry talked to Sir John; but Oldcastle was a learned clerk, which Henry was not; and, after much writing and talking on the point, the King, at once puzzled and vexed over a coil which his wit could not smooth, left the swordsman and the gownsman to fight their fight.

Arundel cited Oldcastle to appear at Canterbury and purge his fame. Oldcastle replied by manning the walls and strengthening the gates of Couling Castle; since the Lord Primate, a baron of the realm, no less than a prince of the Church, was likely enough, on his second citation, to send archers and halberdiers to enforce his will. The crafty Primate took a surer way. He caused John Butler, one of the King's servants, to go with his own man to Couling, where he was challenged by the guard, and refused admission within the gates. Butler had no business there; but the fact of his being sent away was adroitly presented to the King as an act of disloyalty on the part of Sir John. Quick in temper, Henry gave orders to arrest his friend, who was seized by a royal messenger, and given in keeping to Sir Robert Morley, then Lieutenant of the Tower.

Sir Robert lodged the King's old friend in the Earl of Warwick's chamber; then the most stately and commodious prison in his charge; the Lieutenant's house not being erected until the reign of Henry the Eighth.

In this chamber, which people began at once to call Cobham tower (a name which clings to it still), he was visited by his fast enemies, the monks and friars, who put him through his catechism, and got logically cudgelled for their pains. But Arundel felt that he had his foe in the toils. A prisoner of the Church had no friends; and a man on whom Henry frowned was not likely to meet with mercy from a bench of priests. A synod met on his case in St. Paul's, which Arundel adjourned to an obscure Dominican convent on Ludgate Hill. When Oldcastle was brought to this convent by Sir Robert, he found among his judges, over whom the Primate sat in state, the priors of the Augustine and Carmelite friars. In fact, the denouncer of monkish abuses was now to be tried for his life by a board of monks.

Oldcastle's answers to his accusers struck the folks who afterwards heard of them like steel on flint. Wycliffe himself had never put the new lore in a finer light. He declared that the Bible was his rule of faith; that every man had a right to the sacred guide; that the bread and wine were typical, but not actual, body and blood of Christ. 'What!' cried one of the judges; 'this is flat heresy.' 'St. Paul, the Apostle,' answered Sir John, 'was as wise as you be now and more godly learned: and *he* wrote to the Corinthians, "The bread which we brake, is it not the communion of the body of Christ?" He threw out his opinions freely.' 'By our Lady,' cried the Primate, 'there shall be no such preaching within my diocese and jurisdiction—

if I may know it.' The synod, acting on the new Spanish law, condemned Sir John to be burnt with fire until he died.

When that sentence of the court was read, and the culprit was asked what he had to say, he stood up, and spake these memorable words:

'Ye judge the body which is but a wretched thing, yet am I certain and sure that ye can do no harm to my soul. He who created that, will of His own mercy and promise save it. As to these articles, I will stand to them, even to the very death—by the grace of my eternal God.'

Morley led him back from the Dominican convent to the Beauchamp tower, followed by the cries and tears of a whole city, in which his words were repeated from mouth to mouth. A paper in which he wrote down the points of his belief was read in every gateway as Sir John Oldcastle's creed. In his fresh confinement, under sentence of death by fire, he heard from friends of the good cause that reports were being spread abroad of his having changed his mind since his condemnation. To meet these slanders, and to edify the pious, he sent out from Beauchamp tower a paper in the following words:

'Forasmuch as Sir John Oldcastle, knight and Lord Cobham, is untruly convicted and imprisoned, falsely reported, and slandered among the common people by his adversaries, that he should otherwise both feel and speak of the sacraments of the Church, and especially of the blessed sacraments of the altar, than was written in the confession of his belief, which was indicted and taken to the clergy, and so set up in divers open places in the City of London, known be it here to all the world that he never since varied in any point.'

The paper was posted by his friends on church-doors, on blank walls, and on the City gates. But this good service was not all that could be done for him. Four weeks after his sentence had been read at Paul's Cross, William Fisher, dealer in skins, and a band of resolute citizens, came down to the fortress on a dark October night, the vigil of St. Simon and St. Jude, forced their way into Beauchamp tower, drew out the popular hero, got away from the gates without being pursued, and carried him in safety to his town house in Smithfield.

Henry took no active steps against the escaped heretic, who remained for nearly three months in his town house, safe in the armed city against all that could be done by monks and friars. But Arundel was not a man to slacken his grip on an enemy's throat. Of himself he could do nothing against a peer so strong in popular support. Only the King could cope with Cobham. Now, Henry would never stir against a brave soldier, at the suit of a turbulent priest, unless some danger should appear to threaten his crown and life. Then, indeed, the primate knew that his passion would be fierce and his movement swift. How could an appearance of danger be brought about? No man then living had enjoyed a longer experience than Arundel in popular tumults, in civil war, in the deposition of kings. He knew the art of goading the Commons into discontent, and turning their discontent to his own account. Even the great place which he held in the Church had been won as a gambler wins his stake, by a lucky chance.

The Lollards helped him. Either prompted by cunning spies, or moved by reckless councillors, the men who shared the new light resolved on making a grand display of strength. They spoke of holding a meeting in St. Giles' Fields; they said their general, as they called Sir John, would appear amongst them; and they promised to muster at his call a hundred thousand strong. Such a meeting of the Commons, in a field near London, was not to Henry's mind, and his Christmas revels in the country were troubled by the spectre of this coming Lollard day.

Arundel seized his chance. The King was away at Eltham, keeping the festival of his faith, when the Lord Primate sent him word that an army of fanatics was about to encamp in front of Newgate; that these pestilent fellows meant to pull down kings and bishops, and set up a devil's commonwealth, with the heretic, Sir John Oldcastle, as regent of his realm. Henry flushed into rage; yet even in his fury he acted like a master of events. No one read alarm upon his brow. The palace revels were kept up; but on Twelfth Night coming, his horse was brought to the door, and he rode away towards London. If the captain who had smitten Burgundy were in the field, with a hundred thousand commoners at his back, the task before him might be rough and sharp. So he called his barons to his side, shut up the City gates, stuck a white cross on his banner, such as knights put on who were going to die for Holy Church, sallied from the city before it was yet dawn, marched into St. Giles' fields, and occupied all the lanes. The Lollards were completely caught. As the bands came in from the country, they were seized and brought before the King. 'What seek ye?' was the sharp question. 'We go to meet our General,' said the foremost, scarcely knowing to whom he spake. 'Who is your General?' 'Who is our General! Who should he be save the Good Lord Cobham?'

Oldcastle was proclaimed; a thousand marks set on his head; and privilege offered to the city that should yield him bound to the King. All these rewards were cried in vain. Leaving his house in Smithfield, he roamed about the country; now in Wales, anon near London, afterwards in Kent; in every place hearing of the thousand marks, and of the privilege to be won by his arrest; finding, in every shire, men and women eager to brave ruin and death in his defence. As a man cast out from the Church, it was a mortal sin to feed and shelter him. Every monk whom he met was a spy; every priest whom he saw was a judge; yet for more than four years he defied the united powers of Church and Crown; sheltered from pursuit by poor folk whom he had taught, and by whom he was madly loved.

Once he was near being taken. Lodging in a farm-house near St. Alban's, on a manor belonging to the abbey, he was seen by some of the abbot's men, who quickly ran to inform their lord, and came back to the farm with a force to arrest him in his bed.

Oldcastle was got away; but his books were seized; and some of his stout defenders, who were taken by the abbot's men, were hung as a warning to the rest. On the books being opened they were found to be religious works; but the abbot of St. Alban's was shocked to see that the heads of all the saints had been either torn out or defaced.

William Fisher, the dealer in skins, who had conducted Oldcastle's rescue from the Tower, was seized in his house, and tried at Newgate before Nicholas Wotton, and three other judges, on a charge of breaking into the Tower, and carrying off the King's prisoner. Fisher, found guilty by a packed jury, was sentenced by Wotton to be hung at Tyburn, to have his neck chopped through, to have his head spiked, and exposed on London Bridge.

After a chase of more than four years, the friars, who could not persuade the commons to betray Sir John, were base enough to buy him from a Welsh fellow named Powis; a wretch of some local weight, who had won the friendship of Oldcastle by adopting his views about the monkish order and the Bread and Wine. The friars who got hold of Powis plied him with money to betray his master, until his virtue finally gave way, and he consented to act the part of Judas, on receipt of such wages as Judas got. He came upon Oldcastle by surprise, accosted him as a friend, and took him prisoner by a desperate fight.

Wounded and weak, Sir John was brought to the Tower; and, the King being absent in France, the clergy gave themselves no trouble about a second trial; but, taking the old sentence of death to be sufficient, they sent him to the gallows and the stake; to the first as a traitor against his King; to the second as an apostate from his Church. He was burnt in Smithfield, in front of his own house; the first man who was given to the flames on that famous spot. Such is the story of a gallant warrior, a pious gentleman, and a faithful knight.

Now, what is there in such a man to suggest the idea of Falstaff—a braggart, a coward, a lecher, a thief?

Shakspeare was not the first to put this insult on Sir John. When the young poet came to London, he found the play-writers using the name of Oldcastle as synonymous with braggart, buffoon, and clown. As Fuller says, Sir John Oldcastle was the make-sport in old plays for a coward. Finding the name current (just as a comic writer finds Pantaloon—a degradation of one of the noblest Italian names—on our modern stage), Shakspeare adopted it in his play.

This false Sir John was the creation of those monks and friars against whom the true Sir John had fought his manly fight. Those friars composed our early plays; those friars conducted our early dumb shows; in many of which the first great heretic ever burned in England was a figure. Those friars would naturally gift their assailant with the ugliest vices—for how could an enemy of friars be gallant, young, and pious? In this degraded form, the name of Oldcastle was handed down from fair to fair, from inn-yard to inn-yard, until it took immortal shape on Shakspeare's stage.

Now comes a personal query:—the significance of which will not be overlooked by men who wish to learn what they can of Shakspeare's life.

Why, after giving to the Oldcastle tradition that immortal shape, did Shakspeare change the name of his buffoon to Falstaff, and separate himself for ever from the party of abuse?

The point is very curious. Some motive of unusual strength must have come into play before such a course could have been taken by the poet. It is not the change of a name, but of a state of mind. For Shakspeare is not content with striking out the name of Oldcastle and writing down that of Falstaff. He does more—much more—something beyond example in his works—*He makes a confession of his faith.*

In his own person, as poet and as man, he proclaims from the stage—

OLDCASTLE DIED A MARTYR!

That was a sentiment which Raleigh might have held, which Cartwright would have expressed. It was the thought for which Weever was then struggling in his 'Poetical Life of Sir John Oldcastle;' for which James, the friend of Jonson, if not of Shakspeare, was compiling his 'Defence of the noble knight and martyr, Sir John Oldcastle.'

The occurrence of such a proclamation suggests that, between the first production of 'Henry the Fourth' and the date of his printed quarto, Shakspeare changed his way of looking at the old heroes of English thought.

In the year 1600, a play was printed in London with the title, 'The First Part of the True and Honourable History of the Life of Sir John Oldcastle, the Good Lord Cobham.' The title-page bore Shakspeare's name. 'Sir John Oldcastle' is now regarded by every one as a play from other pens; in fact, it is known to have been written by three of Shakspeare's fellow-playwrights; but many good critics think the poet may have written some of the lines and edited the work. This drama was a protest against the wrong which had been done to Oldcastle on the stage by Shakspeare. The prologue said:—

'It is no pampered glutton we present,
Nor aged councillor to youthful sin;
But one whose virtue shone above the rest,
A valiant martyr and a virtuous peer.'

These lines are thought to be Shakspeare's own. They are in his vein, and they repeat the declaration which he had already made.

OLDCASTLE DIED A MARTYR!

The man who wrote that confession in the days of Archbishop Whitgift was a Puritan in faith.

CHAPTER XI.

KING AND CARDINAL.

WHEN the Wars of the Roses came to an end, the royal stronghold ceased to be a general prison, and opened its gates to few save men of the highest class. Down to the Tudor times, offenders of rank had been lodged in the Banqueting hall, while those of inferior state had been flung into Little Ease. But poetry and art were touching men's souls into softness, and a rival in politics was no longer regarded as a wretch unworthy to live in the light of heaven.

Under the Belfry, in the south-west corner of the royal ward, King Henry the Eighth built a Lieutenant's house; a house of many chambers; opening into the lower and upper rooms of the Belfry; and having a free passage, on one side into the Garden, on the other side into the Beauchamp tower. This house was flanked by two smaller buildings; warders' houses, one under the west wall, another under the south wall. The latter, standing in the Lieutenant's garden, was called the Garden house. None of these places were built as prisons; and none were used as such under Henry the Eighth, except the Belfry and the Beauchamp tower.

A bare stone vault, pierced for archers and balisters, who from this high post could sweep the outer works with shaft and bolt: such is that upper chamber of the Belfry, which is known in old records as the Strong Room.

Two points about this room, beyond the fact of its amazing strength, soon catch the eye. In the first place, it has no stairs; no entrance from below; no passage into the outer world, except through the Lieutenant's house; in the second place, it is provided with a private closet, called in old English a 'homely place.'

The man who made the Strong Room famous, not by his age, his eminence, and his sufferings only, but by his gaiety, his humour, and his stoutness of spirit, was John Fisher, Bishop of Rochester, Cardinal in Rome.

Cardinal Fisher's story takes one back to an age when England was becoming what Spain has always been,—a country governed in a high degree, not by the nobler spirits of her church, but by ignorant monks and superstitious nuns. The offence by which Fisher fell was the half smiling, half earnest siding which he took with Elizabeth Barton, the Maid of Kent; a crazy young girl, subject to fits and ravings, who lifted up her voice against the divorce of

Catharine and the marriage of Queen Anne. The Maid sent her prophecies to both Wolsey and the King. Henry was only moved to mirth. 'Why,' said he, in effect, to Cromwell, 'these are rhymes, and very bad rhymes; this is no angel's work; but such as a silly woman might do of her own poor wit.' Afterwards he read her rhymes in a darker spirit; but this change of humour was wrought in his mind by the Maid herself.

The Spanish party in the Church, prone to accept irregular aid from heaven, soon saw the use which might be made of this crazy girl. Placing her in a convent, they gave her five monks of Christ Church, of whom Father Bocking was the chief, to be her guides and secretaries. Under their eyes, the Nun made startling progress in divine lore; speaking words which priests and prelates who wished them to be true, received with a thankful heart. Wolsey was puzzled by the Maid; but Wolsey was then trying to play two games. Fisher wept with joy; but Fisher agreed with what Father Bocking was making his Nun put forth. Many of her sayings were dark enough; but when need arose for plainness, she could be curt as a Hebrew seer. She declared that Heaven was against the divorce. She called on the King to abandon his great design. She admonished him, as he loved his soul, to put Anne away and take Catharine back. These words from the Maid of Kent were scattered through the land; copies being sent from Christ Church through the province of Canterbury, and the mendicant friars employed to report them in every village ale-house, and in every convent-yard from the Medway to the Tweed.

One day, under Father Bocking's lead, the poor Nun overshot her mark, and brought down ruin on her master and herself. In true Spanish style, she sent a message to the King, not only denouncing his divorce, but declaring that if he put Catharine away, he would die in seven months, when his daughter Mary, though degraded to the rank of bastard, would ascend his throne.

Such a threat was no theme for mirth. Henry swept the whole brood of darkness—Nun, priest, friar, doctor—into the Tower, on their way to Tyburn. The poor girl confessed with her last breath that she was a simple woman, who had only done what the fathers told her to do for the love of God and the service of Holy Church.

A room over Cold-harbour gateway, in which the poor Maid was lodged, was for many years known as the Nun's bower.

Fisher, it is not denied, played fast and loose with the Maid of Kent; as in our own day we have seen great prelates coquet with nuns, apparently not more worthy of their trust. He hoped that good would come of her delusions; most of all, he fancied that the King, having waited six long years for Anne, might be frightened into waiting a few years more, after which it would be easier for him to change his mind. In some such hope the prelate took the Maid's part, encouraging her visions, stirring up public curiosity about her, implying that her speeches came from God.

When charged with aiding and abetting treason, he replied that he had given his ear to the impostor only on fair grounds, seeing cause for the favour he had shown to her in facts which had come to him on good report. With biting malice, Cromwell told him that the outward facts had not weighed with him one jot. 'My lord,' said Cromwell, not in these words, but to this purport, 'you liked the stuff she uttered, and you pretended to believe it true because you wished it true.'

Of the treason of Father Bocking and the Holy Maid, no man can feel a doubt; for theirs was a simple act; imagining and compassing the King's death in a way which brought them under judgment of the law. Fisher's crime was far less clear; and many men regard him, not without grounds, as having been made a martyr to his faith. The Cardinal's hat took off the Bishop's head.

Cardinal Fisher, eighty years old, was seized as a plotter, tried for his offence, thrust into a barge, and pulled down the Thames. When his boat slipped under the archway of the Water-gate, he toddled on shore, and turning to the crowd of guards and oarsmen about him, said, 'As they have left me nothing else to give you, I bestow on you my hearty thanks.' Some of the rough fellows smiled, though they must have felt that hearty thanks from a good old man who was about to die could do them no harm. Lodged in the Strong Room, he suffered much from chill and damp. The Belfry not only stood above the ditch, but lay open to the east wind and to the river fog. Fisher told Cromwell, in piteous letters, that he was left without clothing to keep his body warm. Yet the fine old prelate never lost either his stoutness of heart or his quick sense of humour. One day, when it was bruited about the Tower that he was to suffer death, his cook brought up no dinner to the Strong Room. 'How is this?' asked the prelate, when he saw the man.—'Sir,' said the cook, 'it was commonly talked of in the town that you should die, and therefore I thought it vain to dress anything for you.'—'Well, said the bishop, 'for all that report thou seest me still alive; therefore, whatever news thou shalt hear of me, make ready my dinner, and if thou see me dead when thou comest, eat it thyself.'

Henry and Cromwell would have spared his life, had they seen their way. But Fisher would not help them; neither would his friends help them. First and last, he was a member of the Italian Church, and no thought for his country could for one moment move him to desert the cause of that Church. Even while he was lying in the Strong Room of the Belfry he sent secret messages to the monks at Sion, hostile to Queen Anne. He kept up a warm correspondence with Rome, and Paul the Third chose that unhappy time to send him, against the express command of Henry, a cardinal's hat. On hearing of this hat being on the way from Rome, the King exclaimed, 'Fore God, then, he shall wear it on his shoulders.'

The death-warrant reached the Tower at midnight, and the Lieutenant, Sir Edmund Walsingham, went into the Belfry at five o'clock, to let the Cardinal know his fate. 'You bring me no great news,' said Fisher; 'I have long looked for this message. At what hour must I die?'—'At nine,' said Walsingham.—'And what is the hour now?' —'Five,' answered the Lieutenant. It was June, and of course broad daylight, even in the Strong Room, at five o'clock.—'Well, then, by your patience, let me sleep an hour or two; for I have slept very little. Walsingham left the Cardinal, who slept until seven, when he rose and put on his finest suit. On his servant wondering why he dressed so bravely, the old man answered, 'Dost thou not mark, man, that this is our marriage day?'

Taking a New Testament in his hands, he walked from the Strong Room, through Walsingham's house and the Bye-ward gate to Tower Hill; a vast crowd pressing round him, some of whom could see his lips moving in prayer, and hear the words issuing from his mouth. As he gazed on the closed Gospel in his hand, he prayed the Lord that he might find in it some special strength in that mortal hour; and as he prayed for this strength, he paused in his walk, opened the sacred volume, and read the passage on which his eye first fell—'This is life eternal, to know Thee, the only true God, and Jesus Christ whom Thou hast sent.'

Comforted by these words, he went lightly on, mounting up the steep hill, repeating, 'This is life eternal,' until he came to the scaffold, where he spoke a few words to the people, and laid his white head upon the block.

CHAPTER XII.

THE PILGRIMAGE OF GRACE.

In the hot war which the new learning had to wage against the ancient Church—a war of life and death—a war which, under new names, and with a new line of battle, carried forward the great feud of the Red Rose against the White, the Beauchamp tower was choked for many reigns with those who on either side went down in that pitiless fight.

Some of these men wrote records of their passage on these walls; not men of the first rank always; not the prime leaders in bloody fields, but mostly their companions in defeat—men who in happier days would have pricked their names into the stones of the Colosseum and the Great Pyramid. Much true history is graven on these walls; for even though the tablets may have been wrought by men of the second rank, the chiefs, no doubt, stood by while the artists toiled. The inner eye may catch in yon deep recess by the window-sill the figure of some spent hero, scarred from either Flodden Field or Nevill's Cross, standing apart from his fellows, dumb with pride, and gazing with scorn and pity on such work.

One of the early groups contains the names of three men who fell into trouble through that wild passage in our contest with the Italian Church called the Pilgrimage of Grace.

Cut into the wall as with a sword we read:

SARO: FIDELI:
INGGRAM PERCY
1537.

The author of this record was Sir Ingram Percy, third son of Algernon, fifth Earl of Northumberland; a younger brother of Henry the Unthrifty, once a lover of Anne Boleyn; and of Sir Thomas Percy, the dashing knight who bore the banner of St. Cuthbert on the Don.

Also cut into the wall we read:

WILLIAM BELMALAR

And in another place:

RAVLEF BULMAR
1537.

Sir William and Sir Ralph Bulmer (the name was spelt in a dozen ways) were border chiefs. The head of their house was that stout Sir William, a cousin to Lord Dacre of the North, who had served on the Duke of Richmond's council, and held the Lord Warden's commission as Lieutenant of the Eastern March. Stout Sir William Bulmer had two sons, John and William; men who followed the profession of arms, as that profession was understood in the border lands. The old knight had given his boys a start in life by getting them knighted, and put in a way to earn their bread. Sir John, the elder, had been sent to the Irish Pale; Sir William, the younger, had got the command of Norham Castle, a fortress on the great north road. The King's favour had descended to the son and to the son's son. Sir Ralph, a son of Sir John, was made an officer on the border, with a company of fifty mounted men.

Elsewhere on the wall we read:

ADAM : SEDBAR
ABBAS : JOREVALL
1537.

Adam Sedburgh was the last reigning Abbot of the great Yorkshire Monastery of Jervaulx (pronounced Gerviss) in the north riding; a monastery which was famous for its beauty even in the shire of Bolton and Fountains, and which is still gratefully remembered in the county for having beaten the whole world in two great Yorkshire arts—the breeding of horses and the making of cheese.

These men bore a part in the Pilgrimage of Grace. The names of Robert Aske, Lord Darcy, and Sir Robert Constable, are not found on these walls; neither are those of William Thirske, Abbot of Fountains, Sir Thomas Percy, Sir John Bulmer, and Madge Cheyne, the wild fanatic who is sometimes described as Sir John's paramour, sometimes as his wife. All these personages were brought into the Tower; but they passed through it and left no sign.

The Pilgrimage of Grace was a rising in the rude northern shires against the reforming King, Council, and House of Commons, in favour of the Spanish princess and the Roman Church; a movement set on foot by idle speeches from Lord Darcy of Darcy, Lord Dacre of the North, and other great barons; but which passed out of their cautious hands into those of ignorant clods, and hardly less ignorant country squires; men who stood by their priests and friars, and who, had their strength been equal to their will, would have thrown down their country at the feet of Spain.

The divorce of Queen Catharine and the bull of Paul the Third had produced among the lower ranks in these northern shires a ferment for which the men of Kent and Essex were unprepared. In the home counties, opinion was with the King. In London, and in all the provinces lying near

London, the creed and the cause of Spain had fallen at a word—had fallen at once, and for ever; the decrees which were to frame a true English order in the family and in the church, having been issued by the commons long before they were put into legal phrase by Parliament and King. Not so in the north. The partition of England into two church provinces was in the reign of Henry the Eighth, but echo to an actual fact. The Trent was like the Tweed; a border line between counties jealous of each other; counties apt to fall out, and when they fell out, to fight. The two provinces had a different custom, in some things a different law. York was a great capital; Yorkshiremen spoke with contempt of the city on the Thames; and most men living beyond the Trent thought shame of the King for not holding his Court and Parliament in York. Yet, in every point of culture and civility, the northern shires were a century behind those of the south and west. All that made England great, all that was helping to make her free, was found in that reign, not on the Humber and the Tyne, but on the Severn and the Thames. The thinkers who were moulding her mind, the poets who were fixing her speech, the politicians who were shaping her laws, were men of the southern race. Below the Trent, the peasant was better clothed, the gentleman was better served, the parson was better read, than their fellows above that stream; and any fight for sway between north and south was in fact a conflict of the brooding darkness against the growing light.

Those silent changes in the state of public thought which made the first great acts of the reforming council—the defiance of Spain and Rome, the establishment of an English church, the suppression of monks and friars,—so welcome in the south, had no true counterpart in the shires beyond the Trent. In those counties there was hardly any public thought to change. In Yorkshire and Northumberland, men saw few travellers and read no books. They roamed through their native dales, they tented on their native wolds, from youth to age; loud of oath, and fierce in fight; proud of their dogs, their horses, and their wives; ready for either a bout of sticks or a bout of ale; but chained to one place, at feud with the world, dependent on the wandering friars, with never a thought in their great strong heads. Coarse in manner and rude in speech, they were not so shocked as southerners by the immoralities of their spiritual guides. They owed a good deal to monks, and they had much to learn from priests. In an age when few men could read and cypher, it was a benefit to the grazier to have a learned man call at his house, who could cast up his tallies and see that he got his own. The friars who dwelt in these dales were perhaps of better and stouter stuff. Certainly the cloisters of Jervaulx had no such evil reputation as the cloisters of St. Augustine. When a Yorkshire man mentioned Jervaulx, he spoke proudly of the fine horses and the good cheese to be found in that abbey. When a Kentish man mentioned St. Augustine's, he spoke bitterly of the insolent Abbot and his dissolute monks. While the laity of Kent were rejoicing over the ruin of St. Augustine's, the friars of Jervaulx were regarded by the laity of York as the peasant's best friends.

Hence, when Darcy of Darcy, and Dacre of the North, gave tongue on the changes being made in London, the common folk took up the tale with a clatter of hoofs and pikes which echoed through the land.

Some old political feeling mingled with the fray. York was still sore on account of Bosworth Field. In the last struggle of the Red and the White Roses, she had gone down in her armour, while the victors on that field had been her masters ever since. She burned to avenge that shame. King Henry, it is true, united in his person the claims of both Lancaster and York; and but for his change of belief and the bull of Pope Paul, no man, however hot for blows, would have dreamed of questioning his right to reign. But he was quarrelling with their lord the Pope. He was tampering with their ancient laws. He was separating them from the universal Church. Under such conditions, it was right to tell him, in no doubtful terms, that his safety lay in harking back, in taking his old wife, in keeping to the ancient lines. If he refused good counsel, the heavens might fall upon his head and leave them free. Should he fight and fail, the settlement made after Bosworth Field could be reversed. Then a Lancastrian prince had taken a White Rose to wife; now a Yorkist prince might marry a Red one. A prince of the line of Edward the Fourth would not be far to seek. There was Courtney, there was Pole; either of whom, by marrying Queen Catharine's daughter, the Princess Mary, would unite the rival houses in a second bond. With either of these princes on the throne, Yorkshire would be satisfied, and religion would be saved.

When the royal decree for putting down monastic houses reached Yorkshire, mobs rose upon the King's commissioners; hooting them from the towns, tearing up their proclamations, and in more than one town clubbing them to death. In place of standing by the law, the gentry looked on in silence. Show of authority was gone. The magistrates fled; the citizens snatched up pike and bill; and the barons, whose foolish clatter had roused this storm, retired to their fortified houses, on pretence of guarding those strongholds for the King. Northumberland lay at Wressil, Darcy at Pomfret. All the border was in uproar, and no man knew what he ought to do. Then, the monks came out and made their game. Fathers sallied forth from the abbeys of Fountains, Jervaulx, Hexham, and Lannercost, calling on the people to rise up in defence of the King and Holy Church. They laid the blame of all evil at Cromwell's door. Cromwell, they said, was putting down convent and abbey in order that he might levy a tax for the King on marriages, births, and deaths. Cromwell was a devil, and the first demand of the saints must be Cromwell's head. This rising must be a Pilgrimage of Grace. The stout Yorkshire lads must march on London; deliver their king from his evil councillors; restore Queen Catharine to his bed and board; hang Cromwell like a dog; revive the religious houses; and see that their father the Pope got his own again. These friars supported their appeals with prophetic tales. The Prior of Maldon told the story of an ancient man, who had said the Church would suffer dole for three years and then flourish as before; also of another ancient man, who had said the King would be forced to fly from his realm, and on coming back from beyond sea would be glad to reign over two-thirds of his former land.

These dreamers were going back to the Heptarchy; and thinking of a new Catholic kingdom on the north of Trent.

The friars prepared an oath, which they put to every man they met; a pledge to stand by the King and Holy Church. Vast crowds were taking up the cross, and sticking on their breasts the pilgrim's sign; a scroll displaying the five wounds of Christ. But as yet the Catholic host was without a general; the great barons would not descend from their castles into the streets; and the mob, after yelling through twenty courtyards 'A chief! a chief!' began to seize on leaders by force and chance. These louts believed that if they could catch a man and put him to the oath, he would become their own for weal and woe;

bound by a compact from which he could never break. More than once, it was proposed in their camp to make a dash into Norfolk, carry off the Duke, Anne Boleyn's uncle, and put him to the oath.

One Robert Aske, a gentleman of middle age, was riding home to London from a hunting-party at his cousin Ellerkar's place in Yorkshire, when he was seized by a band of pilgrims near Appleby, put to the oath, and saluted Captain of the host! The choice seemed droll enough. Aske was a London lawyer, who knew nothing about war, and had never seen a camp. Yet here he was, on a Yorkshire wold, with a general's staff, in the midst of a swarm of men; some of them mounted, most of them armed, all of them hot with passion; clamouring to be led on London in defence of the King and Holy Church.

Aske, thus suddenly armed with power for either good or evil, looked around him. A man of the north, he felt with the louts and churls who had thrust the sword into his hand; but he knew, as a northern man, that for any any rising of these commons to have a chance, it must be led by the ancient lords of the soil; by the Percies of Alnwick, by the Darcys of Darcy; not by an unknown commoner like himself. These captains he made up his mind to seek. New men were coming daily into camp; Bulmers, Danbys, Tempests, Moncktons, Gowers; and the great barons, even those who held the King's commission, were supposed to share in the general hope. Why was not Percy in the camp?

Henry Percy, sixth Earl of Northumberland, was the man of highest rank and power then living beyond the Trent. In the antiquity of his line, in the fame of his fathers, in the extent of his possessions, he stood without a rival. Lord of Alnwick, Wressil, Leckinfield, and other strong places, he kept the state and exercised the power of a prince; having his privy council, his lords and grooms of the chamber, his chamberlains, treasurers, purse-bearers, some of which offices were hereditary in gentle houses; together with his dean of the chapel, his singers, his scribes, and no less than ten officiating priests. He was the King's deputy in the north; Warden of the East March and the Middle March; the fountain of all authority in the border lands. If any man could be made a prince of a new kingdom of the north, Percy was that man.

Like his neighbours, Percy had been slow to follow the great changes then going on in London. As yet, the names of Catholic and Protestant had not been heard in Yorkshire. Those who were now in arms for the King and Holy Church had risen in favour of old ways and old things; in favour of Queen Catharine, of monks and friars, of religious houses; points on which the Earl took much the same view as his tenants and friends. But Henry was unthrifty; a weak and ailing man, who had never got over his love for Anne Boleyn; and who was mourning in his great house at Wressil, on the Derwent, her starless fate. When Aske and a body of riders dashed into the courtyard of Wressil, shouting 'A Percy, a Percy!' the King's Warden of the Marches slipped into bed, and sent out word that he was sick. The Pilgrims would not take this answer. They wanted a Percy in their camp; Earl Henry if it might be; so that folk could say they were marching under the King's flag, with law and justice on their side. Aske sent fresh messages into the sick room; either the Earl or his brothers, Sir Thomas and Sir Ingram, he said, must join the camp. Now these young knights were only too quick to obey his call. Henry made a feeble protest; and after they were gone, he revoked the commissions which they held under him as officers in the East and Middle Marches. Catharine, their mother, widow of the fifth

Earl, detained them with tears over what she felt would be their doom. She came of a house which had known the Tower and the block too well; her uncle being that Duke of Somerset who was executed by Edward the Fourth; her great-grandsire, that Earl of Warwick who had given his name to Beauchamp tower; but her sons, though they paused for a moment at her warning cries, soon leapt to horse, and, clad in flashing steel and flaunting plume, rode forward into camp, where the Pilgrims received them with uproarious joy. That shining steel and that dazzling plume were afterwards cited as evidence that they had joined the Pilgrims by deliberate choice; and his fine attire caused one of the brothers to lose his head.

Some thirty thousand Pilgrims of Grace began their march towards London, where they meant to hang Lord Cromwell, and give the Pope his own. York, after short parley with the Captain, opened her gates. On entering the chief northern stronghold, Aske, now master of the country beyond Humber, announced that all monks and nuns who had been driven from their houses should be restored, and that the King's tenants, to whom abbey lands and buildings had been let, should be expelled. Few of the King's tenants waited for his bands to oust them; but leaving, for a time, the fields which they had ploughed, and the granaries which they had stored, they fled for safety beyond the Trent. Aske advanced on Pomfret Castle, the surrender of which by Lord Darcy gave him the command of Barnsdale up to the gates of Doncaster. Darcy, captured at Pomfret, was put to the oath, and hailed a leader; as were also Sir Thomas Percy, Sir Ingram Percy, Sir John Bulmer, and many more; though the rank of Captain still remained with Aske.

At Doncaster bridge the Pilgrims came to a halt; the Duke of Norfolk, a great soldier and an able councillor, the hero of Flodden Field and Wissant Bay, having been sent up north by the King, to seize and hold that passage of the Don. Aske was extremely strong in horse. Sir Thomas Percy, glittering in steel, and bearing St. Cuthbert's banner, was followed by five thousand mounted men. The borders sent as many more. In all, twelve thousand horsemen waited the signal to advance. The Duke, though his force was weaker in numbers, kept a firm front to the north; waiting for his reserves to come in; negotiating with the chiefs; sending heralds through the towns; tempting Darcy to his side; and operating everywhere for time.

Before his reserves had come up, the campaign was over. The Duke had beaten the lawyer in a game of words, ending in a treaty of peace, which the two parties were left free to understand in a different sense.

The Captain thought he had gained his point; the Duke felt sure that *he* had gained *his* point. In the meantime, the northern men, on laying down their arms, received a king's pardon, and rode off to their several homes. In a few days, the rebels were scattered to the four winds, never to meet again in strength; while the King's forces kept the field, as lawful guardians of the public peace. The Yorkshiremen fancied the King had agreed to govern in the old spirit; to hold a Parliament in York; to receive complaints from his disloyal subjects; to restore the religious houses; to put away Cromwell; and to give back all that he had taken from the Pope.

Thus ended, in delusion and doubt, the Pilgrimage of Grace. The ruin caused by that rising in the north was yet to come.

CHAPTER XIII.

MADGE CHEYNE.

When the three Bulmer knights, Sir John, Sir William, and Sir Ralph, rode into the Pilgrim camp, they brought with them a wild creature, who was sometimes called the wife, oftentimes called the paramour, of Sir John. Her name was Margaret Cheyne, bnt in the rough border speech she was only known as Madge. She talked of herself as Lady Bulmer, and in loose border fashion she may have gone through some rite which made her believe she was a lawful spouse. But in the legal process taken against her afterwards in London, she was described with the coarse accuracy of an indictment as Margaret Cheyne; all claim to the rank of Lady Bulmer being set aside. Sir John had a second wife, either living or dead, in Ann Bigod of Musgrove, who was the mother of his son Sir Ralph.

In those times, the border laws as to man and wife were vague and feeble; good enough for trolls and callants; not of much force when applied to women of spirit and men of wit. Madge was a woman of very high spirit; and Sir John, though he could not be called a man of wit, was one who lived by that coarse substitute for wit—his sword. Neither of the twain could boast a very clean record in the past. Mad blood ran through the lady's veins. She was a love-child of that Edward, Duke of Buckingham, who had left the Tower as Lord High Constable of England, to come back poor Edward Stafford. Sir John had not only missed his chance of fame, but covered himself with the obloquy which a soldier would rather die than bear. Lord Surrey, the Lord Lieutenant, had broken him and dispersed his troop. Coming back to his eyrie in the Cleveland hills, a place on the slope of Eston Nab, called Wilton Castle, remote from roads and men, and suiting, in its savage beauty of marsh and fell, the soreness of his spirit, the border knight was still further tried by the loss of his old and profitable command on the Tweed.

But the news which year by year came down from London to Sir John and his partner Madge, news brought into the Yorkshire dales by wandering friars, were not of a kind to vex his soul; for they told him of things being wrong at court, of doubt and strife in the council, of messages going and coming between King and Pope, of prophecies uttered by the Maid of Kent; and all these signs of trouble in the south had given promise of employment to the border-man. William, third Lord Dacre of the North, his cousin, was sore in spirit like himself, owing the court a grudge, not only on religious, but on personal grounds. From Lord Dacre, Sir John took up the tale of sedition, and when the Pilgrimage of Grace began, he was one of the first gentlemen in the dales to march. But hate had more to do with his resolve than love; for the Duke, who was coming up north against the Pilgrims, was the very man who had broken him as a soldier and branded him as a coward. Eager to break a lance with Norfolk, Bulmer rode into camp, attended by his son, his brother, and his faithful Madge.

Now Madge, who was a devout woman, if not an honest wife, brought with her into the Pilgrim camp not only her high blood and her bickering tongue, but Father Stanhouse, her family priest. Madge, like Sir John, had her grudge against the Duke. Norfolk was her kinsman; she said her brother-in-law, since he was married to her sister, the Lady Elizabeth Stafford; and many others besides Madge

Cheyne thought he might have done more to save the Duke, her father, from Wolsey's malice. Madge thought herself equal to her enemy, since her father was a duke, like Norfolk, and her father's daughter was Norfolk's wife. All that lay between them was, in her opinion, a phrase, and a ring. But the day was now come for vengeance. Many other females put on the pilgrim's badge, but no woman in the crowd disputed the foremost place assumed by Madge. The woman was equal to all demands upon her. If any hard thing was to be said, she was prompt with the cruel word. If any bad deed was to be suggested, she was quick with the fatal hint. She roamed through the Pilgrim camp, crying out for blood. She wanted Cromwell's blood. She wanted Norfolk's blood. At first, the death of these two noblemen would have slaked her thirst; but as days went on and difficulties rose in her path, she cried out for other and humbler blood.

When the Pilgrims went home from Doncaster, and the leaders were invited to lay their complaints before the King, Madge spurned the offer, preferring the solitudes of Eston Nab before the gaieties of a faithless court. Aske rode up to London, where he saw the King, and almost fell a victim to his courtly grace. Sir John sent up his son, Sir Ralph, to feel the ground, meaning to join him in London if all seemed well at court. But Madge would neither go nor allow Sir John to go. 'Ride to London!' she exclaimed; 'she would never ride to London until Cromwell and the Duke were hung.' At Wilton Castle she had her confessor, Father Stanhouse, a man of like grit with herself; a wild and passionate fellow, who tramped through the dales and towns, taunting the gentry with the shame of living as pardoned rebels, telling them that Norfolk was now master of every man's land and life, calling upon them to stand by the Spanish princess and by Holy Church.

Father Stanhouse was only one of many priests who raised their parable against what they called the deception of Doncaster. From Fountains, Jervaulx, and Hexham, bands of friars came forth; men who had been turned out of their stalls; and these men spread themselves through the country, preaching against Cromwell and Norfolk; whispering in too willing ears that the pardon was a snare, that the King was forsworn, that no parliament would be held in York, that no petition from the Commons would be received, that the whole north would be lost when the King had thrown his garrisons into Newcastle, Scarborough, and Hull, towns on the coast which could be victualled and supported from the sea. Under such preachers of sedition the dalesmen were prepared for some new Pilgrimage of Grace.

The new movement preached by these monks was to differ from the first in this grand point—it was to be a movement of the Commons. The knights and squires had played their game; they had been beaten and must stand aside. Some voices called them traitors; others branded them as cowards. What was the upshot of their parley with the Duke? A pardon, which was not a pardon, but a sentence. Nothing had been gained. The Pilgrims had been checked at the bridge only because Darcy was afraid to march, and Aske was ignorant of war. That day was lost; but the north was still strong in numbers and stout in faith. Of the sixty thousand brave lads who had sworn the Pilgrim's oath, not a hundred had gone over to the King. All that was now wanting to success was a movement of the Commons.

Adam Sedburgh, Abbot of Jervaulx, and William Thirske, Abbot of Fountains, lent the weight of their names and offices to these appeals.

Hardly less ominous than the tone adopted by the Commons and the friars was the attitude taken by the defeated gentry. Knight and squire, after marching proudly to the Don, could not be made to see that the treaty had left them in the position of pardoned rebels; of men who had forfeited their ancient standing and their ancient rights. They found their neighbours in no easy mood; and many a squire who had been hard and high in his former state was taught to feel how weak even rich and big men may become when they cease to have law and power upon their side.

No two gentlemen north of the Trent had more rebuffs to bear than Sir Thomas and Sir Ingram Percy. When they set out on the Pilgrimage of Grace, Earl Henry, their brother, as Warden of the East and Middle Marches, had recalled their commissions of lieutenancy in the border lands, giving them to Robert Lord Ogle, and Sir Raynold Carnaby, gentlemen of the county who stood well affected to the King. Ogle, a kinsman of the Earl, was made his lieutenant in the Eastern March; Carnaby, a gentleman of his bedchamber, was made his lieutenant in the Middle March. But this transfer of the border power was one of those changes which Sir Thomas and Sir Ingram could not accept. When the conference on the bridge broke up, Sir Thomas rode back to his house at Pridhow, and called to his side the men of Hexham and Tynedale; while Sir Ingram rode to Alnwick Castle, whence he summoned the local gentry to meet him at Rothbury. To these acts of the pardoned rebels, Lord Ogle and Sir Raymond Carnaby objected in their capacity of lieutenants to the King's warden, whose commission they held; on which Sir Thomas and Sir Ingram Percy railed in all places against these officers—most of all against Sir Raynold, whom they treated as a mere lacquey in their brother's house. Sir Thomas sent a gang of dalesmen into Sir Raynold's lands—fellows who laid waste his farms, entered his house, and stole his plate.

At the same time, in defiance of the border lieutenants, Sir Ingram Percy began swearing the gentry of Alnwick and Rothbury to stand by each other, shoulder to shoulder, for the honour of God and the good of Holy Church.

Poor folk were at their wits' end. No man could tell on which side lay the law; for, while Carnaby asserted in a meek voice that *he*, lieutenant of the Middle March, was the only man to speak in the King's name, Sir Thomas Percy declared that *he*, and he only, was the warden's true representative in those parts. The loud voice and the haughty bearing won the day. Most men believed Sir Thomas must be right; and Carnaby, who could do nothing save complain to the sick warden, had to hide himself in Chillingham Castle from the attacks of his turbulent foe.

Men were in these cross humours when news came down from Sir Ralph Bulmer, warning his father to look well to himself, as things were going all wrong at Court. Madge leapt to her feet. 'If only one man will stir,' she screamed, 'the whole country will be up.' Father Stanhouse supported her. 'Now,' cried the priest, 'is the time to rise—now or never.'

Norfolk was on his way to the north; some said with a great army to waste the land; others said with a free pardon in his pocket, and the writs for a new Parliament to be held in York. Which was the true report? Abbot Adam, of Jervaulx, sent his man Simon Jaxon, into Lincolnshire, on pretence of collecting rents from the abbey farms; but with instructions to observe the state of things; to see whether men were standing for king or pope; to lie about Newark until the Duke should come; and then bring news of the King's army, whether his company was large or small.

Lord Ogle, as lieutenant of the East March, called a court of the border, by proclamation, at Morpeth; but Ogle proved to be as feeble in presence of these rough Percies as poor Carnaby himself. Sir Thomas sent forth a counter-proclamation, declaring that Lord Ogle had no right to hold a border court, and calling on his friends and tenants to meet him in Morpeth and resist the attempt by force. Sir Ingram put himself in harness; called on his men, and rode from Alnwick Castle into Morpeth on the appointed day. Ogle now fell back—afraid, as he said, in excuse, of blood being shed, until the King should send him his orders what to do. Sir Ingram had some show of the law on his side, which his brother Sir Thomas had not; a lucky fact for him when the transactions in which they were now engaged came under the eyes of twelve impartial men. Sir Ingram had persuaded the Abbot of Alnwick, a man devoted to his Church, to ride over to Wressil, in Yorkshire, and get from the sick Earl a commission for Ingram to act as a deputy warden in the eastern March. The Abbot rode to Wressil and saw the Earl, to whom he told a lying story of Sir Ingram being now a true liegeman to the King; one who could do his grace high service in the unsettled borders, if he could only have a writing to that effect under his brother's hand. Henry, who heard this tale with pleasure, gave the Abbot such papers as he desired, naming his brother deputy and sheriff; though he made it a condition that Sir Ingram should serve for that year without pay, since the King had been already put to the full amount of his border charge.

Sir Ingram sent no answer as to whether he would act or not; but he kept the papers, which bore the warden's signature and seal, in order that he might silence any man who should challenge him for preventing Lord Ogle's court.

When news was brought from Newark by Simon Jaxon that Norfolk was coming with a strong army, the whole border began to throb with life; church-bells were rung, and a fire was lighted on Eston Nab. Some rioters seized on Beverley, a town in which the Percy tenantry were strong. Sir Francis Bigod raised the banner of Holy Church. 'Now is the time,' cried Madge to her sluggish lover; 'now is the time; Bigod is in the field; up, up and join them.' Bigod was the brother of Bulmer's wife. But the country was too much cowed for this revolt to grow, and an attempt which was made on Hull not only failed, but compromised Aske. The spirit of the first Pilgrimage could not be revived; for no one could now be deceived by the cry of King and Holy Church; and every man who took up arms was well aware that he was putting a halter round his neck.

Henry the Unthrifty rose from his sick bed and went to York, hoping to save his brothers and to serve his King. There Sir Ingram joined him, in the mad belief that the dying man could be persuaded to throw in his lot with the commons who were dreaming of a second Pilgrimage of Grace. Henry was sad and stern; Ingram hot and silly. 'Cromwell,' cried the young knight, 'should be hanged as high as men could see;' and when his brother turned on him in pity, the madman added, 'Yes; and be I present, as I wish to God I may be, I will thrust my sword into his belly.'

The Earl, too weak to arrest his brother on the spot, as he should have done, if only to keep him out of harm, revoked the warrant which he had given him as deputy and sheriff, so that Ingram had no longer a shadow of authority for what he was about to do. But the withdrawal of his warrant was not yet known beyond the gates of York, and he made it his first affair to prevent the news from going north. Of course, his brother would write to Lord Ogle and his other deputies; and he laid a plan for intercepting his brother's letters. Some of his men were planted in the king's highway, along which the messenger would have to ride; and when the carrier came up they seized his bridle, tumbled him from his seat, rifled his sack, and opened the letters which they found. It was a dáring crime, for the warden was the king's deputy, and his servant, travelling on public duty, was regarded by the law as the king's own man. To stop him by force, and break open his sealed despatches, was an offence for which the penalty was death. The criminals were baffled. Either the man had no letters for Lord Ogle, or he suspected foul play, and put them out of sight.

Much of the border was now up; the oath was again put to men at the sword-point; and every one who refused to swear it had to fly into some place of safety until calmer times. Carnaby and his friends shut themselves up in Chillingham Castle; a very strong place on the Till, which Sir Ingram tried to reduce, but with no success for the want of heavy guns. These guns he made an effort to obtain from the King's magazine of arms in Berwick; by representing that he held a legal commission, and needed artillery for the King's service. The falsehood of his assertions was found out in time.

Sir John Bulmer was not the last to declare himself, though his slowness to appear in the field drove Madge to despair. He wished to see the Commons out in force. 'If the Commons will not rise,' cried Madge, 'let us begone; let us flee away into another land.' Sir John took counsel with his priests. The clergy who heard the confessions of their flocks must surely know the state of men's minds; and the cause being that of Holy Church, he had some right to know, from those who held all such secrets in their keeping, what the churls would do. So he sent Stanhouse to Father Frank, a popular priest, and Robert Hugill to the Vicar of Kirkby, to ask whether the dalesmen would rise against the King or no. 'If they will not rise,' said Madge, 'let us take ship for Scotland.'

When Norfolk crossed the Ouse, the commotion began to droop. One day after mass in the chapel of Alnwick Castle, Sir Ingram said to his brother: 'I am afraid the King and Commons will agree.' 'Nay,' replied Sir Thomas, 'that will not be so; for the Commons have promised me never to agree without my knowledge.' Ingram felt sore. 'Tut,' cried his elder, 'they will never agree, without a pardon for all offences done; therefore let us do what we think, and that whilst we may.' But their little hour was gone. While they were talking in the chapel, the officers of justice were on their track; not a pike was lifted by the Commons in their defence; and the splendid young knights were soon on their way to the Tower.

One wild scheme came into the crazy pates on Eston Nab. Sir John and Madge proposed to descend from their hold into the towns; to raise the men of Guisborough, among whom the monks had much sway; and try a dashing blow at the ducal camp. If they could seize the Duke, and carry him by force to Wilton Castle, they fancied that something good might come of such a deed. They could either sell him to the King, or send him to the devil. But while they were dreaming of this bold attempt the officers were at hand, and in a few hours Sir John and Madge were also marching south.

William Thirske and Adam Sedburgh, abbots of Fountains and Jervaulx, were also on the road.

The procession of Pilgrims was long and doleful; but the foremost offenders were only too soon at Tyburn tree.

Darcy, Aske, Bigod, Constable, were quickly put away. Sir Thomas Percy and Sir John Bulmer pleaded guilty. Madge did the same. They were all condemned to die; poor Madge by fire. The bill against Sir Ralph was dropped.

Adam, abbot of Jervaulx, pleaded not guilty. He had not willingly joined the rebels. He could not deny that he had fed them from the abbey larder, and that he had given them money; but the meat was given in charity, and the money for services in tending the abbey sheep. Neither could he deny being out with the Pilgrims; but he explained to his judges, that when the rebels knocked at the abbey gate and called upon him to come forth, he slipped away by a back door and hid himself for three days and nights in Witton fell; but being tracked by scouts, he was brought into the camp by force.

A jury brought him in guilty, and he was hung at Tyburn, in company with Sir Thomas Percy, Sir John Bulmer, and William Thirske.

Sir Ralph Bulmer was pardoned in the following year, and restored in blood by Edward the Sixth, when he went back to Eston Nab, a wiser and a poorer man.

Sir Ingram Percy, like Sir John Bulmer, had lived with a woman in the lawless border way. When he died, in the year of his pardon, he left a daughter by this paramour, for whom he made special provision in his will. Two centuries after they were dead and gone, the story of this lawless love, and this illegitimate child, came to occupy public attention for many years. Sir Ingram was the ancestor from whom Percy the Trunkmaker derived his claims.

Madge Cheyne met the most terrible fate of all. The wild daughter of Buckingham was sentenced to die by fire; and being carried in a cart to Smithfield, she was placed in the centre of a pile of faggots, and on the very spot where the Good Lord Cobham had been burnt, her passionate life was licked up by the flames.

CHAPTER XIV.

HEIRS TO THE CROWN.

Sixteen years after the Pilgrims of Grace had been hung and burnt alive for standing by the old faith, men and women were being hung at Tyburn and burnt at Smithfield for standing by the new. A queen had risen who could not walk in her father's way; she was a Spanish, not an English, queen; and the men who had done her father's will were now being paid for that service to her house with a pile of faggots and a length of rope.

A roll of drama now unfolds itself in the Good Lord Cobham's chamber; the romance of three Queens, the epoch of English thought; the opening scene of which drama was a contest for the crown.

On what may be called the opening day of this new reign, the Beauchamp tower and some adjoining rooms and vaults, never until that day used as prisons, received into their embrace a family group; for one of whom a fair and innocent girl, the world has never ceased to feel that sad and tender passion which a father nurses for the child whom he has loved and lost.

That family group consisted of John Dudley, the proud Duke of Northumberland, Lord President of the Council; John, Earl of Warwick, a youth of twenty-three; Lord Ambrose Dudley, a younger son; Lord Robert, a boy of twenty, but already the husband of Amy Robsart; Lord Guilford, and Lord Henry still in their teens; and that young wife of Guilford Dudley, who is known as the Nine Days' Queen. These noble folk were scattered through the Tower; Duke John in the Gate house, then called the Garden tower; Lord Ambrose and his youngest brother, Lord Henry, in the Nun's bower; Queen Jane in the deputy-lieutenant's house; Lord Robert in the lower tier; Lord Guilford in the middle tier of Beauchamp tower.

John, Earl of Warwick, a laborious carver, left the work of his knife in many places on these walls. Some of his pieces are light and jesting; all

'The sadder that they make us smile.'

On the north side of the chamber, just above the name of Adam Sedbar, abbot of Jervaulx, stand these four letters:

JANE.

On the same side of this room, but on the inner jamb of the recess, this name occurs a second time.

These things are not her doing. Lady Jane never lodged in this chamber; and after her nine days' reign was over, she never assumed the style of queen. They are the work of her partner in greatness—Lord Guilford; a youth who was always whining to be king.

From this family group of prisoners, two men and one woman were taken to the block; an old warrior, a young bridegroom, and a lovely bride. All three made a good end of life; though neither the stout soldier, nor the gallant youth, adorned the stake with so much patient beauty as that girl of seventeen summers, who had come to the end of her nine day's reign.

The crime which sent her to the block was her royal blood; and her story is a part of that great contention for the crown which brought so many princes of her family to the Tower.

When Edward the Sixth died, the keenest wit in England could not tell in whom the right to succeed him lay. Law was thought to be on one side, right on the other side. Parliament had been asked to settle, unsettle, and resettle the order in which the throne should go, so often, that every point of law and of fact had become confused, except that which seemed to lie in the power of nature and of habit. Every man said the sceptre *ought* to descend upon the true heir. But who was that true heir? Those who had the best claims by blood appeared to have very poor claims by law.

As King Edward left no issue, his crown fell back; first, upon his father's heirs; next, upon his grandfather's heirs; then upon the heirs of Edward the Fourth; afterwards, upon the heirs of George Plantagenet, Duke of Clarence; finally, upon the heirs general of Edward the Third. These lines were represented by claimants more or less able to make good their right.

The front rank consisted of not less than eight pretenders; all of whom were women? Of these eight women, not one had a clear title; two of them being aliens, while six were blemished in their birth. Here, then, was a situation for the opening drama; — eight females fighting for a crown which had never yet been worn on a female brow!

I. Princess Mary.

II. Princess Elizabeth.

The two sisters of Edward the Sixth had been set aside by acts of Council, acts of Parliament, acts of the Church, and so far as state decrees could put the King's sisters out of court, they were out of court. Their mothers had been cast away on the ground that they had never been lawful wives; their birth had been assailed; their titles had been quashed; their rank had been reduced; their rights, as king's children, had been extinguished. These public acts had never been repealed. In his old age, their father had in some sort owned his daughters; but the act in which this show of justice had been done was of doubtful force, since the previous statutes which defined their bastardy were left untouched. Indeed, his act for regulating the succession had only named them, in so far as they *were* his children. They were not restored in blood; they were not declared to have been lawfully born; they were not adopted into the regal line, except as additional heirs, and with the risk of being excluded by a final will. Whether they had been excluded, or not, could only be known to the King's executors, who were supposed to have been sworn to secresy during King Edward's life.

III. Mary Queen of Scots.

IV. Princess Margaret.

After the luckless sisters of King Edward, the Crown would pass to the heirs of Henry the Seventh. Now, Henry the Seventh had left behind him two daughters—the Princess Margaret and the Princess Mary, both of whom had issue living when he died.

Margaret, the elder sister, had been married to James the Fourth, King of Scots, to whom she had borne a son, afterwards James the Fifth, father of Mary, the Queen of Scots. This Queen Mary, born on a foreign soil, was excluded from her natural place in the order of succession by the Alien Act. But her mother, Queen Margaret, had left a second child.

That field of Flodden, which put James the Fifth on his father's throne, made his mother, Queen Margaret, a widow—young enough for love, and ready enough to fall into dangerous ways. A very handsome fellow, Archibald Douglas, sixth Earl of Angus, caught her eye. He had a wife and daughter living; but the Scottish queen (true sister of Bluff Harry) cared little for law when her passions were on fire; and in less than twelve months after the great disaster of Flodden Field, she took to herself the handsome and wedded thane.

They used each other ill. Margaret was shrewd of tongue; Angus fickle in the point of love. One child was born of this godless union; little Princess Margaret, born within the border, to save her English rights. For a dozen years, Queen Margaret led a wretched life; she quarrelled with her husband; she left his house; she went back to live with him; she found him faithless to her; she left him once again. The court was vexed with her troubles; scandalised by his amours. At length the Queen procured a divorce from Rome, by which her marriage was declared null and void, on the ground that Angus had a wife alive when he took the Queen.

This decree would have made poor little Margaret illegitimate; but a brief was brought from Rome to the effect that, since the mother had gone through the form of marriage in good faith, the child, though born in adultery, should be considered as lawful heiress of Archibald and Queen Margaret, just as though they had been actually man and wife! Rome could do much in those days; but Rome herself could not prevent rivals from laughing at a declaration which made a tavern jest of both law and fact.

V. Princess Frances.

VI. Lady Jane.

Mary, the younger child of Henry the Seventh, had been married to Louis the Twelfth, King of France (son of Duke Charles the Poet), who died, as it were, in his honeymoon. Within a few months of the King's demise, Queen Mary had been secretly united to her first lover, Charles Brandon, afterwards created Duke of Suffolk. By this second husband the Queen had issue two princesses—Frances and Elinor—to the first of whom her eventual rights descended, though not without legal flaw; since, at the time of the Queen's marriage with Brandon, that nobleman had a wife alive. Frances had in turn been given to Henry Grey, Marquis of Dorset, a man of high birth, and of austere life; but weak in character, short in vision, apt to go wrong when the reason for his going wrong seemed good; a man of order and ideas, without will of his own, and with very little sense; a man not born to mate with princes and fight for crowns. Here, again, that demon doubt was in a royal house; for Grey, like Brandon, had a wife alive when he had wedded Frances: Lady Catharine Fitz-Alan, sister of Henry, seventeenth Earl of Arundel; a woman whom he had wedded in his early youth, and from whom he parted in view of the more brilliant bride. By his separation from Lady Catharine, Grey provoked the undying enmity of Lord Arundel, once his brother-in-law and dearest friend; an enmity which lived through a score of years, which fed itself in secret, never dying out, until Arundel stood on Tower Hill gloating over his old friend's headless trunk.

Created Duke of Suffolk on account of his royal spouse, Grey imagined he could forget the wrongs which he had done to Lady Catharine—the insult which he had cast upon her house. Three daughters blessed his union; Lady Jane, Lady Catharine, and Lady Mary; all of whom as well as their mother Frances, were alive when King Edward died. The princess was a lady of meek temper and austere life; humble, affectionate; with little desire to shine in courts. Such pretensions as belonged to her blood she passed on to her children: first of all, to Lady Jane.

VII. Catharine Pole.

The Poles, or De la Poles, went back to Princess Margaret, daughter of George, Duke of Clarence. This lady, who had been married to Sir Richard Pole, left four sons

—Henry Lord Montagu, Sir Geoffrey Pole, Arthur Pole, and Reginald Pole. Reginald was the able and restless intriguer known as Cardinal Pole. Lord Montagu had been caught in some plot, of which his brother, the cardinal, was the secret mover, and sent to the block, leaving an only child, Catharine, who had now become the wife of Sir Francis Hastings, Earl of Huntingdon, to represent his mother's line.

VIII. The Infanta Isabel.

A more remote, and perhaps a more menacing claim was that of the Infanta Doña Isabel Clara of Spain—a lady who traced her line through the kings of Portugal to Princess Philippa and John of Gaunt.

Besides these ladies, there lay in the Tower, in some forgotten cell, a male pretender in Edward Courtney, a youth whom nobody had seen since he was a child of twelve. He had no friends in power, and nobody fretted about his right; yet he was a grandson of Princess Catharine, youngest daughter of Edward the Fourth, and thus he represented the cause of York.

All these claimants had their partisans; though the main interest gathered around the Princess Mary and the Lady Jane. Duke John, President of King Edward's Council, thought the legal right either lay with Lady Jane, or could be given to her by force. Jane was young, beautiful, accomplished, popular; and if she came to her own, he, John Dudley, who had heard his father hooted through the streets, and seen him butchered like a dog, might live to hail a grandson on the throne. This bold, bad man had four sons living; all young and of handsome presence; fellows who could draw, and dance, and play the lute, as well as they could ride, and joust, and run the ring. Three of these youths were already sealed away; but Guilford, a boy of seventeen, was free; and when the

Duke perceived that the King would die, and leave no heirs, he began to scheme for marrying Lord Guilford to Lady Jane. Mary was unpopular in London. Let Edward now die, and as every rein of the government would be in Dudley's grasp, Jane might become queen in her mother's right, without much cavil from Mary's friends. Such an event would be hailed as a triumph of England over Spain.

The old schemer had not much trouble with Grey and his wife. These feeble folk were only too glad to put themselves and their child into the Duke's strong hands. To them, the Duke was not only the greatest man in England, but one of the greatest men in Europe. As a soldier he had no equal; as a statesman he was thought farseeing and safe; as a patriot he was held in high esteem. Most men believed him honest in his faith; some went so far as to call him saint. Ridley, Rogers, Knox, and all their followers prayed for him as the soundest pillar of the reforming Church.

Much of this high character had once belonged to the Duke of right, but the lust of power had crept into his blood and poisoned the springs of his religious life.

Lady Jane, a soft and grave, though very lovely girl, who had been pinched and bobbed into learning by her parents, raised few obstacles to their scheme for her union. She had no liking for the Dudleys; she had a little secret of her own; but on hearing that the King, as well as both her parents, wished her to marry Guilford, she took her wedding with this youth like a lesson in Greek, or any other trial; bowed her sweet head, and went with him, a child like herself, to church. On Whit-Sunday the youth and maiden were united in holy wedlock at Durham house in the Strand, in the presence of many people; the bride being dowered with Stanfield Hall in Norfolk; a house which even then had an ominous fame; but the bride and groom were both so young, that when the rite was over, Lady Jane begged as an act of grace, that she might go home with her mother to Suffolk House, in Southwark, until she and her husband were of riper age.

Her wish was law; but that riper age was not to come for either Guilford or Lady Jane. Six weeks after this parting of youth and maiden at the altar in Durham House, the King was dead, the throne was empty, and the hour for which Duke John had schemed was come. Now was to be found, through rough and ready tests, that 'true heir to the crown' which Acts of Parliament were powerless to unmake.

CHAPTER XV.

THE NINE DAYS' QUEEN.

KING EDWARD died on the summer night of Thursday, July 6, at Greenwich Palace, so calmly, that the fact could be kept a secret all that night and all the next day, while Dudley matured his plans. The council were of his advice, the fleet and army at his back. On the city he could count for passive assent; but passive assent was not enough. On Saturday morning he sent for Sir Thomas White, Lord Mayor, six aldermen, and a score of the richest merchants from Lombard Street, to whom he showed the King's body, and papers which he called the King's letters-patent, fixing the order of succession to the crown. These papers, which gave the sceptre to Lady Jane, Dudley got the Lord Mayor and citizens to sign. The Londoners were told to keep the King's death and the contents of these letters-patent secret, until the lords should make them known. Dudley's plan was, that Edward's death should not be noised abroad until Mary had been lodged in the Tower, and Jane was ready to announce herself as Queen.

When Edward was dying, Mary had been called to his bedside by the council, and she had come so near to Greenwich as the royal lodge of Hunsdon, twenty-five miles distant. So soon as the King was dead, Lord Robert was sent off by Dudley with a party of mounted guards to bring her in. Once in the Tower, the unpopular princess would have found few knights to strike in her behalf.

Dudley himself rode down to Sion, near Isleworth, his house on the Thames, to which Lady Jane had repaired. When Dudley summoned the Princess Mary to Greenwich he sent his wife to Suffolk House for Lady Jane. Frances, her mother, refused to give her up; Jane herself preferred to stay in Southwark; until the Duchess of Northumberland fetched her son, who begged her, on her duty as a wife, to depart with him. Not liking to begin her married life by an act of disobedience, Lady Jane went with the Duchess and her son to Chelsea, where they locked her up till Sunday, on which day Lady Sydney, her husband's sister, brought her a request from Dudley to repair at once to Sion, and await a message of highest moment from the King. She was not aware that Edward had been dead three days!

The two ladies took boat at Chelsea. When Lady Jane arrived at Sion, the House was empty, but the great lords soon came dashing in; the Duke himself, President of the Council; William Parr, Marquis of Northampton, Grand Chamberlain, and brother of Queen Catharine Parr; Francis Hastings, Earl of Huntingdon, husband of Catharine Pole; William Herbert, Earl of Pembroke, husband of Anne Parr, the Queen's sister; Henry Fitz-Alan, the smiling and deadly Earl of Arundel; accompanied by the Duchess of Northumberland and the Marchioness of Northampton. Arundel and Pembroke fell on their knees, and were the first to kiss Lady Jane's hand as queen.

By help of these men and women the first and fatal part of Dudley's work was done. Jane fainted when they told her she was queen. She had loved King Edward with a sister's love; read with him, played with him, shared his secrets and his hopes; and when she heard that he was dead she swooned and sank upon her face. They told her she was queen by Edward's will, according to the Acts which vested the succession in the king. Pembroke and Arundel, who were famous soldiers, swore by their souls they would shed their blood and give their lives to maintain her rights. Then Lady Jane stood up before the lords, saying she had never dreamt of such greatness being thrust upon her, but that if she was called to reign, she prayed for grace to act as might be best for God's glory and His people's good.

The next day, being Sunday, she remained at Sion, surrounded by her husband's family; the Duke giving orders of many kinds, instructing heralds, sending out proclamations, writing to the lords and sheriffs, and acting generally as protector. That night, the interregnum was to end, the new reign to begin.

First Day.—On a bright July morning, Queen Jane embarked in the royal barge at Sion, and followed by a cloud of galleys, bright with bunting, gay with music, riotous with cannon, dropt down the river, making holiday along the banks, passing the great Abbey, calling for an hour at Whitehall Palace, and for another hour at Durham House, and shooting through the arches of London Bridge. She landed at the Queen's stair about three o'clock, under the roar of saluting guns, and was conducted, through crowds of kneeling citizens, to her regal lodgings by the two Dukes, the Marquises of Winchester and Northampton, Arundel, Pembroke, Paget, Westmoreland, Warwick; all the great noblemen who had made her Queen. Her mother, Frances, bore her train; and her husband, Guilford, walked by her side, cap in hand, and bowing low when she deigned to speak. The Lieutenant, Sir John Brydges, and his deputy, Thomas Brydges, received her majesty on their knees. At five o'clock she was proclaimed in the City, when the King's death was announced and his final testament made known.

But the day was not to end in peace; for after supper was over, and the Queen had gone to her rooms, the Marquis of Winchester, lord treasurer, brought up the private jewels, which he desired her to wear, and the royal crown, which he wished her to try on. Jane looked at the shining toy, and put it from her, saying, 'It will do.' Winchester told her another crown would have to be made. Another crown! For whom must another crown be made? For the Lord Guilford, said the Marquis, since he was to be crowned with her as king! Crowned as king! Surprised and hurt by what the treasurer had let fall, she sat in silent pain, until Guilford came into her room, when she broke into a fit of honest wrath. The crown, she said, was not a plaything for boys and girls. She could not make him king. A duke she had power to make, but only Parliament could make a man king. Guilford began to cry, and left the room. In a few minutes he came back with his mother, still whimpering that he wanted to be king, and would not be a duke. The Queen was firm; and after a hot scene the Duchess took her boy away, declaring that he should not live with an ungrateful wife.

Second Day.—Bad news came in from the eastern shires. When Lord Robert had got to Hunsdon his prize was lost; no man could tell him how or why; but the lodge was empty, and the Princess gone. Mary had been well served; for while Dudley was drawing a curtain round the bed, the false Arundel and the honest Throckmorton were both intent on letting her know that King Edward was no more. Sir Nicholas rode to London, told his three brothers the dread news, and took counsel with them as to what should be done. The four men, sitting in a dark room, whispering in hot words that summer night, were but the types of four millions of English subjects. They were loyal men, stout of heart, and true in faith; men who feared that Mary might be led astray through her confessors and her Spanish friends; but who chose to risk that evil rather than confront the perils of a civil war; a war which seemed likely, if once begun, to prove longer and fiercer than the strife of the Red against the White Rose; seeing that the weaker party could always count on the support of Spain and Rome. Their first thought was to do right. Mary was the true heir to her brother's crown, and they could not stand aloof when powerful and unscrupulous men seemed bent on driving her from her father's realm. As Sir Nicholas put the case in his doggrel rhyme:—

And though I liked not the religion,
  Which all her life Queen Mary had profest,
Yet in my mind that wicked motion,
  Right heir for to displace I did detest.

After long debate the four brothers agreed to mount their horses, to leave London by different roads, to spur with all speed for the royal lodge, to inform the Princess of her brother's death, and warn her to fly from Hunsdon before the arrival of Lord Robert's company of horse. Arundel's man confirmed the news. A night ride saved the Princess, who sent out letters to the shires and cities, calling out her people, and then rode swiftly through the Suffolk flats towards Kenning Hall, a strong castle on the river Waveney, where she proclaimed herself Queen.

Missing his prize at Hunsdon, Lord Roberts was ordered to gallop hard upon such track as he might find; and, to aid his search, Lord Warwick was sent out with a second company of horse. These young men had their father's orders how to act, and there is reason to suspect his orders would have justified them in putting Mary to death. Of course, she could be called a suicide, and three or four frightened servants might have been got to swear they had seen her either mix the drug or plunge the knife into her heart. Dudley, who already contemplated sending Bishop Gardiner, Edward Courtney, and the Duke of Norfolk, to the block, was of opinion that the throne would be all the more stable if it were red with blood.

Third Day.—On Wednesday morning, while the lords were sitting with Queen Jane in council, news came to the Tower that Mary was at Kenning Hall; that John Bouchier, Earl of Bath, was with her; that Henry Ratcliffe, Earl of Sussex, was on his way to join her; and that sons of Lord Wharton, and Lord Mordaunt, with many gentlemen of note, were up in arms.

Kenning Hall belonged to the Howards, whose tenants and followers hated Dudley and all his tribe; partly for the wrongs which his party had done the Duke; still more for the ruthless manner in which he had scourged their country in pursuit of Kett. The Queen was safer than she knew among these Norfolk men, who not only flocked to her banners the moment they were raised, but threatened to put every man's land under fire who should dispute her claim. Knights and squires kept pouring in, hot with the summer sun, and grey with the summer dust; and the curfew rang that Wednesday night on what promised to be strife between the English commons and the English nobles; squire and yeoman striking for Queen Mary, while duke and earl were striking for Queen Jane.

.The council sitting in the White tower now felt that the time had gone by for such feeble warriors as Lord Warwick and Lord Robert to do their work; and the question rose, as to which of the great lords would go forth in arms against the rival queen? If Norfolk had been free, and of the council, he would have been the man to send. Not a pike in East Anglia would have been raised against the Lord of Framlingham and Norwich, the hero of Flodden, the suppressor of the Pilgrimage of Grace. But Dudley had kept the Duke a prisoner, and the Duke's tenantry were now arming in Mary's name. Some one else must go. The council fixed on Grey; an unwise choice, if fighting was to come, since Grey had never yet led an army in the field. Jane would not consent. She begged the lords to make a second choice. She needed her father's counsels; she prayed them, tears in her eyes, not to send him from her side. Arundel turned his serpentine eyes on Dudley. He was the soldier of their party; he had led an army into Norfolk; he had quickened men's minds with a lively terror; and he knew the county as a general ought to know his ground. These facts were urged upon him by the lords, who seemed to think his presence in the shire would be enough to drive the Princess Mary into France.

'Well,' said the Duke, 'since you think it good, I and mine will go, not doubting of your fidelity to the Queen's majesty, whom I leave in your hands.'

From the Council chamber in the White tower they passed through the chapel into the Queen's apartments, where Jane thanked the Duke for leaving her father by her side, and, wishing him a speedy return, bade him good night.

Fourth Day.—Early on Thursday morning, men, horses, guns, and carts began to block up the Strand in front of

Durham House, the Duke's residence near Charing Cross. Dudley called for his suit of steel, and tried it on. He sent for cannon from the Tower, with waggons of powder and shot and many field-pieces. After breakfast, he begged the council to prepare his commission, as the Queen's Lieutenant, forthwith, and to send on his instructions by mounted messenger to Newmarket, as soon as they could be drawn up. To the peers who came to Durham House to dine with him and see him off, he made a speech; in which he told them, that he was going forth in the common cause; that he left the Queen in their hands; that he felt no doubt of their faithfulness; that they were all engaged in God's work; that any man who faltered in the cause would come to grief. At this moment dinner was brought in, on which Dudley concluded in a few words, 'I have not spoken to you,' he said, 'in this sort upon any distrust of your truth, but have put you in remembrance. . . . and this I pray you, wish me no worse God speed than ye would have yourselves.' To which one of the lords replied, 'If you mistrust any of us in this matter, your grace is much deceived.' The Duke made answer, 'I pray God it be so; let us go to dinner.' Then they sat down.

After dinner, Dudley rode down to the Tower and took his leave of the Queen. As he came back from his audience into the Council chamber, he met Lord Arundel, who prayed that God would be with his grace, saying he was sorry it was not his luck to be going into the field with him, as he wished no better end than to fight in his cause and die at his feet. A page, named Thomas Lovel, was with the Duke. 'Farewell, gentle Thomas,' said Arundel to the boy, 'farewell, with all my heart.' The lords came down the spiral stairs, and stood upon the green for a last greeting of their fellows; the Duke of Northumberland first, then the Marquis of Northampton, Lord Grey of Wilton, and many more; after which final greeting they took boat on the wharf, and went back to their houses in the Strand.

Fifth Day.—On Friday morning the Duke rode proudly forth, with his first train of guns, a body of six hundred men, and a magnificent staff. If great names and officers could have given the victory to Queen Jane, she might have slept in peace. Besides the Lord General, Dudley himself, went the Lord Admiral, Edward Lord Clinton; the Marquis of Northampton; the Earls of Warwick, Huntingdon, and Westmorland; Lord Grey of Wilton, Lord Ambrose Dudley, Lord Robert Dudley, with most of the men whose steel had been tried in actual war. But they were Generals without troops; Admirals without ships; Lords without following. Clinton and Huntingdon were enemies in disguise. As they pranced along Shoreditch, the Duke observed with a soldier's eye that the crowd which flocked to see the martial array go past, in all its bravery of steel and plume, looked sad and curious, and turning to Lord Grey, who was riding at his side, remarked, 'The people press to see us, but no man cries, "God speed you!"'

Yet Mary feared to wait their coming at Kenning Hall; a place too near the capital, too far from any port; so she leapt to horse, and, with a long train of riders, dashed across country towards Framlingham Castle, the Duke of Norfolk's stronghold on the Ore; riding so hard that she made no less than forty miles in a single day. Once that day she was in peril, for in part of her road she fell foul of the companies led by Warwick and Lord Robert. But on the first shout of the onset, Jane's troops went over to her side, and Dudley's sons escaped becoming Mary's prisoners only by the fleetness of their steeds.

Later in the day, a messenger from Bucks brought word

to the Council in the Tower that Lord Windsor, Sir Edward Hastings, and other gentlemen, were raising men in that county in Queen Mary's name.

Sixth Day.—On Saturday a train of waggons left the Tower, with arms, supplies, and cannon for the Duke, who found himself in presence of a thousand troubles on which he had never counted. The commons gave him no help; for no one liked him; and as he advanced into East Anglia he found himself in the midst of active foes. When he heard bad news from the front, he halted. Mary was now in Framlingham Castle, surrounded by a guard, which was strong in number, if not in discipline and arms. She had been proclaimed in the market-place of Norwich, from which city a band of gentlemen had ridden to her court. Worst of all, some ships which Clinton had sent from London to the Norfolk coast, on the pretence of arresting Mary's flight, should she try to leave the country, had gone over to the Queen, and supplied her with guns and stores. From other shires, the news was equally dark and fitful. Bucks and Beds were stirring; Lord Derby was up in Cheshire; and the midland counties were about to march. Dudley, who knew his business as a soldier, saw that these changes must be met; and sending in hot haste to London for fresh troops, he pushed on for Cambridge, which he reached that night.

Seventh Day.—The summer Sunday dawned on a country wasting with a passionate pain. In every city, the crowd was for Mary, while the higher class of thinkers and reformers was for Jane. Nicholas Ridley, Bishop of London, walked down to Paul's Cross, and preached an eloquent sermon against the Scarlet woman; while John Knox was thundering forth his prophetic warnings at Amersham in Bucks. From a thousaud pulpits England was that day warned that a house divided against itself must fall.

In the palace of the Tower, a cry of defection rose, but the garrison was too prompt in action for the evil spirit to get abroad. About seven o'clock, the gates were suddenly locked, and the keys carried up to the Queen's room. The guards were told that a seal was missing; but in fact, the missing seal was the Lord High Treasurer. Pembroke and Winchester had tried to leave the Tower privately; Pembroke had been watched and taken; but Winchester had got away. The first thought of every man was that he had carried off his money; and some archers of the guard were sent after him to his house, with orders to arrest and bring him back. They seized him in his bed, and delivered him at the Tower wicket to Sir John Brydges, the Lieutenant, as the clocks were chiming twelve.

Eighth Day.—Monday brought fresh sorrow to Queen Jane. Her house was divided against itself: the Duke, her father, had no confidence in the Duke, her father-in-law; the Duchess of Northumberland was quarrelling with the Duchess of Suffolk; and the foolish Guilford was going about whimpering that he wanted to be king. Her council was also divided against itself. Dudley was absent; Pembroke and Winchester were little more than prisoners; Paget and Arundel were false; Bedford was suspected; and Cranmer, if true to Jane, was acting as a councillor with the faint heart of a man who feared that he was doing wrong. Her country was divided, too, but in no equal parts. Jane was popular, yet the people were mainly on Mary's side; and no thunders of Ridley and Knox could make common folk understand that a woman ought to lose her civil rights because she held certain opinions about the Keys and the Bread and Wine. As yet there had never been a prince on the throne of hostile creed; and the people had yet to read in the light of Smithfield fires the sad lesson of a country divided in its body and its head. The Commons felt for Mary, and they fancied she could do no harm. Single and sickly, she was not likely either to leave a son or even to live long. Her sister,—strong and beautiful as a pard, was English in blood, and English in thought. What the Spanish weakness of Mary might put crooked, the English strength of her sister could set straight. They would rather bear with Mary's monks for a time—a very short time—than start on a new contention of Lancaster and York. Wise men might forecast the future in another way; but in days of turmoil, wise men do not shoulder pikes and brandish broadswords; and while the thinkers were weighing arguments for and against the two queens, a hundred thousand men, moved by their hot blood only, were bearing Queen Mary to her father's throne.

Ninth Day.—On Tuesday morning the game was seen to be up. The Queen's Council were nearly of one mind. Cranmer and Grey were true; but of the noble crowd who elbowed them at the table, every other man was false. Most of them, Winchester, Arundel, Pembroke, Paget, Shrewsbury, had made their peace, and kept their places in the Council only to betray the girl whom they had forced to ascend the throne. The army was as rotten as the Council. When Dudley marched on Bury, his soldiers mutinied on the road, and forced him to fall back on Cambridge, which was already filling with Queen Mary's friends. In fact, when he took up his quarters in King's College, he was a prisoner, though suffered to sleep without the appearance of a guard.

Next day, the Council left Queen Jane in the Tower alone; Queen Mary was proclaimed in Cheap and in St. Paul's Churchyard. The nine days' reign was over.

When the archers came to the Tower gates, demanding admission in Queen Mary's name, Grey gave up the keys, and rushed into his daughter's room. The Summer Queen was sitting in a chair of state, beneath a royal canopy. 'Come down, my child,' said the miserable Duke; 'this is no place for you.' Jane thought so too; and quitted her throne without a sigh.

CHAPTER XVI.

DETHRONED.

PEMBROKE had been the first to salute Queen Jane: he was now the first to proclaim Queen Mary. Pembroke was a bold man, a good soldier, a rich baron, able to put twenty thousand pikes in the field. Dudley excepted, no one had higher motives for supporting Jane than Pembroke; since his eldest son, William Lord Herbert, had been united to Lady Catharine Grey, Jane's sister and heiress. But he saw how the tide was flowing; and he was more concerned to save his head from the axe, than to enjoy the prospect of a matrimonial crown for his son.

The Council left the Tower, the gates of which were now open to them, for Baynard's Castle—not the great hold which John had ravaged, but a palace built on the site by Henry the Eighth—to which they called Sir Thomas White, Lord Mayor, with some of the City merchants, in whose presence Arundel announced that Mary was the true Queen and Jane a mere usurper of the Crown; on which Pembroke drew his sword, and flashing the steel in their faces cried—'This weapon shall make Mary Queen.' Sir Thomas and the citizens were hurried off from Baynard's Castle to Cheapside, where Pembroke read the proclamation of Queen Mary, threw his cap into the air, and flung a handful of coins among the crowd. Paget and

Arundel leapt to horse, and rode at night towards Framlingham Castle, were they were joyfully received by the Queen, who heard from them the minutest details of the work which they had done for her in London. Paget was detained by the Queen as her adviser, while Arundel set out for Cambridge to arrest the Duke.

Dudley was sore in mind. He saw that his scheme had failed, and knew that his blood was forfeit to the law. When news came to him by a private hand, that Jane had been abandoned in the Tower, and Mary proclaimed Queen in Cheapside, he called for a herald, and going into the market-place with Northampton and Warwick, he read the proclamation and threw up his cap. But his loyalty was too late. Roger Slegge, the Mayor of Cambridge, followed him to King's College, and took him prisoner in Queen Mary's name.

One chance of escape was thrown into his way. Late in the evening letters arrived in Cambridge from the Council that every man should go to his own place. The object was to get the Duke's force disbanded and dispersed. Dudley drew Slegge's attention to these orders. 'You do me wrong,' he said, 'to withdraw my liberty. See you not the Council's letters, that all men should go away as they list?' Slegge was puzzled, and withdrew his men. If Dudley had sprung to horse, and ridden off that moment, he might have found a boat, and escaped beyond sea. He let the moment slip. Warwick drew on his boots, called for his horse, and got himself ready to ride away; but the Duke hung on, as though he were hoping, like a desperate gambler, for some sudden change in the game. Late in the night, he heard that Arundel was coming to his rooms; then his heart sank within him; and going forth to meet him in the outer chamber, he knelt at the Earl's feet, and prayed him to be good to him for the love of God. Arundel was cold. 'Consider,' said the Duke, 'I have done nothing but by consent of you and the whole Council.'

'My lord,' said Arundel, 'I am sent hither by the Queen, and in her name I arrest you.'

'And I obey,' replied the broken Dudley; 'and I beseech you, my lord of Arundel, use mercy towards me, knowing the case as it is.'

'My lord,' quoth the earl, 'you should have sought for mercy sooner; I must do according to my commandment.'

They were still in the outer room of his lodging in King's College, now filled with knights and gentlemen, to whom Arundel gave the Duke in charge, and then withdrew. For two hours, Dudley chafed and stamped about that room, in the midst of strange and angry men, without the comfort of his page and servant to attend him. When he wished to go into his bedroom, the guards prevented him. Then he looked out of his window, and, seeing Arundel go by, he called—

'My lord, my lord of Arundel, a word with you.'

'What would you have, my lord?'

'I beseech your lordship,' cried the Duke, 'for the love of God, let me have Coxe, one of my chamber, to wait upon me.'

'You shall have Tom, your boy,' said the bitter earl.

'Alas, my lord,' whined the Duke, 'what stead can a boy do me? I pray you, let me have Coxe.'

Arundel turned away; but in going, he sent orders for Tom and Coxe to have access to their master.

Warwick was taken in his boots, and along with Lord Robert Dudley, the Marquis of Northampton, Sir Thomas Palmer, and Sir Henry Gates, was brought to the Tower, of which Arundel was now made Constable. All the prison rooms being full, they had to be crowded by Sir John

Brydges into chambers never up to that day used as prisons—such as the Garden tower, the Garden house, the deputy's house, and the Develin tower. The Duke was lodged in the Garden tower; Sir Thomas Palmer in the Garden house; the Marquis of Northampton in the Develin tower, behind St. Peter's church. Jane was in the house of Thomas Brydges, brother and deputy of Sir John.

Warwick and his brother Guilford were lodged in the middle room of Beauchamp tower; where they began to carve their misery on the walls. Lord Warwick made a puzzle of the family names, so subtle that no wit of man has yet been able to guess his secret. Two bears and a ragged staff, with his own name under them, stand in a frame of emblems; Roses, Acorns, Geraniums, Honeysuckles; which some folk fancy from the initial letters, may mean Robert, Ambrose, Guilford, and Henry; an explanation much too easy to be the true one. The rose may mean Ambrose; the oak, no doubt, is Robert. A sprig of oak, Lord Robert's own device, appears on another side of the room. Guilford could not forget that his wife was Queen; and solaced his captivity by carving the name of Jane.

Lord Robert was lodged in the lower room, on the ground-floor, while the Earl of Warwick and King Guilford, as men of higher note, were lodged in the upper room. During this period of separation, Lord Robert dug into the stone:

ROBERT DVDLEY

a name which may still be read near the door; cut into the wall by Amy Robsart's lord. After his trial, perhaps after Guilford's death, he was promoted to the upper room; on the wall of which he also left his mark, in the shape of an oak-branch with the letters

R. D.

Jane was alone with her gentlewomen, Elizabeth Tylney and Mistress Ellen, in the upper room of deputy Brydges' house; where she spent her days in reading the Greek Testament, and in grieving for her sire, whose love for her had brought his venerable head within reach of the fatal axe. Of herself she hardly thought, and of Guilford only as a starless boy, whose fate was married for a moment to her own. She had no such love for him, as she felt for her parents and her sisters. She had known him a few days only; she had married him as an act of obedience; she had never lived with him as a wife. She was little more than a child in years; but in six such summer weeks as she had now gone through, the characters of men are ripened fast. We know the Dudleys; and what was there in them for a girl like Jane to love?

Mary was now the Queen; and her triumph was understood as the victory of Spain. Renard, the crafty agent of her cousin, Charles the Fifth, became her chief adviser. Arundel, Pembroke, Paget, were consulted by the Queen, but the actual power was in Renard's hands. The blood to be shed was poured out, not on an English, but on a Spanish scale.

The Duke, the Marquis, and Lord Warwick, were brought to Westminister Hall for trial, where the aged Norfolk, white with years and sorrows, now restored in blood, and freed from bonds, presided as Lord High Steward, and pronounced the sentence of death on his cruel foe. Dudley, who could not deny that he had been in arms against Queen Mary, pleaded his commission under the Great Seal, and protested against the lords who had signed that commission judging him to death. Every one felt that he had made a point; but the peers were not open to legal points;

and when he had made his protest, Norfolk declared that he must die.

Warwick and Northampton were also condemned to death. Warwick displayed a manly pride. Asked by Norfolk what he had to say in excuse of his treason, he answered that he stood by his father, that he accepted his doom, and had nothing to ask save that his debts might be paid out of his lost estates. Next day, Sir Andrew Dudley, the Duke's brother, Sir John Gates, Sir Thomas Palmer, and Sir Henry Gates, were tried. They pleaded guilty; all except Palmer. 'Can you deny that you were there?' asked the judge. 'No,' answered Sir Thomas. 'Then you are culpable,' returned the judge. 'If that be so,' said Palmer, 'I confess the same.' They were all condemned.

Monday, August 21, being named as the day on which the Duke must die, the guards were drawn up, the block was got ready, and the headsman waited with his axe. But the Duke made a feint, which put off the evil hour. He felt sore of mind on account of his change of faith; he had a great desire to hear mass, as in his boyish time; he begged to receive his Maker from the hands of a priest. Here was a change! To gain a few hours of life, the proud enemy of Rome was willing to become her slave. Arundel, who had never ceased to be a Catholic, snapped at the Duke's hint; sent for the Tower priest, and bade him prepare the altar in St. Peter's church. He also sent into Cheapside for twelve or fourteen merchants—Hartop, Newse, Baskerville, and others—to appear in the Queen's chapel by nine o'clock. This was to be a morning of sweet revenge. When all was ready, and the people seated, Sir John Gage, the old Constable, went to the Garden tower for the Duke, while Sir John Brydges, the lieutenant, went to Develin tower for the Marquis; and Thomas Brydges, the lieutenant's deputy, went to the Garden house for Sir Thomas Palmer. The Duke and Palmer had to pass under Lady Jane's window; and this young girl, who saw them go by, between the guards, heard with pain and shame, that to save their lives for a few hours these heroes of twenty battle-fields were going to hear mass.

When they were placed in the church, the priest began; saying his office in the usual way, with *Pax*, and blessing, and elevation of the host. On the wafer being offered to him, the Duke turned round to the people and said: 'My masters, I let you all to understand that I do most faithfully believe this is the right and true way.' Then he knelt before the priest and took the wafer into his mouth.

Those who had been fetched to see Dudley's act of humiliation, went away from St. Peter's church saying to each other, 'Wist ye, friend, that it is forty-four years this day, since his father was put to death?'

Warwick, on hearing that his father had been to mass, sent for a priest and reconciled himself with Rome. Mary would probably have spared their lives; but Renard would not listen to her plea of mercy. Next day, the Duke, Sir John Gates, and Sir Thomas Palmer, were marched to Tower hill. At the block they declared themselves good Catholics; Dudley, most of all, appealing to the Bishop of Winchester, Nicholas Heath, who stood by him near the rail. They were buried in the Tower chapel; Dudley beneath the altar, the two knights at the west end.

Seven days after their execution, a citizen was dining with Thomas Brydges, in the Tower, when the Lady Jane chanced to come down stairs, from the upper room in which she lived, and seeing the good folks at table, said she would sit and dine with them. Her youth, her modesty, her tenderness took the stranger's eye, yet not so strongly as her piety and steadfastness took his heart.

'I pray you,' asked Lady Jane, 'have they mass in London?' 'Yea, sooth,' he answered, 'in some places.'

'It may be so,' sighed Jane; 'it is not so strange as the sudden conversion of the late Duke. For who would have thought he would have so done?'

'Perchance, he thereby hoped to have had his pardon.'

'Pardon!' she flashed out; 'pardon? Woe worth him! He hath brought me, and our stock in miserable calamity by his exceeding ambition. Hoped for life by his turning! Though other men be of that opinion, I am not. What man is there living, I pray you, that would hope for life in that case:—being in the field against the Queen in person? Who was judge that he should hope for pardon?'

These good people, fired by her holy wrath, looked at the girl in love and wonder. 'What will you more?' she cried. 'Like as his life was wicked, so was his end. I pray God, that neither I nor friend of mine, die so.' And then with kindling fervour she exclaimed:

'Should I, who am young and in my fewers (teens) forsake my faith for the love of life? Nay, God forbid. Much more *he* should not, whose fatal course, though he had lived his years, could not have long continued. But life is sweet. . . God be merciful to us! He sayeth, Whoso denieth Him before men, He will not know him in His Father's Kingdom.'

When she rose from table, she thanked Brydges and the stranger for their company, and then retired with her gentlewoman to the Upper room.

Early in September the Tower received a new file of tenants; old rivals and enemies of Cardinal Fisher; three of the most eminent prelates in the English church: Thomas Cranmer, Archbishop of Canterbury; Nicholas Ridley, Bishop of London; Hugh Latimer, once Bishop of Worcester. Latimer had been here before. On the green he met

Rutter, one of the warders, to whom he cried, in that cheery voice which every one liked to hear, 'What, my old friend, how do you? I am come to be your neighbour again.' Latimer was lodged in the Garden house, which the apostate Palmer had now left. Cranmer was placed in that Garden tower, which was supposed to have broken Dudley's pride.

The kinsmen and councillors ot Lady Jane had nearly all conformed to the new Queen's faith. Warwick, Lord Ambrose, and Lord Robert, had given way. Huntingdon and Northampton heard mass daily in St. Peter's church. Some favour was extended to all Jane's captives; Lady Warwick being allowed to see her husband in Beauchamp tower, and Lady Ambrose Dudley to visit her lord in the Nuns' bower. Ambrose had license to walk on the leads over Cold harbour, and Guilford the same liberty on Beauchamp tower.

A priest was sent to Lady Jane, and confident hopes were expressed by those who knew nothing of her high nature, that she would follow the example of her masculine friends.

Time and peace were wanted for such a work; but time and peace were not to be found during Mary's reign. The experiment of converting Jane to the faith in which Dudley died, was rudely disturbed by events in Kent.

CHAPTER XVII.

THE MEN OF KENT.

On the walls of Beauchamp tower, and in the crypt of St. John's, memorials of the Kentish men may still be found. In the slant of the window, looking towards the green, a rude carving on a kind of shield, shows the name of—

THOMAS COBHAM

1555.

This Thomas Cobham was the youngest son of George, Lord Cobham of Couling Castle, a descendant of Joan, wife of the Good Lord Cobham, and a cousin of Sir Thomas Wyat, of Allingtin Castle, Captain of the men of Kent. It is probable that Wyat shared with Cobham the Middle room of Beauchamp tower; from which Lord Robert and Lord Guilford Dudley were removed to the Belfry.

The frolic known as the Kentish rising was a political, not a dynastic threat. Wyat, a son of Sir Thomas of the Songs and Sonnets, a grandson of Sir Henry of the Cat, and of that stout Lady Wyat who had put the Abbot of Bexley in the stocks—is known as Sir Thomas of the Waster; his waster being a great cudgel, made of a brand, a piece of iron, and a length of thong, which the young gallant carried under his cloak, in the hope of laying it on the back of John Fitzwilliam, a wretch who had sent him word that it would be well to get rid of Queen Mary by either foul means or fair means. The Mercutio of the rising was a loyal man.

In youth, he had been gay and fractious; first in his father's house, where he lived in an atmosphere of wit and song; afterwards in France, where he served, not without credit, in the war against Charles the Fifth. The death of Edward the Sixth found him living at Allingtin Castle; a married man, with youngsters at his knee; fond of his hawks, his horses and his dogs; but when Mary hinted that she hoped to contract a Spanish marriage, the flighty passions of his youth rushed back into his veins. Had he not fought against the Spaniards at Landrecy? Was he to put his neck under the feet of a Spanish prince? Never, cried the thoughtless spark. Talking to his neighbours by the yule logs, he found them no less eager than himself to oppose the projected match. Between the dinner and the dance, they put their heads together; and on the morrow these Twelfth Night revellers were a band of plotters moving into camp; Wyat was chosen captain; just as the day before he might have been voted Lord of Misrule.

They fancied that a scuffle and riot would serve their turn; checking the plans of Renard, and forcing the Queen to dismiss her project of a Spanish match. They meant no harm to Mary; they hoped to do her good; nay, they expected her to stand aside, and let the English faction and the Spanish faction fight it out.

Among the first to throw in their lot with Wyat were Robert Rudston, Thomas Culpepper and Thomas Fane, gentlemen of family and estate, who were quickly followed by Sir Harry Isely, Sir George Harper, Cuthbert Vaughan, and many more. Wyat strove to persuade George, Lord Cobham of Couling to join; but Cobham, though a good patriot, was a timid man, who allowed his son Thomas to ride into Wyat's camp, while he sent news to the council of what was being done. George was a Brooke, not an Oldcastle. The rioters, who soon became an army, rang the church-bells in every town, seized Rochester Castle, and mounted guard on the Medway Bridge. Norfolk was now sent down to disperse the mob; but the aged warrior, pale from his cell, was no longer the man of Flodden and of Doncaster Bridge; and when the levies which he led into Kent heard that the Kentish men were up in arms, not against their Queen, but only against the Spanish match, they deserted their general, threw down their flag, and shouting, 'A Wyat, a Wyat!' went over to his side. 'So many as will come and tarry with us shall be welcome,' cried the gay leader, as he rode through the deserters' ranks; 'and as many as will depart, good leave have they.' A few fell back; men of the Queen's guard, who returned to London in wretched plight; their bows broken, their scabbards empty, their coats turned inside out. When these scarecrows passed through the gateway of London Bridge, on their way back to the Tower, the citizens of Cheap, who thought the Queen must surely give way about the match, ran mad with joy.

Renard was now alarmed; and he wished the Queen to leave London; but Mary never had a moment's fear. She had spies in Allingtin and Rochester, in Wyat's house and in his camp, who reported to her council everything that was either done or likely to be done. In place of yielding the match, Mary mounted her horse, rode into the city, harangued the citizens in Guildhall, declared her purpose to proceed, proclaimed Wyat a rebel, and bade the well-wishers of his cause go join him, offering them a free passage through the gates of London Bridge into Kent.

On the day of her proclamation, Wyat was in Dartford, the next day in Greenwich. The game was now close. Early on Candlemas day a gentleman came dashing up the Kent Road, accompanied by a drummer; and being stopped by the picket near St. George's Church, he said he had a message for the Queen's general, the Earl of Pembroke. With a band round his eyes and a drummer by his side, he was led on foot through the city to Coldharbour, Lord Pembroke's residence, where he remained in secret parley until the afternoon, when he was brought out again with the band round his eyes and the drummer by his side, and led back to St. George's Church. No one but the Queen's council knew his name. When he was gone from Coldharbour, Pembroke rode out, attended by Lord William Howard, the Queen's stout deputy of Calais, followed by fifty men; passed over London Bridge; and went up the High

Street, Southwark, as far as St. George's Church. Everything was quiet. They put a number of Lord William's men in the Tabard and other taverns much used by the men of Kent, and then rode back to court.

On her side, Mary offered a pardon to such of her good subjects as would lay down their arms at once, with the four exceptions of Wyat, Rudston, Harper, and Isely, and a reward for any man who would take Wyat, of a hundred pounds a-year to himself and his heirs for ever.

Next day rebel flags were seen from the Belfry and the Keep; the Kentish men marching lightly towards the bridge, two thousand strong, with many good pieces in their train. No attempt was made to stop them. The Queen's troops, posted near St. George's Church, fell back to the bridge, the chains of which were cut and the gates made safe. The men left by Lord William in the taverns, went over to the rebels, and Southwark was surrendered to Wyat without a blow. Sir John Brydges said they ought to go out from the Tower and fight; but Pembroke, who knew his own business, refused to stir.

Panic ran through the City, in which the shops were closed, the church-bells rung, and the gates secured against surprise. Pembroke sent Lord William to the bridge for a parley. 'Wyat, Wyat!' cried Lord William from the gate. 'What would ye with the Captain?' asked a Kentish man. 'I would speak with him,' quoth Lord William. 'The Captain is not here,' said the other; 'but if ye will anything to him, I will show it.' 'Marry, then,' returned Lord William; 'Know of him what he meaneth by this invasion, and whether he continue in his purpose?' In less than an hour the Kentish man came back to the bridge with a purse in his hand, which he threw over the gate, saying, 'There, in that ye will find the Captain's answer.' Wyat required on behalf of the Kentish men no less than that the queen should give up her project of a Spanish match, and that she should yield to him the Tower as a pledge of her good faith. There must have been peals of laughter in the supper-rooms of the Tower that night.

Mary's spirit seemed to rise as the peril pressed around her. She raised on the keep a flag which the diarists describe as a banner of defiance, and gave orders that the morning and evening guns should be fired off as they were fired in times of peace on the change of guard; nay, she affected a sudden tenderness for people who are seldom much cared for by princes in time of war. Poynings, one of her gunners, came to tell her he could beat down some houses across the river, and bury many of the rebels in the crash. 'Nay,' said the Queen, like a queen, 'that were great pity; for many poor men and householders will be undone and killed.' Charity on her side seemed to beget chivalry on the other. A fanatic, named William Thomas, a man of good parts, whom the times had driven mad, made a proposal for taking off the Queen, as the simplest way to get rid of the Spanish match. This proposal was made known by John Fitzwilliam, one of Norfolk's men, not to Wyat, who would have pinked the rascal on the spot, but through third and fourth parties, by whom it came at length to the Captain's ears. Wyat then cut his waster, a thick stick, through which he burnt a hole and fastened a length of thong. With this waster in hand, he sought a whole day for the rascal who talked of laying hands on his Queen. Failing to find Fitzwilliam, Wyat gave the cudgel to a servant, and bade him seek the fellow out, saying, 'Bob him well, for the knave is a spy, and therefore be bold to beat him.'

In this lightsome and generous spirit he acted from first to last. When he heard that the Queen had promised a hundred pounds a-year for ever to any man who should take him, he wrote his name in big letters on a scroll and gaily stuck it in his cap.

A flight of romantic pity led to his ruin. One of Sir John Brydges' men was passing down the river in his barge, when a waterman whom he knew, a poor fellow from Tower stairs, called to him from the bank to take him on board. Now, passage from one side of the Thames to the other was forbidden, and when the Kentish gunners saw the Tower barge taking a man on board against the agreement, they fired a volley into her, and the waterman fell dead. Brydges, maddened by what he thought an insult to his barge, opened fire from the keep, the Devil's tower, and the Water gate, not only against the wooden houses on Horsleydown, but against the steeples of St. Mary's Church and St. Olave's Church. The poor people whose sheds were rattling into pieces, ran to Wyat; the men in rage, the women in tears; and begged him to save them from destruction. 'Sir,' they cried in terror, 'we shall be utterly undone for your sake; our houses, which are our living, will be thrown down, our children will be slain, this borough will be desolated; for the love of God, take pity on us!' Wyat is said to have paused for a long time. What they asked of him was to give up all the advantages of his position, in order to save the Queen's subjects from the violence of her Lieutenant. A soldier would have packed them home with an oath; a statesman would have sent them to the Queen. But the light-hearted Captain could not stand a woman's tears. 'I pray you, my friends,' he said, 'content yourselves a little, I will ease you of this mischief. God forbid that ye, nay the least child here, should be hurt in my behalf.'

Wyat had only one choice; either to fall back on Rochester, confess his failure, and wait for some luckier moment; or, by a forced and fatiguing march to Kingston, get across the Thames higher up, and march on the capital by the northern bank. He chose the more dashing plan.

Paying every one his due, so that no man lost a penny by his bands, he marched his forces through the marshes of Lambeth and Wandsworth, towards the old Saxon town, which he reached the same night; to find the bridge broken down, the boats all moored on the Middlesex side, and the passage secured by two hundred of the Queen's troops. What was he to do? He could not pause; neither could he fall back. Southwark was occupied in his rear. What was in front, he could not tell; but come what would he must now push forward. Two of his guns were trailed to the bridge, and the soldiers swept away. Three or four Medway swimmers sprang into the flood, swam across the stream under fire, unfastened the boats, and paddled them over to the Kingston bank. Into these frail craft a few of the Kentish men leapt—only a few, and these had to leave their horses and artillery behind. Yet Wyat could not wait. On foot, half armed, and panting with fatigue, some broken companies pressed on through that dark February night. Before day they were at Brentford—hungry, worn, and sleepless, with a royal army in their front.

The Queen was in high spirits; for these masquers who were falling into her nets, might be used to involve in treason personages whom she wished to strike and could not reach.

Drums were beaten in the streets at four o'clock, and London was astir that winter night from Westminster to the Tower. A thousand preparations had been made, and every point of the City, from Islington ward to St. James' Fields, was bristling with pikes and guns. Renard urged the Queen to keep out of peril. The citizens were known to be with Wyat; but the chief men were being watched, while common folk were deceived with lies and overawed with force. From the Tower to Charing cross the series of positions were strongly manned. Lord William Howard, a stout soldier, was at Ludgate with his guards; Lord Chidiock Pawlett, son of the Lord Treasurer, held Fleet street and the bridge with three hundred men; John Sir Gage, the Lord Chamberlain, was at Charing cross with a thousand pikes; Pembroke, the Queen's general, was at Whitehall, under the Palace window, with his line of battle fronting St. James's park. If these men were true, all would be well; but Renard was fearful that they would play their Mistress false.

Faint in limb, but high in spirit, the Kentish men pushed on from Brentford to Hyde Park corner. Some of their great pieces, which had been lugged across the river, came up, and, being planted on Constitution-hill, opened fire on Pembroke's lines. With a few brave words to his men, Wyat, and his cousin Cobham, pressed forward on foot down the old lane by St. James's Church, marched along the front of Pembroke's horse, who sat motionless in their seats, until they arrived at Charing cross. There they met Sir John Gage, who fired upon them and fell back. Wyat pushed up the Strand, his object being to reach the Tower. In Fleet street he met Lord Chidiock and the Queen's troops, who suffered him to pass. The rout went on, and the Lord of Misrule seemed coming into actual power. At Ludgate he found himself in a trap, where the deputy of Calais plucked from his temples the paper crown.

With a loud clatter the Kentish men came up to Ludgate. 'A Wyat! a Wyat!' they cried to the guards. Lord William stood upon the gate, and to his questions they replied—'Here is Wyat, to whom the Queen hath granted our requests.' 'Avaunt thee, traitor,' cried Lord

William; 'thou shalt not come in here.' Wyat had no guns to force the gate. Dying with hunger and fatigue, he sat on a stone near the Belle Sauvage for awhile; then, jumping to his feet, he marched his men back over the Fleet bridge, as far as Temple Bar, where the Queen's troops were drawn up. A fight began, which lasted a few minutes only; for William Harvey, the herald, in his coat-of-arms, coming forward, said to Wyat—'Sir, you were best to yield; the day is gone against you. Perchance the Queen will be merciful, the rather if ye stint the flow of blood.' Wyat turned to his men, who said they would fight it out; but he saw that the play was over, and gave up his sword. Sir Maurice Berkeley took him up behind on his horse, and carried him to Whitehall.

At five o'clock, Wyat was at the Tower gates a prisoner. Taking him through the wicket, Sir John Brydges, flourishing his blade in his hand, cried, 'Oh, thou villain and traitor, if it was not that the law must pass upon thee, I would stick thee through with my dagger.' The Captain was very quiet. 'It is no mastery now,' said Wyat, in scorn, and passed into his cell. He wore a coat of mail, with rich sleeves; a velvet cassock, covered with yellow lace; high boots and spurs; and a velvet hat, adorned with very fine lace. The sword and dirk were gone. Cobham, Rudston, and Fane were brought into the Tower; and a few days later, Thomas Culpepper, Sir Henry Isely, and many more, including Edward Courtney, the White Rose of York.

CHAPTER XVIII.

COURTNEY.

Edward Courtney, the White Rose of York, was born to a captive's fate. From the age of twelve, when he was first removed from his father's house to the Tower, until he died in Padua at the age of twenty-nine, he had only twenty months of freedom.

Courtney's father, Henry, Earl of Devon and Marquis of Exeter, was born too near the purple for his peace; being a son of Princess Catharine, daughter of Edward the Fourth. These Courtneys had been a splendid race; robbers, crusaders, paladins; bearing the arms of Boulogne, and tracing their lineage to the blood royal of France. Some members of this great house had been Counts of Edessa, Kings of Jerusalem, Emperors of the East. One had married into the house of Capet, another into that of Plantagenet; but the Courtneys had never yet made a royal and imperial match without down bringing the skies upon their house. They dated their decline in France from the day when they gave one of their daughters to a son of Louis the Fat. Peter of Courtney's union with Yolande of Constantinople, though it brought the purple to three princes of the house, put an end to their greatness in the East. When William Courtney, eighteenth Earl of Devon, took the Princess Catharine to wife, he provided for all who were to follow him a dark inheritance—the Tower, the headsman's axe, and the poisoned bowl. William had passed seven years of his married life a prisoner in the Tower. Henry, Princess Catharine's son, had been executed, along with his cousin, Lord Montagu, for his share in the plot of Cardinal Pole. Edward, his boy, then twelve years old, was left a prisoner in the Tower.

When the great party of York, which had been stunned, but not killed, at Bosworth, began to raise its head once more, it had found in Henry Courtney, Earl of Devon, Marquis of Exeter, grandson of Edward the Fourth, young, dashing, handsome, one of those men who cannot help being made a rallying sign. Exeter was a Catholic, a friend of Reginald Pole. In secret he was called the White Rose of York; nay, it is probable—as Henry the Eighth alleged—that he had dreamt of one day wearing a royal crown. Indeed, his claims were strong; for he stood next in order of succession to the King and his sisters; and thus he had come to be regarded as a natural chief by all those partizans of the ancient church who could not travel so fast and far as the new primate and the new queen. These partizans were neither few in number nor obscure in rank. A majority of the people were unlettered peasants, and a majority of the great barons were known to be on the Catholic side. The burghers and scholars, with a majority of the freeholders, were on the Reformers' side. In any trial by battle, the issue of a conflict between the two opinions might have been doubtful, and the presence of such chiefs as Henry Courtney and Reginald Pole had made a resort to arms seem easy, and almost lawful in the eyes of turbulent men.

Such a kinsman could only be left in peace, by such a king as Henry the Eighth, on one engagement, and that engagement Exeter either would not or could not take. He must have kept aloof from public affairs. But, far from hiding his light in his own house, Exeter had assumed in London the bearing of a prince, while in his own counties of Devon and Cornwall he had set himself high above the law. Henry grew angry, not without cause ; and on the eve of a movement which threatened to become a general rising in the west, Exeter and his son Edward, a boy of twelve, had been seized and thrown into the Tower; whence a short trial and a shorter shrift had conducted the luckless son of Princess Catharine to the block.

The boy was spared. Shorn of his honors and estates, Courtney underwent the fate which, in those rude times, was known as being forgotten in the Tower.

For fifteen years the grandson of Princess Catharine remained a captive. While he was still a boy, he ran about the garden and the Lieutenant's house. As he grew in years, in beauty, and intelligence, his high blood was put into the scale against him; his freedom was abridged; and the pale pretender to the name of White Rose was lodged for safety in the strong room of the Belfry; where his chief amusement was to watch the gunners fire their pieces, to count the ships going up and down the Thames, to pace the stones on Prisoners' Walk.

He was treated as a man of no high mark; having only a common servant at 6*s.* a week to wait on him; being dieted and lodged at 26*s.* 8*d.* a week; while young men of his quality, such as Guilford and Ambrose Dudley, were dieted at 53*s.* 4*d.* a week, and allowed two servants each.

Not until the two reforming kings, Henry and Edward, had passed away, and his Catholic kinswoman, Princess Mary, succeeded to the throne, was Courtney freed from his confinement in the strong room.

The twenty months of freedom which he was now to enjoy were months of very high favour and very warm hope. It seemed likely that the child on whose early life fortune had shed her darkest clouds would be called to wear a matrimonial crown.

On the new Queen riding down to the Tower, in front of

a proud cavalcade of nobles and prelates, she found at the postern of her citadel a row of kneeling figures. Halting the procession, she got down from her palfrey, and clasped them in her arms. For among these kneeling figures who had been suffered to come forth from their cells, many were dear to her heart and servants to her cause; the aged Duke of Norfolk, the Primate Gardiner, the Duchess of Somerset, the young Lord Courtney. Mary stooped to these applicants for her grace, and kissed them one by one. 'These are my prisoners,' she exclaimed, as she carried them from the outer gates into the royal gallery. The scene was a stage device; but the effect on the popular mind was great. Courtney, for example, had been free for three months; yet he had come down to the gates that day, to receive the royal kiss, and to play his part in a striking act.

A very wild dream now filled the young man's soul with hope. He was popular in the city and in the court, not only on account of his royal blood and his personal beauty, but more on account of the tenderness felt for a youth who had done no wrong, and suffered much pain. The world had been very hard to him; and a generous people wished to make amends for the bitterness of his early life. Pale with long vigils, his beauty had that soft and melancholy cast which takes captive the eyes of women. When he came out of the Belfry, at the age of twenty-six, he found himself high in favour. He was, in fact, the man whom nearly all true lovers of their country wished to see married to their Queen.

Mary herself, though she was nearly old enough to have been his mother, was not blind to her cousin's claims, and she more than once thought seriously of the proposal ere she fixed her mind for good and evil on the Prince of Spain. During her day of doubt she poured favours enough on

Courtney to turn his head. She made him Earl of Devon, Parliament restored the Marquisate of Exeter to his house, and in dress, habit, and hospitality, he was encouraged to adopt a style beyond that of a private person. He gave himself the airs of a prince. He smiled on the Yorkist barons, and allowed his flatterers to call him the true White Rose. Even after Mary had engaged herself to Philip, he fancied the foreign project of alliance would pass away, and that the Queen would accept no husband but himself. To the amusement of men knowing better, he talked of his approaching nuptials, and ordered a magnificent suit of bridal clothes.

His fortunes fell when Mary got a promise from Renard that she should wed the Spanish Prince. She was asked by Renard to make many sacrifices; one of which was the pale and foolish youth who had lived so many years in the Belfry. Mary, left to herself, would have done the boy no harm; but Renard told her that when Courtney ceased to be her lover, he could not help becoming her rival. He stood too near. At first, the Queen could see no peril to her throne in the pretensions of such a youth; but Renard, who knew better than Mary what men were saying in the Cheapside taverns and St. Paul's Churchyard, began to whisper in her ear that after her marriage with Philip the young Lord Courtney would be a dangerous man, if not on his own account, yet on account of her sister, for whom there was a powerful party in her realm. He spoke the truth. So soon as Mary's contract with the Prince of Spain was made known in London, people began to busy their minds about a second union. They married Courtney to Elizabeth. Mary, they said, would have no son; at thirty-nine she was too old; the crown must come to her younger sister; and since Courtney was set up by many as the White Rose, it would be well to end all feuds and heal all sores between White and Red by wedding the Lancastrian princess to the Yorkist peer.

All this tattle was repeated day by day to the Queen. Mary felt that her people were avenging her Spanish match, by proposing to themselves an English match. It was hardly necessary for Renard to hint that a marriage of Elizabeth and Courtney would be dangerous to her throne. Yet he urged it in her ear from day to day. Nothing, he told Mary, could make her mistress of her kingdom, and secure to her the lover she had chosen, but the ruin of these two pretenders to her crown and state.

Unlike her Spanish councillor, Mary had touches of human pity. If she feared to act against her sister, then a young girl of twenty, bright with her first beauty, witty and debonair, she still more disliked to crush with her strong hand the poor boy whom she had loved and kissed. The youth soon helped her to decide. Fancying himself neglected by the Queen, he fell into bad ways; carousing in City taverns, keeping loose company, running after strange faces, hanging on the skirts of men known to be engaged in plots. The austere lady grew angry and ashamed. Courtney repented, and was half forgiven. It is not clear, whether, in some of his pranks, he was not acting a part. Some think he became one of Renard's spies. When Wyat marched on Charing Cross, his conduct was suspicious, if it were nothing worse; and his arrest, along with the crowd of rioters, may have been a blind on Renard's part to conceal the deeper infamy of his course.

CHAPTER XIX.

NO CROSS, NO CROWN.

On the day of her triumph, as she sat brooding in her closet, listening fitfully to Renard, Mary consented to give up her cousin, if not her sister, to the minister of Charles the Fifth. Jane had been sentenced by the court and reprieved by time. Seven months had passed since her nine days' reign was over; the author of her offence had paid the penalties of his crime; and in the recent stir no man had even breathed her name. Her youth, her innocence, her beauty, had won all hearts to her; even those of Father Feckenham the Queen's confessor, and Sir John Brydges the Queen's lieutenant. But Renard called for blood; and Mary was little more than a scribe in Renard's hands.

That day, on the eve of which Queen Mary sat in her closet with her Spanish councillor, was Ash Wednesday; and Mary, on consenting that her cousin should not live forty hours longer, called to her presence Father Feckenham, whom she had just made Dean of St. Paul's and Abbot of Westminster; and bade him go to the deputy's house in the Tower, with news that Lady Jane must die, and see what could be done to save her soul. Father Feckenham, though a coarse man, was not a bad man. As a divine, he was learned and ingenious; one in whose power of dealing with backsliders the Queen had a boundless faith. That he failed with Lady Jane, that he got angry with her, that his speeches to her made him hateful in the eyes of men, were more his misfortunes than they were his faults. A good deal must be allowed to a man who honestly thinks he has power to bind and to loose, in his dealing with those who in his opinion are trifling with the fate of immortal souls.

Feckenham, who brought down his message of death to the Tower, was startled to see that girl receive his news with a sad and welcome smile. It seemed to him out of nature, almost out of grace. He spoke to her of her soul; of the sins of men; of the need for repentance; but he found her calm and happy, at peace with the world, and at one with God. He talked to her first of faith, of liberty, of holiness; then of the sacraments, the Scriptures, and the universal Church. She knew all these things better than himself; and she held a language about them far beyond his reach. With a sweet patience, she put an end to the debate by saying that since she had only a few hours now to live she needed them all for prayer.

The Dean was moved, as men of his order are seldom moved. Convert this girl in a day! Worn as he was in church affairs, he knew that no skill of his would be able in one winter day, to avail him against one who combined a scholar's learning with a woman's wit. If her soul was to be saved—and the Father was anxious to save her soul—that order for her execution on Friday morning must be stayed. With the sweet voice pulsing in his ear, he rowed back to Whitehall, and told the vindictive Queen, with the bold energy of a priest, that her orders for that execution on Friday must be withdrawn. With much ado, the Queen gave way; but she feared the anger of Feckenham even more than that of Renard; and the puzzled Father went back to the Tower, to resume his task. Jane was kind but cold. She had no use for him and his precepts in her final hour on earth. His going to court about her sentence gave her pain. She did not want to die; at seventeen no one wants to die; but she did not like the Queen to add one day to her life, under the hope that she would act as Dudley and Warwick had done, in giving up their faith. That was a sacrifice she could never make. When Feckenham told her the warrants for Friday were recalled, she merely said she was willing to die, if the Queen, her cousin, was minded to put the law in force against her. For the rest, she only wanted to be left alone.

'You are not to die to-morrow,' he persisted.

'You are much deceived,' said Jane, 'if you think I have any desire of longer life.'

When Feckenham returned to the Queen with a report of his second interview, Mary became wild with rage. She bade her secretaries draw up warrants for her death. She sent for Grey, who was a prisoner in the country. There were ways of adding bitterness to death, and Mary studied and employed them all. She could separate the husband from his wife in their last hours on earth; she could march Guilford under Lady Jane's window, as he went by to execution; she could drive the cart with his dead body past her door; she could prepare a scaffold on the open green, under Lady Jane's eyes; she could bring up Grey to see his daughter slain; she could refuse to let her have a minister of her own faith to pray with her; she could send her Jesuits and confessors to disturb the solemnity of her final night on earth. All these things she could do, and she did; and all these things must have been of Mary's will.

Renard required that Jane should be put away; that sacrifice was wanting to confirm the conquest made by Spain; but Renard could have no motive for adding to the bitterness of her death.

The priests sent down by Mary to the Tower were Lady Jane's worst tormentors. They would not be denied; they pushed past her women; and when they got into her chamber, they would not go away.

The long reports which have been printed of their contention with her, may not be exact; but they have that rough kind of likeness to the truth which a common rumour bears to actual fact. When Feckenham was tired out with argument, he is said to have exclaimed, 'Madam, I am sorry for you; I am assured we shall not meet again.' To which Jane is said to have answered, 'It is most true, sir; we shall never meet again, unless God should turn your heart;' not a word of which 'happy retort,' we may be sure, ever passed the lips of Lady Jane.

The tussle on the Bread and Wine was no doubt sharp, for that was the dogma most in dispute. 'Do you deny that Christ is present in the bread and wine?' 'The broken bread,' said Jane, 'reminds me of the Saviour broken for my sins, the wine reminds me of the blood shed on the cross.' She meant to say that Christ was ministerially, but not bodily, present in the bread and wine. 'But did He not say,' put in the Father, 'Take, eat, this is my body?' 'Yes,' she answered, 'just as He said, I am the vine.' It was a figure, not a fact.

Feckenham at length retired, and Jane withdrew into the upper chamber, to compose her mind; to write a farewell to her father, and to wait on God in prayer.

She was not aware that her father had been arrested, still less that he was on his way to the Tower. The tender note which she addressed to him ended in these words:

'Thus, good father, I have opened unto you the state wherein I stand: my death at hand; to you, perhaps, it may seem woeful; yet to me there is nothing can be more welcome than from this rule of misery to aspire to that heavenly throne with Christ my Saviour, in whose steadfast faith (if it may be lawful for the daughter so to write to the father) the Lord continue to keep you, so at the last we may meet in heaven.'

When it was known in the Tower that warrants were out, and that Jane would die on Monday morning, every one became eager to get some token from her, to catch a last word from her lips, a final glance from her eye. To Thomas Brydges, the deputy, in whose house she had lived nearly eight months, she gave a small book of devotions, bound in vellum, containing two scraps of her writing, and a few words by Lord Guilford; one of her notes being addressed to Brydges himself, in words which must have gone to his soul: 'Call upon God to incline your heart to his laws, to quicken you in his way, and not to take the word of truth utterly out of your mouth.'

On Sunday, Guilford sent to ask her for a final interview; but this sad parting she declined, as useless now, fit for stage heroes only, which they were not. She bade him be of good cheer; and seeing how weak he had been, it is only right to say that the poor boy took his fate quietly, like a man. Sunday morning she spent in prayer and reading; her book, a copy of the Greek Testament; in which she observed a blank leaf at the end, and taking up her pen, wrote some last words to her darling sister, Lady Catharine Grey, sad heiress of all her rights and miseries:

'I have sent you, good sister Kate, a book of which, although it be not outwardly rimmed with gold, yet inwardly it is more worth than precious stones. It is the book, dear sister, of the law of the Lord; his testament and last will, which He bequeathed to us wretches, which shall lead you to eternal joy.'

Closing the sacred book, she gave it to Elizabeth Tylney, her gentlewoman, praying her to carry it after she was dead to Lady Catharine, as the last and best token of love. She then composed herself to prayer.

Early next day, before it was yet light, the carpenters were heard beneath her window, fitting up the block on which she was to die. When she looked out upon the green, she saw the archers and lancers drawn up, and Guilford being led away from the Lieutenant's door. She now sat down and waited for her summons to depart. An hour went slowly by; and then her quick ear caught the rumble of a cart on the stones. She knew that this cart contained poor Guilford's body, and she rose to greet the corse as it passed by. Her women, who were all in tears, endeavoured to prevent her going to the window, from which she could not help seeing the block and headsman waiting for her turn; but she gently forced them aside, looked out on the cart, and made the dead youth her last adieu.

Brydges and Feckenham now came for her. Her two gentlewomen could hardly walk for weeping; but Lady Jane, who was dressed in a black gown, came forth, with a prayer-book in her hand, a heavenly smile on her face, a tender light in her grey eyes. She walked modestly across the green, passed through the files of troopers, mounted the scaffold, and then turning to the crowd of spectators, softly said:—

'Good people, I am come hither to die. The fact against the Queen's highness was unlawful; but touching the procurement and desire thereof by me, or on my behalf, I wash my hands thereof, in innocency, before God, and in the face of you, good Christian people, this day.'

She paused, as if to put away from her the world, with which she had now done for ever. Then she added:—

'I pray you all, good Christian people, to bear me witness that I die a true Christian woman, and that I look to be saved by no other means than the mercy of God, in the merits of the blood of His only Son, our Lord Jesus Christ. And now, good people, while I am alive, I pray you to assist me with your prayers.' Kneeling down, she said to Feckenham, the only divine whom Mary would allow to come near her, 'Shall I say this psalm?' The Abbot faltered, 'Yes.' On which she repeated, in a clear voice, the noble psalm: 'Have mercy upon me, O God, after Thy great goodness: according to the multitude of Thy mercies do away mine offences.'

When she had come to the last line, she stood up on her feet, and took off her gloves and kerchief, which she gave to Elizabeth Tylney. The Book of Psalms she gave to Thomas Brydges, the Lieutenant's deputy. Then, she untied her gown, and took off her bridal gear. The headsman offered to assist her; but she put his hands gently aside, and drew a white kerchief round her eyes. The veiled figure of the executioner sank at her feet, and begged her forgiveness for what he had now to do. She whispered in his ear a few soft words of pity and pardon; and then said to him openly, 'I pray you despatch me quickly.' Kneeling before the block, she felt for it blindly with her open fingers. One who stood by her touched and guided her hand to the place which it sought; when she laid down her noble head, and saying, 'Lord, into Thy hands I commend my spirit,' passed, with the prayer on her lips, into her everlasting rest.

CHAPTER XX.

CRANMER, LATIMER, RIDLEY.

The fact of Cranmer having been lodged in the Gate house, once known as the Garden tower, now as the Bloody tower, has not been noted by the thousand and one historians of his age. It was recorded at the time by a resident in the Tower whose diary is still extant; and the fact now tardily recovered from the waste of time, may throw some light on a story which is confessed to be one of the puzzling pages in a great man's life.

From the day of his arrest, Cranmer appeared in a new part. He had never been deemed a coward. Even those who loved him least had given him credit for the virtues and the passions of a genuine man. As a student and a priest, he had been daring and original in a high degree. He had thought for himself. He had thwarted and opposed his clerical superiors. He had been bold enough to marry, not once, but twice. When every one else hung back in doubt as to the best way of dealing with the great divorce, his learning gave the clue, and his spirit supplied the force, by which Henry was delivered from his matrimonial chains. Since that time he had passed through a thousand of those trials which are said to temper and steel men's minds. He had sent brave knights to the block. He had knelt by the feet of dying queens. He had watched the flames lick up the flesh of martyred saints. Nothing in his course of life led any one to suspect that he feared to die. Up to the very hour of his arrest in council, his conduct had been stout; for, knowing how Queen Mary loathed him, he did not falter; and hearing of her march on London he did not fly. What hindered him from passing into France? To the friends who urged his flight, he proudly said, It was fit that he should stay, considering the post he held, and show that he was not afraid to own the changes which had been made in the late King's time.

Yet, from the day when he was seized and clapped in the Garden tower, his stomach began to fail. Brave old Latimer lay in the adjoining Garden house; and in a room which he could see from his window, dwelt the young and innocent Lady Jane. But the soul which animated Latimer and Lady Jane appears to have been scared out of

Cranmer in that hour of need. No doubt the hardships of his cell were great; for the winter months were cold; and though he dined with the Lieutenant, he was probably kept without a fire. Cranmer could not treat his situation as a theme for jokes. How could he tell whether some new Forrest might not break upon his sleep? He heard that the Queen was thirsting for his blood; he knew that Renard, a minister to whom the assassin's knife was a familiar thought, was at her side. Yet seeing that the primate felt no hope, it would have been manlier in him to affect no fear. The Queen, knowing how much he had been her enemy and her mother's enemy, was in no mood to forget her wrongs. Indeed, those wrongs were not of a kind which lonely and unhappy women like Mary can forgive; since they touched the honour of her birth, and the purity of her mother's name. With the dark blood, and the brooding passions of her mother's race, Mary had the strength to bear, but not the virtue to forbear. Nor, in such a case as hers, could a woman be expected to see the merit of an act of grace. Not only had this man's crafty brain suggested the scheme by which Catharine could be put away, but his audacious tongue had summoned that royal lady to his court, and on her failure to obey had given his judgment of divorce against her; branding her child, now queen, as a bastard; telling her, as a man of God, that while she had been calling herself Henry's wife, she had been actually wallowing in mortal sin. Could such an offender be forgiven? Mary told her Spanish adviser that until Cranmer was in the Tower she had never known one joyful day.

In the middle of September he was lodged in the Bloody tower. Winter was coming on; and his health began to droop. In November, he was suffered to leave his cell and walk in the garden below, under Latimer's window.

The winter was so cold, that Latimer sent his servant to tell the Lieutenant, with pathetic humour, that unless he took more care he would give him the slip. When Sir John Brydges, fearing lest the prelate meant to escape, ran from his pleasant fireside to the Garden house, the good old man assured him there was no cause for fear. 'They mean,' he said, 'to burn me; now unless you give me some wood in my chamber I shall die of cold.'

On the arrest of Wyat and the Kentish men, the London prisons were so choked with inmates that many of the city churches had to be used as jails. One church received four hundred captives. The Tower, especially, overflowed. Little Ease was crammed, and many of the Kentish gentlemen were thrust into the crypt. Some clergymen were sent to Newgate, some to the Fleet. Among other changes of cells and prisoners, Ridley and Latimer were put into Cranmer's room in the Garden tower; an opportunity of which they had never dreamt, and of which they made the highest use. Thrown together in the Garden tower, they kept up each other's spirits, by holding conferences on faith and works, which their friends found means to copy down and print. At Sir John Brydges' table, to which they walked by way of the wall terrace, afterwards known as Raleigh's walk, they met the Queen's confessor, Feckenham, who talked to them of the bread and wine, as he had done with Lady Jane, and strove to entrap them by his crafty words. Above all, they searched the Scriptures in their lonely rooms; but instead of finding in Holy Writ the evidence in proof of a bodily presence in the bread and wine, they satisfied their souls that mass could never be offered as a sacrifice for sin.

Yet Mary's end was gained, in some degree. The cold and misery of the Bloody tower broke Cranmer's spirit, as it had helped in some degree to break Dudley's spirit; so that the priest who, in Lambeth, had been little less than a hero, became, when he was removed to Oxford, little better than a craven. Mary felt that in Cranmer she could humiliate the Reformation. And she was right. The high deeds of many years have not sufficed to cover the weakness of a day, when the chosen champion of religious freedom set his seal to a recantation and denial of the most cherished sentiments of his life.

The only excuse that can be made for Cranmer is, that his flesh was frail, that he was greatly tried, that his denial was drawn from him, as it were, on the rack. When he found the Queen obdurate, he withdrew his denial, and met his death like a martyr. Peace to his soul!

Latimer and Ridley also passed through fire to their Father's house.

CHAPTER XXI.

WHITE ROSES.

On the removal of Cranmer to Oxford the Garden tower received Edward Courtney, the hapless White Rose of York.

'You here again, my lord?' said Brydges, as the boat pushed in. 'How is this?'

'Truly I cannot tell, unless I should accuse myself; let the world judge.'

He was placed at once in the Garden tower, to see whether any fact would turn up against him in the Wyat trials. His peril lay in his royal blood; his offence was in Renard's fear; an offence which, only a few days later, brought Elizabeth herself to the Strong Room. Renard insisted on these arrests being made; arrests, he said, which were essential to Mary's peace; arrests, he knew, which were essential to the policy then pursued by Spain.

In the dull seclusion of the Tower, Sir Thomas Wyat had become another man to what he had been at Rochester and Southwark. Gardiner, who had become, next after Renard, the Queen's chief councillor, spoke of him with scorn, as 'little Wyat, a bastard of no substance.' On his trial, Wyat hinted that there were higher traitors than himself; and his words were enough to justify Renard in urging the arrest of Elizabeth. Wyat said he had sent a letter to the Princess Elizabeth, praying her to get as far from London as she could; and that the Princess had sent him thanks for his good will, saying she would act as she found cause. He said he had been in correspondence with Lord Courtney, who had told him to proceed in his course. He said he was called the Captain, but that four or five others ranked above him in the camp.

Who were these others? 'Elizabeth first, and Courtney next,' said Renard. Both were sent to the Tower, in the hope that matter could be drawn from the 'little bastard' which might warrant a jealous Queen in taking both their lives.

For the moment every one turned to Wyat. Sir John Brydges, the Lieutenant, worked upon his love of life and his fear of death; and, sad to say, the dashing young knight, who had once stuck the scroll in his cap, to tempt an assassin's blow, now listened to the Lieutenant's words. Under skilful treatment, he seemed willing to become a tool. He hinted at grave matters. He affected much knowledge. When the council met in the Lieutenant's house, he was brought before them, as one having high secrets in his keeping, which her Majesty ought to know. Before this council he made a charge against Courtney, and raised a suspicion against Elizabeth, which threw these personages into Renard's power.

The Queen was so much pleased with Brydges, that she sent him a baron's patent; calling him to the House of Lords as Baron Chandos of Sudeley Castle, the residence of Queen Catharine Parr.

But his work was not yet done. To strike at Elizabeth, as Renard meant to strike, was one of those acts of policy which could only be dared on the strongest grounds. But the accusation of a dying man, a partner in the crime, who has ceased to be swayed by hope of life and fear of death, is *very* strong ground. Chandos had persuaded Wyat to make a charge in private; he had now to persuade him to repeat that charge in public; and in presence of the man whom his words would involve in guilt. The second part of his work was not so easy as the first. Wyat had hinted secrets in order to save his life; but we now began to fear that he had made this sacrifice in vain. In truth, his death was necessary to Renard's method of proceeding; since the evidence wanted against Courtney and Elizabeth was that of a dying and impartial man. Yet Chandos thought he had gained his point; and on the morning fixed for Wyat's execution, he arranged in the Garden tower a most striking scene.

On his way to Tower Hill for execution, Wyat was halted at the door of the Garden tower, in which Courtney lay, and conducted by Lord Chandos into the upper room, which he found full of great people; lords of her Majesty's council; Sir John Lyon, Lord Mayor, with David Woodruffe and William Chester, Sheriffs; Gentlemen of the Guard, officers and wardens of the Tower; all eager for the few words which he had been taught to pronounce, and on which the lives of Courtney and Elizabeth might be said to hang. To the chagrin of Lord Chandos, to the joy of Sir John Lyon and the Sheriffs, Wyat declared that he had nothing more to say. When he was placed before Courtney, in the midst of frowning councillors and kneeling sheriffs, he proudly called for the death procession to move on, as he had nothing to allege against either Courtney or Elizabeth.

Later in the day, two reports were made by spectators of what had taken place in the Garden tower. Chandos told the House of Lords that Wyat had implored Lord Courtney to tell the truth; and he told his story to the peers in such a way as to suggest that if Courtney had confessed the truth he would have confessed his guilt. The Sheriffs of London told the citizens that Wyat had begged Lord Courtney's pardon for having in his first and false confession brought the names of Courtney and Elizabeth together in connexion with his plot.

The death procession then moved on. A few minutes later, when the axe was gleaming near his eyes, the rebel told a crowd of people who had come to see him die, that he had never accused either the Princess or the Marquis of a guilty knowledge of his plot; that he could not truly make that charge, since they had known nothing of his affairs until the rising in Kent had taken place. 'You said not so before the council,' cried a priest who stood beside him. 'That which I then said, I said; that which I now say is true,' replied the rebel. In a moment more his head was in the dust.

No proceeding could be based on such a confession against the Queen's sister and heiress; but Renard could not think of letting Courtney escape his toils. Courtney was the White Rose; the White Rose was an English flower; and the Pomegranate was the only rose for which Renard cared. Though Courtney could not be put on trial, he was carried to Fotheringay Castle, where he was kept in durance until the marriage of Philip and Mary had taken place, when he was put on board ship, and sent abroad. He wandered about Europe, in what was understood as honourable exile, for a couple of years, and then died suddenly at Padua (not without hints of poison), in his twenty-ninth year. He was buried in the splendid church of Sant Antonio, and his ashes were covered with a sumptuous tomb.

Elizabeth is said to have looked with a favouring eye on Courtney; but his early death, before she came to her own, put an end to all chance of his ever being called upon to wear a king consort's crown.

Dying a bachelor, Courtney's titles of earl and marquis appeared to be gone for ever; but in an old country like England family titles have a charmed life. Ten generations after the pale young Earl of Devon and Marquis of Exeter died at Padua, a discovery was made which led to a revival of the earldom of Devon in the same old line. The patent granted to Edward Courtney on his release from the Tower by Queen Mary, was worded in a peculiar way; perhaps by an error of the copying clerk; for the Earldom of Devon was given to him and to his 'male heirs' for ever; the usual words 'of his body' being omitted from the grant. On the ground of his being one of Edward Courtney's 'male heirs,' the Viscount Courtney of our own day laid a claim before the House of Peers for the earldom of Devon, and having made out his descent from Hugh, the second earl, a remote ancestor of the youth who lived in the Tower and died in Padua, that House resolved that he had established his right and must take his seat as Earl.

On Edward Courtney's death, the honours and perils of the White Rose fell upon Edmund and Arthur De la Pole, the luckless descendants of George, Duke of Clarence; and Beauchamp tower, the prison in which they pined away, shows many a sad memorial from their hands.

In the summer of 1562, when Queen Elizabeth was in the prime of her youth and beauty, an astrologer named Prestal, pretending that he had cast her horoscope, affirmed that she would die in the following spring, when her crown would devolve by right on Mary, ex-Queen of France, and reigning Queen of Scots. When Edmund and Arthur Pole (nephews of Cardinal Pole) heard of this prophecy, they thought it would beseem them, as members of the royal family, to prepare for the coming-in of Mary by raising a body of troops and throwing them into Wales. Mary was young, and a widow; and some one whispered to these poor boys that she might marry Edmund, who would then become king, and make his brother Arthur Duke of Clarence. Burghley seized them at the Dolphin Tavern, on Bankside, near the Globe playhouse, as they were going to take boat for Flanders. Carried before the Council, they protested that they had never sought their sovereign's life, that they had never dreamt of laying hands upon her crown, that their aim, however wrong, had been confined to bringing in the true heir when her throne was vacant. But their name was against them; a jury found them guilty of high treason; and a judge condemned them to die a traitor's death.

Edmund was barely twenty, Arthur about thirty, when they were captured at Bankside. Their youth, and perhaps their folly, pleaded for them with the Queen; who had never yet signed a warrant for any political offender's death. She left the two brothers the consolation of each other's society in the Beauchamp tower; Edmund sleeping in the upper, and Arthur in the lower room. Each has left tracings on the wall; the sadder, as I think, those of the younger and more innocent boy.

In the first year of his imprisonment the young Plantagenet wrote in the stone:

DIO SEMIN
IN LACHRIMIS IN
EXULTATIONE METER.
Æ. 21. E. POOLE,
1562.

Six years later there is a second inscription, now illegible, from his hands. Half-way down the winding stair, in a narrow slit through the masonry, he must have sat very often, with the gay life of the river spread out before him, the ships coming up and going down, the horsemen with their swords and plumes, the children playing on the bank, the country folks staring at the lions, and a little farther off the processions on the bridge. From his seat on the stairs he could see the fatal spot near St. Mary's Church, where, tempted by the lying astrologer, he was taking boat for Flanders when seized by Burghley's men. Unhappy youth! Yet he was less unhappy in the Tower than he might have been elsewhere. He might have been married to Mary; he might have perished, as his cousin Darnley perished, in some Kirk of Field. Even in the Beauchamp tower he was luckier than many other princes of his race. His great-grandsire, the Duke of Clarence, had been drowned in the Boyer tower; his grandmother, Margaret of Salisbury, had been hacked to pieces on Tower green; his father had been executed on Tower Hill. Compared with most of his race—who inherited the curse of his royal blood—his fate was mild; since he fell into trouble in that golden time of Elizabeth's reign, when the land was free from any stain of blood. As in the upper room, so on the staircase, he has left two records of his long imprisonment. In the slit, through which he could see the ships, the river, and the bridge, the church of St. Mary's and the playhouse at Bankside, he has twice inscribed his name.

Arthur also left inscriptions on the wall; inscriptions rich in wisdom and resignation. To wit:

I H S
A PASSAGE PERILLUS
MAKETH A PORTE
PLEASANT
A D 1568
ARTHUR POOLE
Æ SUE 37
A P.

The two princes pined and died in the Tower, when their ashes were laid in St. Peter's Church.

CHAPTER XXII.

PRINCESS MARGARET.

One prisoner in the Tower has the rare distinction of being an actual ancestress of Queen Victoria. Outside the strong room of the Belfry is a small chamber, on the wall of which appear these words:

UPON THE TWENTIETH DAY OF JUNE
IN THE YEAR OF OUR LORD ONE THOUSAND
FIVE HUNDRED THREESCORE AND FIVE
WAS THE RIGHT HONORABLE COUNTESS OF
LENNOX GRACE COMMITTED
PRISONER TO THIS LODGING FOR THE MARRIAGE
OF HER SON MY LORD HENRY DARNLE AND THE
QUEEN OF SCOTLAND

HERE IS THE NAMES THAT DO WAIT
UPON HER NOBLE GRACE IN THIS PLACE.
M. ELIZABETH HOSEY
M. JHAN BAILY
M. ELIZABETH CHAMBRLEN
M. ROBARTE PORTYNGTON
EDWARDE GREYNE
ANNO DOMINI 1566

On a second stone we read—

AS GOD PRESERVED CHRIST HIS SON
IN TROUBLE AND IN THRALL
SO WHEN WE CALL UPON THE LORD
HE WILL PRESERVE US ALL.

The Right Honourable the Countess of Lennox' Grace was the Princess Margaret, daughter of Queen Margaret, and Queen Elizabeth's first cousin of the royal blood.

Margaret's career as a princess living at the English court, may be divided into two parts: The first part records her love affairs until her marriage with her kinsman, Matthew, Earl of Lennox; the second part records the intrigues which led her son, Lord Darnley, to the consort-crown of Scotland, and ended with his murder at the Kirk of Field.

When Margaret came to London, at the age of fourteen, she lived with her aunt Mary Tudor, Queen of France, who, like her own mother, the Queen of Scots, had married again for love. Thence she went to Beaulieu, the house of her cousin Mary, until the birth of Elizabeth, when the King, her uncle, gave her a regular place at court, as first lady of honour to his infant child. She was then eighteen. Like all the ladies of her kin, she was apt to fall in love. While she was yet a girl, some passages between her and Murray had alarmed her friends; and when she met in the house of Anne Boleyn the young and handsome Lord Thomas Howard, she set the court in a flutter by her open preference for this kinsman of the Queen. Howard was encouraged by Anne to press his suit, and Margaret, in her lightsome mood, was very soon tempted into plighting her troth to the man she loved.

That act of devotion cost Lord Thomas Howard his liberty and life. The young lady stood too near the throne for any man to dream of asking her hand, unless with the King's consent to woo and wed. Henry was much perplexed about his crown. His daughter Mary had been tainted in her birth. In no long time his second daughter was to fall under the same dark stain. He had no son; and, in the absence of heirs, his crown would go to the children of his elder sister, the Queen of Scots. These children were James the Fifth and this Princess Margaret. James was barred by the Alien Act; so that Margaret was in fact the King's lawful heir. Had Henry died before his son was born, Margaret would have been called to the throne.

The settlement in life of such a lady was a state affair of hardly less moment than the marriage of Henry himself. When, therefore, the King heard of a contract having been made by Lord Thomas with the young princess, he gave instant order to have the offender quickly seized and safely lodged. Short work was made with him. A bill of attainder passed; and Howard, condemned to die for his love, was left to linger out his life in the Tower, where he slowly pined to death—dying, if his noble kinsman, the poet Surrey, may be credited, for the love of his betrothed.

The Princess Margaret was sent to the convent at Sion, on the Thames, where she was placed under the special care of the lady abbess, with instructions that she should be allowed to walk in the garden by the river side, though in other things she was still to be considered as the King's prisoner rather than his niece.

To this affair of Howard and Princess Margaret we owe the first royal Marriage Act; which made it treason for any man to marry, unless with the King's consent, given under the great seal, any daughter, sister, aunt, or niece of the reigning prince.

By-and-bye the Princess found a fresh adorer in Charles, a son of Lord William Howard; but this affair was less grave, since the lovers exchanged kisses only, and no troth was plighted on the lady's side. Yet Henry thought it well to send Cranmer to his niece with a view to dissuade her from playing, as it were, with fire. Then rose the question as to how a Tudor girl could be hindered from falling into love? Only one way was known; and by good advice this way was followed by the King. At the age of thirty she was given in wedlock to her kinsman Matthew, fourth Earl of Lennox—a man who not only loved her well, but, as a partisan of England, seemed likely to prevent her feet from straying into dangerous ways. So ended, in a happy marriage, the first stage of Princess Margaret's life.

To the Earl of Lennox she bore two sons, Henry and Charles, princes of the blood royal, who were recognised and educated at the English court. King Henry bestowed on his niece that abbey of Jervaulx in which Adam Sedburgh had reared his horses and made his cheese.

Unhappily, Margaret and Elizabeth were not good friends, and when Elizabeth came to the throne the Princess fell out of favour. Many things divided them,—some personal, others political. Margaret is said to have done a wrong to the Princess when a girl, which the Queen could not forget,—put some slur upon her title; a slur which, coming from a woman whose father and mother were described in a papal brief as having never been married at all, the proud girl could not stomach. Margaret was a pretender also; a pretender backed by a large and turbulent party. She was a Catholic, like her niece the Queen of Scots. Her husband was a Catholic; and her sons, Henry and Charles, had been secretly brought up in their mother's faith. Thus the Catholic gentry reaped the large benefit of having a race of English princes on their side. Lord Darnley, the elder boy, was from his cradle the hope and boast of an army of fanatics, strong enough to cause the Queen much trouble, since it was reckoned by very shrewd heads to comprise two out of every three country squires rich enough to hold commissions in the peace.

While these princes were yet boys, they were left in peace; but as they grew in years their mother Margaret began to dream of a crown for her elder son. Lennox adopted her ideas. Their hope was to match Lord Darnley with his cousin the Queen of Scots; a project which they knew that the Queen of England would never brook; but which they trusted by craft and daring to bring about, even though it should drive her wild with rage.

Now the marriage of Mary, Queen of Scots, was one of those topics which no English councillor could ever allow to escape his pillow. Mary stood next in succession to the crown which had been won on Bosworth Field; next in blood, if not in actual law; and the purpose which had been kept in view by the best of Elizabeth's advisers, from the moment when she ceased to think of being succeeded by children of her own, was a union of the English and Scottish crowns on a single head; an object only to be accomplished by uniting them in a descendant of Henry the Seventh, of the Scottish line. Thus Mary's son would be the very next English King. Mary's choice of a second mate was consequently an affair of English policy, in which the English Queen and council fancied they had a right to make their voices heard. Elizabeth wished her cousin to marry a man of English views; if possible, of English blood. Darnley was now known to be a Papist —in her eyes a fatal bar.

On hearing a first hint of this design of putting Darnley on the throne as king-consort, to become the father of an English line, Elizabeth threw Lennox into the Tower, and placed her cousin in a country-house at Sheen. The affair struck Burghley as one of the gravest in which his mistress had ever been engaged. A match between Darnley and Mary would unite the Catholic party in England to the Catholic party in Scotland; a union fatal to the public peace, if not dangerous to Elizabeth's throne. In presence of such a peril the English council had to march with no timid step.

Lennox, lodged in the Tower, was closely watched; denied, as he alleged, both air and exercise; worse than all, he was not allowed to dine and sup at the Lieutenant's board. Thomas Bishop was employed to rake up charges against him; and this scoundrel made out a list both long and black. Lennox, if not his wife, could see at no great distance a vision of the axe and block; and they saw the policy of working by another line. The Earl submitted; on which Sir Edward Warner, the Lieutenant, invited him to dine and sup with the other prisoners of his rank. The Countess threw herself on the Queen's compassion; and Elizabeth, who liked to do her kinsfolk good, when she could serve them without peril, let the penitent Earl rejoin his wife at Sheen.

Margaret and Lennox had only yielded to gain time. They had given their word, but they had never thought of holding to the pledge. In fact, they meant to play their game, and win the English crown by either fair means or by foul. If the Queen of England were against them, the Queen of Scots was on their side. Elizabeth was proposing Lord Robert Dudley, the handsomest man in Europe, to her cousin; offering as the bait of this English match the instant proclamation of Mary as her heir. The Queen of Scots, unable to see her duty with English eyes, refused the match. Darnley was a Catholic like herself; a descendant of Henry the Seventh like herself; and though he had none of the personal advantages of Lord Robert, she resolved to take him for her mate.

Burghley, deceived by Margaret's penitential airs, imagined that Lennox, who seemed to have given up every thought of the match for his son, might be employed as an English agent in the Scottish court. Lennox wished to go north on his own account; but he wished to go north as the representative of English credit and English might. Now, Burghley desired to have a man of high rank, in whom he could trust, near the Queen of Scots, until she should have Lord Leicester as a husband by her side. Lennox proffered his service, professing a strong desire to see Leicester married to the Scottish queen. If Lennox had been true to his word, no safer agent for his purpose lay within Burghley's reach. The English had yet to learn that he was not true to his word.

Supplied with pistoles to spend, and trinkets to give away, Lennox went north, leaving Margaret and the two boys in London. He was armed with letters of acceptance from Burghley, from Leicester, and from the Queen. He bore a confidential note from the Queen of England to the Queen of Scots. His reception at Holyrood was kind. The Queen received him in her chamber; the three Maries smiled upon him; David Rizzio gave him welcome. He sent the news of his reception by his wife's niece and her court to Leicester and to Elizabeth. His own affairs, too, were prospering; but some difficult point of Scottish law required that his son, Lord Darnley, should be present when certain deeds were being signed. He begged her Majesty's license for his son to make a short trip into the north, in order that no legal doubts might afterwards arise. Burghley, still believing in the Earl, allowed the young gentleman to start. Lennox became still more intimate with the Queen of Scots. Mary went with her ladies to sup in his room, where she danced, and played dice, and lost a jewel to the Earl. Backed by the whole English party in Mary's court, as well as by Mary herself, Lennox made rapid way in his suit; and his son had scarcely appeared in the palace of Holyrood, ere he announced to his private friends in Scotland that there was such love between the royal cousins as would end in a match.

On this report reaching London, orders were sent by Burghley for the prompt return of Lennox and Darnley into England. Then came the blow which all along Lennox had meant to deal at the English Queen. He refused to obey, cast off his allegiance, and defied her Majesty's power. He and his son were beyond her reach.

This revolt in her own family not only vexed but alarmed the Queen, who saw her wise care for her kingdom crossed by the humour of a vain woman and the folly of a petulant boy. She arrested Margaret; and her younger son, Charles, a child of nine, was placed in the charge of Lady Knyvet, while his mother was being escorted to the Tower.

Elizabeth hoped that the plot was checked. Knowing Lord Darnley and the Queen of Scots, she felt that this boy of nineteen was no husband for this widow of twenty-three. Boding evil of every kind from such a match, she set her face against it, even though she could not punish either the reckless boy or the wilful queen. Lennox pressed his suit. Darnley made a friend of Rizzio; and Mary, in face of the remonstrance of her brother Murray, the best man in her court, gave her hand to the youth who, of all her suitors, was the most objectionable in English eyes.

When news of their private marriage, which took place in Rizzio's chamber, reached London, the Queen could not believe it. Then came the public rite; the revolt of Murray; and the thousand troubles which followed in their train. More than once the thought of sending an army across the border came into Elizabeth's mind, but the Queen controlled her temper, and left the Scottish drama to end in its own dark way.

Margaret's confinement in the Tower, though close, was far from being harsh. The best rooms in the Lieutenant's house were given up to her use and that of her attendants, and were furnished anew with arras, tables, stools, and plate. A firepan was put into her room; which was supplied with ewers and drinking cups becoming her estate. Two ladies, a maid, one gentleman, and a yeoman, were received in her train, and lodged at the public cost in the Lieutenant's house.

In this state, the daughter of Queen Margaret lay in the Tower. News came to her from her son. She heard of the private marriage in Rizzio's room; of that scene in the kirk where Knox inveighed against the rule of women and boys; of the flight of Murray; of the quarrels of Darnley and Mary; of the murder of Rizzio; of the ominous reconciliation of Murray and the Queen; and of the perilous situation of that son for whom she was enduring her sharp restraint. Few rays of comfort ever reached her cell. Lennox neglected, Darnley forgot her. Of course, she found her situation bad. Her rooms were small, her means were scant. When her cries reached the throne,

Elizabeth sent her Lord Treasurer, the Marquis of Winchester, to look into her case and make things straight, if the royal lady would show him the way to do it. Margaret would not help the Marquis. In truth, her case was not one to be met by a few honied words and a few trifling cares. Her misery was that she had married a faithless husband, that she had borne a foolish son, that she was made the pledge of an unpopular cause.

Darnley, now king consort beyond the Tweed, offered himself as a chief to every man living south of that river who disliked the Queen; and more than once, in his madness, he proposed to cross the border into England, raise a new Pilgrimage of Grace, and drive her from the realm by force.

Thus, the two royal cousins watched the course of events beyond the Tweed, in which they felt an equal passion; one from her apartments in Whitehall, the other from her chamber in the Tower.

One event occurred which might have made them friends; the birth of a prince. That child would be the next English king. In him, therefore, the two women had a common interest; the first as her official heir, the second as her natural heir. Elizabeth melted towards the lady in the Tower, whose son and husband were rejoicing in their Scottish capital over this auspicious birth; but the folly of Lennox and Darnley would not suffer her to express her feelings in acts of grace. The daughter of King Henry and the daughter of Queen Margaret were still to sit apart; watching events beyond the Tweed; and peering through the distance into that cloud of tragic gloom.

Then came the blow which was to end their strife. Darnley was murdered at the Kirk of Field; the victim of his beautiful and perfidious wife. On this news reaching London, the Queen sent down to her Lieutenant, and set her captive free. All the evil which she had feared was come to pass; and though she could never love her cousin, she would not add the misery of confinement to the agonies of a breaking heart.

After Queen Mary had been driven out of her kingdom, and Murray had been shot, Lennox was appointed Regent. Like Murray, he fell by an assassin's hand. Margaret, who stayed in London, sank into poverty and obscurity; only broken by fresh troubles in the marriage of her second son, Charles, to Elizabeth Cavendish. She died at last so poor, that her funeral had to be conducted at the Queen's expense; when she was borne in a state procession to the great Abbey, where she lies among the kings and princes of her race.

When the Princess died, her elder son's only child, James Stuart, was a young man; her younger son's only child, Arabella Stuart, was a little girl. The boy, a dull fellow, was to wear the English crown; the girl, a fair, bright creature, was to be one of that dull boy's captives in the Tower.

CHAPTER XXIII.

PLOT AND COUNTERPLOT.

Sixteen months after Darnley's murder in the Kirk of Field, Queen Mary, his wife and cousin, was a fugitive from justice on English soil. She had married his murderer and lost her crown.

At this moment of her career, the situation of Mary Stuart seemed lonely enough to subdue the wildest spirit. She had lost, not only her crown, but her reputation and her child. The half-brother who had been her companion in youth, was in arms against her. The thanes who had stood around her throne, had flung her into jail. The parliament of her kingdom had set on her brow the brand of murderess. What was she to live for more? At twenty-six she had exhausted every passion of the soul. She had reigned as Queen since she was six days old. She had been adored by poets, warriors, and musicians. She had married three husbands; and these three husbands she had lost by death, by murder, and by captivity. She had enjoyed every luxury of earth, and she had suffered every bolt from heaven. At an age when good women are beginning to taste the flavour of life, she was already separated from her partner in crime, and seeking on a foreign soil a refuge from her country, her brother, and her son.

Such a fugitive might have been expected to live in quiet, to shun the public eye, and to devote her days and nights to making her peace with God. But this was not the view which Mary Stuart and her friends—most of all her clerical friends—were disposed to take of her duty towards the land into which she had come. Granted she was a great sinner; yet sinners have their rights in the law as well as saints. She was a queen, and queens are not to be punished for offences like the rank and file. David, said her divines, was an adulterer and a murderer; yet his people had not risen against him, and taken away his crown. The commons have no authority to judge their kings. If kings go wrong, the Lord will chastise them with rods of steel. They must be left to God; but they must be left to God in hope and charity, not in wrath of spirit. Even from the Scottish pulpits, in the midst of people to whom the details of her life were known, these doctrines were put forth. 'St. David was an adulterer, and so was she,' cried Alexander Gordon, Archbishop of Athens and Bishop of Galloway; 'St. David committed murder, and so did she. But what is this to the matter?' In Gordon's view it was hardly anything at all.

From the hour of her stepping on English soil, Mary Stuart began to plot against Elizabeth's peace, and in all her plots she had the personal sanction and service of John Leslie, the able and learned Bishop of Ross, who became her agent, her confessor, and her spy. This bishop was a divine of the Italian and Spanish type; supple, tolerant, unscrupulous; a man of courts and of affairs; easy with fair sinners, facile with great; never afraid of lying and deceit; and bent on serving his church, even though he should have to do so at the peril of his soul. The plots and counterplots of this crafty woman and her yet more crafty priest, have no examples, except in the Spanish and Italian comedy of intrigue.

To any other woman than Mary Stuart, to any other bishop than John Leslie, the events which had driven the Queen of Scots from Holyrood, and of which her English cousin, in giving her shelter from her foes, was bound to take due notice, would have seemed sufficient to cancel her claim on the English crown. She had no rights in London which she had not in Edinburgh; and the highest court in Scotland had deprived her by solemn acts of all those rights. Found guilty of murder, her very life stood forfeit to the law. In England, too, she was a stranger, excluded from succession by the Alien Act.

But all these facts and laws were nothing to the Queen of Scots, and to her spiritual adviser the Bishop of Ross. She had the example of her cousin, Mary Tudor, before her eyes. Mary Tudor had found no favour in the law; yet law and power united—the letters-patent, the fleet, the army, and the council—had not been able to sustain the nine-days' Queen against the higher force which lay in her rights of blood. Ross pretended that a right of nature is not to be lost by personal offences; and he cited his favourite case of David on the house-top in Zion, and Uriah in the fore-front of the war at Rabbah. Neither Mary Stuart nor her priest could quite forget the points which, in comparison with Mary Tudor, told most fatally against her claims. Unlike her English cousin, the Queen of Scots was an alien, a murderess, and a fugitive. She had no great friends abroad, and not a single friend at home. But she had weapons, and they knew it, such as Mary Tudor could never boast; bright eyes, a velvet touch, and a wheedling tongue. The Bishop himself, though he had professionally renounced the devil and all his works, could not escape the charm of Mary's smile. No woman in the world had so much power of making fools of men. Besides her dazzling beauty, she had a wide experience in the ways of love, and knew the arts by which men's senses are enslaved. No poet, warrior, troubadour, had yet been able to resist her wiles; the best and worst had fallen equally at her feet; for when her grace and radiance failed of their proud effect, she could throw into the charm by which she drew men to her the lustre of her royal birth and her expected crown.

With such advantages of face and birth, how could Mary Stuart want for friends? Among the English lords who were coming to York with power to judge between her and the Scots, was no man open to the flash of peerless eyes? If Mary could find a lover on the bench of judges, she might rebuke her brother, the Regent Murray, and weaken the position of her cousin the English Queen.

From the lords sent down to York on the Scottish business, she selected as her prey, with the assent of her Catholic counsellor, that stern reformer, Thomas, fourth Duke of Norfolk, the richest noble and strictest Protestant in her cousin's court. It is not likely that she would have gone so far as to marry him; for he was crabbed in temper, weak in purpose, ugly in figure; even if the sour but honest Duke could have been persuaded to take her as a wife, while her husband, Bothwell, was yet alive. But short of actual marriage, a clever woman might do much; and Mary's misfortune was that her brain was only too prompt to suggest the way of doing any bad thing on which she set her heart.

Norfolk was not the only conquest which she deigned to make. Thomas Percy—son of Sir Thomas the Pilgrim—a man who, on the fall of Dudley, had been restored by Philip and Mary to the ancient honours of his house, as seventh Earl of Northumberland, and Warden of the East and Middle Marches—was in cross humour with the Queen. He thought himself ill used. Elizabeth had taken from him the great power of Warden of the Marches, and given this power to William, Lord Grey of Wilton, a man whom Percy regarded as inferior to himself in birth and rank. Percy's confessor found fault with the policy pursued by Burghley; and Percy had begun to think that the old religion and the old families would never fare well in England until the dynasty was changed. The Queen of Scots had an easy conquest in the Earl.

But Percy was one of her minor cards; to be played or not, as fortune should suggest; her game was to be made on Norfolk, whom she had drawn to her side in body and soul. 'Have a care, my lord, on what pillow you lay your head,' said Elizabeth slyly to the Duke. Poor Duke, the only pillow to which Mary Stuart could lead him was the block!

For a time, the coming over of Norfolk and his party to the Queen of Scots gave a lively turn to her affairs; leading to many wild hopes in the north, and to much correspondence with the courts of Brussels and Madrid. For the conveyance of this dangerous correspondence, Leslie, —who had been received by Elizabeth as an ambassador from the Queen of Scots—had to find out trusty agents; men who were willing to risk their lives for either a purse of money or a bishop's thanks. Where a fanatic could be found, he was naturally preferred.

Among the shrewdest of the many agents employed by the Bishop of Ross, in going and coming between London and Brussels, was a young Fleming, known as Monsieur Charles, who seems to have been a messenger and spy to Signor Ridolfi, the secret minister of Pius the Fifth. Clever with pen and pencil, speaking four or five languages like a native, a good Catholic, poor, and of no family, attached to Mary Stuart as to a royal saint, professing boundless reverence for his Church, the young Fleming, Charles Bailly, was just the man for conspirators like Ridolfi and the Bishop of Ross. He knew the country and the Continent. In Scotland a Scot, in Italy an Italian, in Flanders a Fleming, in France a Gaul, he could go anywhere, and pass for anything. One day he might be a merchant, a second day an artist, a third day a courtier. Cobham, then Lord Warden of the Five Ports, was keen of scent, yet Monsieur Charles crossed and recrossed from Dover without exciting his jealous quest. Not until he and his packet of letters fell under Burghley's scrutiny was the young Fleming caught in the trap, and made to give up the secrets which he knew.

Norfolk was led to fancy that he could wed the Queen of Scots, and carry her back to Edinburgh with the help of Spanish gold and English steel. Leslie thought so too. Not that the Duke and Bishop regarded Mary as a royal saint, whom it was a sacred duty to assist in recovering her lost throne. They knew her too well. Howard, while he was offering her his hand, believed in his heart that she had been privy to Darnley's death; and Leslie, who knew her as only a priest could know her, believed that she had not only taken off her second husband, but her first. But the fact of Mary being a bad woman was of no account to men with purposes like theirs. She was a Queen. In her veins ran the blood of Stuart, Tudor, and Plantagenet. Her children, thought Howard, will wear two crowns; her advent in London, thought Leslie, will serve the universal Church. The two men thought of Mary as a tool which they could use for purposes of their own. Norfolk persuaded himself that he was not a boy, to be put aside like Darnley; and the Bishop of Ross repeated to himself that even when David had taken Uriah's wife he had not been wholly cast out from the fold of God. The Duke thought himself a wary man; young in years, but ripe in knowledge; with an experience of married life equal at least to that of Mary, since he had buried three duchesses of Norfolk before he was thirty-one years old. The Bishop must have laughed under his cope at the Duke's pretence of being able to control the Queen of Scots.

Elizabeth sent for Norfolk. In the gallery at Whitehall she rated him for trying after a match with her cousin, a pretender to her crown, without coming to her for leave. The Duke made light of the affair; he cared nothing, he said, for the Queen of Scots; he had nothing to gain by the alliance; his own estates in England being worth little less than the whole kingdom of Scotland. Words so haughty must have struck the Queen. The foolish fellow added that when he stood in his own tennis-court in Norwich he felt himself a prince.

What wonder that the Queen was cold to him after that memorable day? Norfolk felt that he was losing favour; and to make things worse for him he withdrew from court without taking leave; retiring to Kenning

Hall, his great castle on the Waveney, which was linked in every one's memory with the advent of that other Catholic Queen. But Elizabeth was not Jane. Norfolk was soon arrested and in the Tower; though not in peril of his life until Ross and Mary began to stir up friends in the north, sons of the old Pilgrims of Grace, to make a diversion in his favor by a sudden appeal to arms.

Percy, Earl of Northumberland, rose at once. Joined by Charles Nevill, Earl of Westmoreland, he donned the Pilgrim's badge, a cross, with the five wounds of Christ; entered Durham at the head of his armed followers; declared the Catholic Church restored to her ancient rights; attended high mass in the Cathedral; and then marched forward to Clifford Moor, on which he encamped with six thousand horse and four thousand foot. The rebel Earls proposed to advance on York, and raising the country as they went along, push onward for the Don. If they could reach Tutbury, on the Dove, where the Queen of Scots then dwelt, and carry her back to Scotland on their shields, Percy might hope for some sweet reward, and both the Earls could defy Elizabeth's power. But while Percy and Nevill were dreaming, Sussex, Clinton, and Warwick, were rushing on their lines with overwhelming power. The rebels retreated across the border; whence Nevill escaped to Flanders, where the Countess of Northumberland joined him; while Percy himself, unable to get on board a vessel in the Firth, was seized by Murray, and flung into Lochleven castle, the strong and lonely pile from which Queen Mary had escaped.

CHAPTER XXIV.

MONSIEUR CHARLES.

The game seemed passing out of Leslie's hands; but the Bishop of Ross knew far too much of what was passing out of sight to feel discouraged. His friend Ridolfi, the Papal agent, had drawn up a list of men in the English court on whom the Pope could rely; and this list, of which Leslie had a copy, included many of the most ancient barons of the realm. What was going on in Rome was to bring a change over Mary's fortunes. A Papal bull was to be launched; Elizabeth was to be cast down; all good Catholics were to be charged, on peril of their souls, to rise up against her. The Queen dethroned, who was to take her place? That was Leslie's care.

Under the name of 'A defence of the honour of Mary, Queen of Scotland,' Leslie wrote a book which he sent Monsieur Charles abroad to get printed for him at the Liège press; a dangerous book to own, since it dealt, in a very bold spirit, with the whole question of Mary's claims to the English crown. In his own mind Leslie had formed a perfect plan; the first part of which was to get Norfolk freed from the Tower, so as to have all his forces in the front. In this feat he succeeded, at the cost of some lying and much pledging on Norfolk's part. Norfolk being free, Leslie sent Monsieur Charles to Liège for copies of his book, so as to be ready to act when the Papal bull arrived. Events, he hoped, would take the following course. The world would read his argument on the title, and be convinced. When men were ready for the truth, the Papal bull would arrive. He would then announce that the Queen was deposed, that the Church had cut her off, that the Catholic powers had declared war against her, that the whole country was up in arms. On this the Catholic lords would seize the Tower; Norfolk would march on Tutbury; and in a few weeks Mary would be crowned in Westminster, the Spanish party would come into power, and the Universal Church would be restored.

The plot was a very fine plot on paper; but Leslie's instruments failed him, and, in truth, he failed himself. A raid of some English troops into the Western Highlands piqued him into a premature publication of the Papal brief. The barons were not ready; and as the London citizens read the bull and passed on laughing, the great conspiracy ended like a farce, except to Leslie and his agents.

Monsieur Charles was leaving Brussels for London with copies of the Bishop's book, and letters from Lady Northumberland, Lord Westmoreland, and other exiles, when the Italian minister, Ridolfi, gave him a packet of three letters addressed to the Bishop of Ross. Landing at Dover, Monsieur Charles was overhauled by the Lord Warden's men; and the books and letters being found in his bag, he was carried up to London for examination by Lord Cobham himself. The books were in English, and the offence of bringing them into England was no trifle; but the three letters, as Monsieur Charles knew only too well, were far more serious than the books. On his way to Cobham's house in Blackfriars, he contrived to send news of his arrest to the Bishop of Ross.

Monsieur Charles and his bag were examined by William Brooke, Lord Cobham, and his brother Thomas, once the companion of Wyat. The letters were in cypher, and two of them were addressed to 30 and 40. The young

Fleming said he knew nothing about them; he was only a messenger; he could not read the cypher; nor had he any clue to the numbers. But on closer search of Monsieur Charles's clothes, a key to this cypher was found sewed up in his coat; by means of which key Lord Cobham and his brother were soon aware what perilous stuff Monsieur Charles had brought to Dover in his bag. Cobham felt that he must carry the books and papers to Burghley; but his brother Thomas, now become a Catholic, catching a sign from Monsieur Charles, opposed this course; urging that the moment these books and papers came into Burghley's hands, their friend, the Duke of Norfolk, would be a dead man. Cobham could not see it, nor could Monsieur Charles explain to him how the Duke was touched. But in fact, as Bailly knew very well, number 30 meant the Duke of Norfolk, number 40 meant Lord Lumley; and the letters addressed to them by the Pope's agent contained treason enough to bring twenty heads to the block, even under a Queen who had never yet shed one drop of traitor's blood.

Cobham got into his boat, and pulled for Burghley's house; but on the way he softened towards his brother's prayer; the more so, as he thought despondingly of much that had passed between Ridolfi and himself. For Cobham was one of the barons in Ridolfi's secret list. Yet, what could he do? The bag had been seized at Dover; Monsieur Charles had been openly brought to town; the searchers had seen both his books and letters; and not many hours would elapse before Burghley would have reports from his spies. Concealment was vain. Something might be done under the plea of accident, to save the Bishop and the Duke. Perplexed in mind, he left the books at Burghley's house, and took back the letters to his own; where he sealed them up afresh and sent them over to the Bishop of Ross, with a request that the prelate would come down next day to Blackfriars and open the packet in the Lord Warden's presence.

Leslie understood his hint. Breaking the seal, and taking out the dangerous missives, the Bishop slipped away to the Spanish embassy, where he told Don Geran his bad news, and begged assistance in his trouble. The ambassador saw that the packet must be taken next day to Cobham's house. They knew it would be sent on to Burghley; and that if Burghley saw those papers, the Bishop would be ruined, the Duke would be executed, and the Queen of Scots overthrown. Could they keep back the papers? Could they foist a false packet of news on Burghley, yet prevent him from guessing that he was tricked? Bishop and ambassador thought they could. Burghley would know that letters had been seized; he would want to read those letters; he would expect to find treason in them. All might be arranged, if Leslie and Geran were left alone. Locked in a private closet, the Scottish prelate and the Spanish minister spent the long night in forging papers; concocting a series of cyphered letters, tinged, indeed, with treason to throw Burghley off his guard, but away from the matters which were truly under hand. Some of these papers they wrote in the cypher found in Monsieur Charles's coat. They threw in the Papal bull; and the packet was then carefully sealed. Before daylight came, their work was done.

The true letters from Ridolfi were now sent on to Norfolk and Lumley; the forged letters and the brief were taken to Cobham's house in the bag; and, when they were safely delivered, the Bishop ventured, with consummate craft, to write a letter to Burghley, complaining that his servant, Bailly, had been arrested, and that some letters, which he was bringing over from Brussels, were detained.

Leslie, who took the high tone of an ambassador, begged his lordship to give orders that his servant might be released, and his letters restored. The Bishop felt no scruple in adding that he could not say what these letters contained; but could and would say that not one word in them would be used by him except as Burghley should see fit.

For a moment Burghley was deceived by these artful lies; but he was cautious enough to send Monsieur Charles to the Marshalsea, where he would be watched by very sharp eyes. In the Marshalsea, Monsieur Charles found one of the suffering saints: William Herllie, a kinsman of Lady Northumberland; a man who had fallen with the family fortunes, and was now the occupant of a wretched cell. Herllie, who was known to the Bishop of Ross and to the Spanish ambassador, was regarded by his fellow Catholics as a victim to Burghley's Protestant zeal, since he was often put into irons, locked in a close room, and fed on bread and water. Every one pitied him—every one trusted him. Women, who saw him pass by pale and shivering, said he could not live; and men, who had a firmer hold on life, were anxious to obtain the consolation of his blessing and the profit of his advice. Yet this suffering saint was in Burghley's pay; and six nights after Bailly's arrival at the Marshalsea, Burghley held in his hands some clue to the Bishop's plot.

Leslie had tried to open a direct communication with Monsieur Charles in prison; but Burghley had taken care that he should fail; and, on the failure of his first attempts, he tried what could be done through the suffering saint. Through William Herllie his letters were passed on to Monsieur Charles, and answers from Monsieur Charles were duly received by the Bishop of Ross. But the adroit and unscrupulous prelate was not aware that his letters, and the answers to them, passed through Burghley's hands, and were copied by Burghley's clerks. Being in cypher, these letters told Burghley no more than that the Bishop was in clandestine correspondence with the prisoner. More was wanting to justify Leslie's arrest; and the suffering saint was employed to get a copy of Bailly's cypher. But here the impostor failed; and Monsieur Charles discovered, through a luckless blunder on the part of Herllie, that the suffering saint, and cousin of Lady Northumberland, was a common cheat and spy.

Other and sharper courses were now adopted. Burghley sent for Monsieur Charles, laid the copies of his letters to the Bishop, with the Bishop's replies, before him, and bade him instantly read them out. Bailly pretended that he could not read them—he had lost the cypher, and could not recall the signs. Burghley told him he was lying, and that the rack should make him tell the truth. Monsieur Charles was sent to the Tower, and Sir Owen Hopton lodged him in the good Lord Cobham's room, on the walls of which he scratched at once this warning:

I. H. S.
1571
Die 10 Aprilis.
Wise men ought
circumspectly to se what
they do, to examen
before they speake, to prove
before they take in hand,
to beware whose companey
they use, and abouve al
things to whom they
truste.

Charles Bailly.

Yet his own hard lessons had been poorly learnt. During the months of April and May he was often questioned by Sir Owen; sometimes, though not severely, on the rack; and as he felt no wish to be a martyr, he complained to the Bishop of Ross: who, in mortal fear lest he should tell what he knew about Ridolfi's letters and the books printed at Liège, sent him such comfort as he could find; beds to lie on, food for his table, good advice for his soul. Most of all, Leslie begged Monsieur Charles to get strength in his travail by thinking of what holy men had often suffered for the truth.

Burghley got at the poor Fleming's secret, without having to break his bones.

There happened to be lying in the Tower in those days, a man whom all his fellow-Catholics regarded as a genuine saint. This man was John Story, Doctor of the Canon Law; a man who had been bred to conspiracy, who had renounced his country, who had been naturalized in Spain. Story had been kidnapped in Flanders, brought to London, lodged in the Lollards' tower, tried for his offence, and sentenced to death. Elizabeth's desire to keep her reign free from political executions, had heretofore saved him from the gallows.

This man had formerly been a tenant of Beauchamp tower, on the wall of which he had carved his name:

1570
JOHN STORE
DOCTOR

But he seems to have been removed before Bailly came in; as the success of Burghley's humane and humorous contrivance for making Monsieur Charles confess, turned upon his not being acquainted with Story even by sight.

Since the open war began between Rome and London

with the Papal brief, it was understood that the law would be allowed to take its course; and as Story lay under sentence, he was reverenced by his fellow-Catholics as a man who was about to die. What Story said was Gospel; and Monsieur Charles, like every other Catholic prisoner, was anxious for his good advice. Great, therefore, was his joy when he opened his eyes one night on a tall, thin figure which stood beside his pallet, and answered to the name of Story. In the face of his own warning on the wall, Monsieur Charles took the stranger's word; opened his ears to the words of an impostor, and consented to act a part, the outline of which the impostor sketched for him. 'Pretend,' said the false Story, 'to enter Burghley's service and to play the spy on Leslie; that is the way to be of use to Mary and the Church. Burghley has got the bishop's cypher: but you may make a merit of giving it up. You will tell him nothing, and gain his confidence, by reading the letters.' A sudden light seemed to flash on Monsieur Charles. So good a man as Story must know best. On the morrow he was to be racked again. Here, then, a door was opened by which he could escape Sir Owen and the torture, and yet do service to the Bishop and the Church. In the morning he rose to confess whatever he knew, and was greatly surprised to find that when he had told his tale, he had betrayed his master and done himself no good.

Monsieur Charles's revelations showed how vast a conspiracy had been organized by Leslie and the Spanish party against Elizabeth's crown. The danger in which the Queen was placed by the Bishop's plot and the Papal brief, was used as an argument for removing her scruples against taking life. Pressed on all sides by foes, the Queen at last gave way; and the iron age of her reign set in. Story was hanged. The Bishop of Ross was seized. The Duke of Norfolk was lodged in the Tower once more.

In the fall of that year Monsieur Charles inscribed a new set of morals on the wall of Beauchamp tower:

I H S

PRINCIPIVM SAPIENTE TIMOR DOMINI.

BE ENNEMYE TO NONE.

XPS.

Anno D. 1571 10 Sept.

The most unhapy
man in the world is he
that is not pacient in ad-
versities. For men are not
killed with the adversities
they have: but with ye impa-
cience which they suffer.

Tout vient assoient quy peult attendre
Gli sospiri ne son testimonie veri dell' angos-
cia mia

Charles Bailly

æt. 29.

BE FREND TO ONE.

HOEPENDE, HERT PACIENTE.

CHAPTER XXV.

BISHOP OF ROSS.

At first, John Leslie, Bishop of Ross, was visited in his own house by Lord Sussex, and put under question as to the correspondence with Monsieur Charles, the mission of Ridolfi, and the letters addressed to 30 and 40. He told a new set of lies, and Burghley knew that they were lies. Bailly's confessions had told him much, and Mary's answers to questions, the object of which she could not guess, completed what the Fleming had left unsaid.

Yet even now, with proofs of Leslie's treason in her hands, the Queen would not consent to lodge him in the Tower. He was an ambassador, the minister of a sovereign prince. Up to this moment Elizabeth had refused to recognise the state of things in Scotland, and to receive at her court an ambassador from king James. She had treated Mary as the actual Queen of Scots, and although that royalty was a mere shadow, Elizabeth would not agree to depress her cousin's party in the north so much as would be done by the arrest of her agent in the English court.

But the plot was coming out shred by shred. Norfolk's servants confessed to much, and Norfolk himself, when locked in the Tower, told all the rest. Lord Cobham, too, alarmed by what he saw going on, came forward to confess having kept back the letters brought over by Monsieur Charles. The secret numbers were discovered to mean Norfolk and Lumley. When these facts were known, the case was again submitted by Burghley to the Queen. Who could answer for the public safety while the chief director of these plotters remained at large? Elizabeth saw the need for action, yet even now she would have gladly seized on any excuse for leaving the Bishop of Ross alone. She said the crown lawyers should be consulted on a case. Burghley obeyed her hint, and in a short time reported that the crown lawyers were of opinion—in the first place, that a prince who had been lawfully deposed like Mary Stuart, had no sovereign rights at all; in the second place, that an ambassador who had been concerned in a conspiracy like John Leslie, forfeited his rights of representation. On reading these reports, Elizabeth gave way so far as to allow of the Bishop being lodged in the Tower, in the rooms which had been occupied by Cranmer, but she would in no wise consent that he should be either put to the rack or threatened with the rack.

By a lucky chance, these merciful limitations of Burghley's

powers were not hinted to the Bishop, who might have held out longer had he known that his bones were safe. But in his chamber in the bloody Tower, he heard from day to day of men being racked until they told the truth, and when Burghley rejected his first confessions as idle talk, and gave him forty-eight hours to consider what he would say, his strength of will broke down. When the judges sent for him on the third day, Leslie answered the questions put to him with the frankness of a man who has done his best and worst, and looks back on his course with consuming scorn. Never was a foul heart emptied of more perilous stuff. He explained the secret history of Norfolk's doings in York; the part which he had taken in Northumberland's rising; the plot for seizing the Queen, for raising an insurrection in East Anglia, and for bringing the Walloons into Essex. He confessed for Mary Stuart as well as for himself. He spoke of her privity to Darnley's murder, and he accused her of meaning to kill Bothwell also. Finally, as a Catholic prelate, he wrote an admonitory letter to his royal mistress, warning her not to meddle with plots in the time to come, but to trust in God and in her good sister the English Queen.

Mary was profoundly moved on reading Leslie's words. 'The hand is Esau's hand,' she murmured, 'but the voice is Jacob's.' After the rising of Percy and Nevill, Mary had been removed from Tutbury to Chatsworth, Coventry, Wingfield, and Sheffield, in the last of which places she was lying when made aware of her most serious loss. On finding that she had not only lost her ambassador, but found in him a critic and perhaps a foe, she burst into sullen rage. 'He is a flayed and fearful priest,' she cried, 'he has done what they would have him do.' All this was true enough, but the royal lady's wrath could not help her to a servant equally adroit. Norfolk was the first to suffer from these confessions. Leslie told enough to slay him, but William

Herllie, the suffering saint of the Marshalsea, found out a good deal more. The Duke's servants and secretaries, thrown into the same ward with Herllie, were soon in the saint's confidence, and every night reports of what they told him were sent over the water to Burghley's house. No man in English story had more evidence of guilt to fight against than Norfolk. Would Elizabeth put him to death? To the last moment she said nay.

No Queen had ever such good reason to hold her own in the way of mercy; for since the day of her sister's death not a drop of blood had been shed on Tower Hill.

The fact is one without example. For two hundred years the axe on Tower Hill had never been at rest; it is doubtful whether in all the reigns from Richard of Bordeaux to Mary Tudor, a single year had escaped the stain of political murder. The reddest reign of all was that of Mary; a reign which lasted five years only; yet filled the land with mourning, and smeared the page of history with blood. It is Elizabeth's glory that she put an end to this feast of death; that for twelve years of her golden prime she never signed a political sentence; that, until Mary Stuart came into England, and the Papal bull was issued, she banished from English life the old dark image of the headsman and his block.

What wonder that the poets called her country Merrie England!

While the Queen was debating what to do, the Scottish prelate was making the best of his situation in the Bloody tower. Being called a Bishop, Sir Owen Hopton, the Lieutenant, had begun by treating him as an English baron, supplying him with food, fire, and lights at the rate of 53*s.* 4*d.* a-week for diet, and 6*s.* 8*d.* a-week for fuel. He had his own servant, Cuthbert Reid, a Scot, to wait upon him. But some of his indulgences were in time withdrawn. Reid, his servant, left him. Hopton informed him that he must provide his own food and fuel; for the allowance made to prisoners was made from estates which had been seized to the prince's use; but Leslie had no estates to seize. In the winter he fell sick of cramp and ague, a common disease in the Bloody tower, and he wrote to ask Fénélon, the French Ambassador, for five hundred crowns to pay his weekly bills. As some solace in his misery, Leslie employed his knife in carving a record of his captivity in the Bloody tower. A long Latin inscription, which is unhappily worn by damp and years, concludes with this name and date:

JO. EPS. ROSSEN. SCOTVS
1572

In the spring of this year a prospect of deliverance opened upon Leslie, which was perhaps more terrible to him than the chambers of the Bloody tower. Since the day when Percy crossed the border into Scotland, Burghley had never ceased to press the ruling Regents, Murray, Lennox, and Mar, for his surrender as a rebel to his Queen. Of course, the Regents had declined to meet him; yet Percy had been kept a prisoner in Lochleven Castle, under the charge of Sir William Douglas, a Highland chief. More than once, the Scottish court suggested the policy of an exchange; of giving up the Earl of Northumberland, and taking in his place the Bishop of Ross; but to such an act of barter the pride of Elizabeth could not stoop. Nor was the Court of Scotland eager to give up the Earl; since a rebel of so much consequence on the border was a capital hostage to hold for the English Queen. But Leslie never could be sure that Burghley and Mar would not come to terms; and he knew that once he were given up to Mar, his shrift was likely to be short. At the end of May, he heard, to his great delight, that Percy was in English hands, having been sold by Sir William Douglas to Lord Hunsdon, Governor of Berwick, for two thousand pounds.

This sale being made, the Bishop felt safe enough, for no English rebel of rank was now in captivity beyond the Tweed; and from his chambers in the Bloody tower he could watch with comparative comfort the dance of death.

Norfolk was the first to die; and the fact that he was the first political offender since her Majesty's reign began, occurred to him on the scaffold; adding, as it would seem, a pang to the bitterness of his remorse. He died denouncing the Pope's religion, and humbly begging his pardon of the Queen. 'I am the first in her Majesty's reign to suffer; may I be the last!' he cried. The assembly sobbed, 'Amen.'

A few days later, Northumberland was put to the axe in York. Lord Hunsdon tried to save him; thinking him a better man than his heir, Sir Henry, second son of Sir Thomas the Pilgrim. The title, entailed on this Sir Henry, could not be withdrawn for his brother's offence; yet Hunsdon, who knew the northmen well, sent Burghley word that the new Earl would be far more dangerous than the old. But Burghley saw no way of pardoning such a man as Percy; the leader of a great revolt and a great apostasy; and towards the end of August, Leslie heard in the Bloody tower, that the second of his illustrious victims had laid his head upon the block.

For Northumberland, it is not likely that Leslie cared; but Norfolk was his confidential friend; and he must have felt that his plots had brought the unhappy Duke to his untimely end. Perhaps he consoled himself with the reflection that Norfolk might have done worse than die without knowing what Mary Stuart was. Any way, he made to Thomas Wilson, doctor of divinity, a confession which that clergyman reports to Burghley in these words:

'He said further, upon speech I had with him, that the

Queen his mistress is not fit for any husband: for first, he saith, she poisoned her husband, the French king, as he hath credibly understood; again, she consented to the murder of her late husband, the Lord Darnley; thirdly, she matched with the murderer, and brought him to the field to be murdered; and last of all, she pretended marriage with the Duke, with whom, as he thinks, she would not long have kept faith, and the Duke would not have had the best days with her.'

The English clergyman who reports the Bishop's words, can only add, in comment: 'What a Queen! and what an ambassador!'

As nothing more could now be got from Leslie, he was suffered to depart from the Bloody tower, on the understanding that he was to live abroad, and trouble her Majesty no more.

CHAPTER XXVI.

MURDER OF NORTHUMBERLAND.

The Bishop of Ross left his chamber in the Bloody tower to the third of his illustrious victims; to that Henry Percy who succeeded the Lochleven fugitive, as the eighth Earl of Northumberland.

Like all the great border chiefs of the Tudor age, Percy had been much employed against the Scots; though he was known to be one of those sticklers for the old creed who bowed with only a sullen and disdainful mind to the new order of things in Church and State. As a soldier he seems to have done his duty; fighting his friends the French as fiercely as he fought his enemies the Scots; and standing by his mistress, even when his brother, the seventh earl, had joined with Lord Westmoreland against their queen.

But the Jesuits in whom he trusted led him astray; and the man who had fought so gallantly at Leith against the Scots, became, under their guidance, one of Mary Stuart's staunchest friends. To what reward for his services he looked we can only guess. Norfolk aspired to her hand; why should not Northumberland? To the last Mary was a siren; a being with the beaming eye, the wooing voice, which take the senses captive. But whether hope of piety led him on, Percy began to waver in his faith; and the English council, who had spies in his closet, and knew what he was saying and doing, even in his private moments, commanded him, as an act of safety, to keep his house.

This order, meant as a warning to him, was not strictly kept, since he was allowed to live at Sion, his princely seat on the Thames, and to ride down when he listed to Petworth, his fine estate on the Sussex downs. Yet chafed by a show of restraint, he listened more eagerly than ever to the tempter's voice. The Jesuits who had gained his ear, soon made of him their tool. In what he thought the seclusion of his own gallery at Petworth, he held midnight interviews with Charles Paget, one of the most subtle and dangerous of the men employed by those who conducted the permanent conspiracy against their queen. Paget came over from Dieppe, landing on a lonely part of the Sussex coast; where he met William Shelley, of Michelgrove, one of the Earl's Catholic friends; and was housed by Percy in one of the lodges of Petworth Park. Here Thomas Lord Paget joined them; and in their cups the three Catholic gentlemen talked a good deal of nonsense about the Pope, the Duc de Guise, and the Queen of Scots. Percy meant no harm. Had the Guises come over, he was likely enough to be the first afield against them; but, like all the old Percies, he was a man of odious temper and imperious habit; one who could ill endure to see such upstarts, as he called Hatton and Burghley, basking in royal favour, while barons of lofty lineage like himself were left in the shade.

Much of his foolish prate with Paget and Shelley was woven by cunning hands into a net, which closed upon him when the time was ripe. To what extent, if any, he was guilty of actual treason we shall never learn; his death cut short all process against him; and the plausible story which was told by Hatton after his murder must be taken with a good many grains of salt.

One of the plotters, Francis Throckmorton, had by his own confession, done his worst to persuade the Duc de Guise to throw an army into Kent. The arrest of that conspirator warned the braggarts of their danger; and Northumberland persuaded Lord Paget to fly the realm. Lord Paget being the most eminent man who knew of his parley with the agents of disturbance, Percy supposed that his secret would be safe so soon as Paget was beyond the sea. But he found, to his dismay, how little his cunning could contend against Burghley's craft. Paget got away; but the meshes were drawn about the humbler associates of his crime; and when Percy, to his great astonishment, found himself lodged, under care of Sir Owen Hopton, in the Bloody tower, he heard that his friend Shelley was not only lodged in a neighbouring vault, but had already been made to confess his offences on the rack. Percy sent a message to Shelley, begging him to be firm; to which the poor gentleman replied that it was easy for a great baron, protected by his nobility from torture, to advise him to be firm; but he, a country squire, had been twice on the rack, and he could not bear it. In fact, on being questioned once more, in the presence of Lord Chief Justice Anderson, as to the coming and going of Jesuits, as to the lodging of agents in Petworth Park, as to the conversations held in the Earl's book-room, Shelley told what he knew, and perhaps more than he knew. Men stretched on the rack became pliant to the judge; answering in their pain as the questioner wished; crying yea and nay, just as the cords were strained and the joints were torn. By Shelley's account, Charles Paget brought news to Petworth that the Pope had sanctioned a crusade against the Queen, that the Duc de Guise would conduct the landing of foreign troops, and that the Church expected the Catholic barons to be ready. Shelley was made to confess that the Earl was a party to these schemes. Paget, in a letter to the Queen of Scots, denied the second part of Shelley's story. It was probably not true. Burghley made no efforts to bring Percy before the courts. A year passed by; yet Percy remained under Hopton's charge; a prisoner, awaiting his trial by the peers. That trial he was not to have.

On a summer Sunday noon (June 21, 1585) Hopton, the Lieutenant, received two orders from court; the first to arrest the Earl's three servants—men who had always waited on him—and to lodge them in close custody for the night; the second, to place in the Bloody tower, as sole attendant on the Earl, one Thomas Bailiff, a gentleman, who brought the orders for that service. By two o'clock the new arrangements had been made. Palmer, Price, and Pantin, Percy's old servants, were caged in their own cells; and Thomas Bailiff was housed in a room adjoining that in which the Earl ate and slept.

When supper time came, Bailiff was at his post. At nine the Earl retired in his usual health. About twelve o'clock an old fellow, who lay in an outer room, heard Bailiff shouting, and called the watch. On the watch coming up, Bailiff sent him to rouse the Lieutenant and beg him to come at once to the Earl of Northumberland's door. Hopton was soon there; and passing into the chamber found the Earl in bed, undressed, with his clothes in perfect order, and the bed-quilt decently drawn about his limbs. He was dead.

On turning down the sheets Hopton saw that the bed was full of blood; that the body had a wound under the left breast, which seemed to have been made by a knife. He left the room for a few minutes, locking Bailiff inside, while he wrote an account of the Earl's death, which he described as having been caused by the plunge of a *knife*. When he returned to the chamber, Bailiff drew his eye to a pistol lying on the floor, about three feet from the bed, which he had not seen before.

Sir Christopher Hatton, who managed the whole affair, set up a theory that Percy, overwhelmed by those proofs of his guilt which had been drawn from Shelley on the rack, had destroyed himself, in order to escape a trial, a traitor's doom, and the forfeiture of his family honours and estates. A theory of self-murder would not square with death by a knife, since three or four warders, who rushed into the room on the first alarm of foul play being raised, had seen the bed in which Percy lay a corpse. No man could stab himself to death, and then draw the sheets about his limbs, as they had been found in Percy's bed. But might he not take a pistol into his bed, fire it under the clothes, and die without a struggle? Such was Hatton's explanation of an event which filled the taverns of Cheapside and the aisles of St. Paul's with wonder and alarm. An inquest on the body, held by the Tower coroner, a mere court official, failed to appease the public mind. Thousands of tongues accused the council of foul play, and to put an end to these bruits in the City, the Government was compelled to act and to explain. Hatton's line was taken in the affair by Burghley.

The first letter, in which Sir Owen spoke of the *knife*, was kept back. A Star Chamber Council was convened, at which the Lord Chancellor Bromley made a long statement of the Earl's offences, of his imprisonment, and of his suicide. Finally, a pamphlet was put forth, in order, as was said, to calm men's minds and to silence malicious tongues, in which Percy's servants were made to give evidence tending to suggest that the Earl had meant to kill himself, while the tale told by Bailiff and Hopton was given in such a way as to show that he had carried out his plan. Pantin, it was said, confessed that the pistol belonged to his lord; that it was bought from Adrian Mulan, a gunsmith, living in East Smithfield; that Price, his fellow-servant, carried it into the Tower; that the Earl concealed it in the chimney of his room; but fearing it would be found in that place and taken away, he had slipt it into the mattress of his bed. Bailiff was made to say that when the Earl supped and sent him away that night, he came to the door and bolted it inside, saying, he could not sleep unless his door was made fast. After that, said Bailiff, all was quiet until the hour of midnight, when he heard a great noise, as of a falling door, and springing out of bed, cried, 'What is that, my lord?' Finding the Earl made no answer, he went on calling and crying until the old fellow in the next room answered him, when they called the watch, sent for Sir Owen, broke into the room by force, and found the Earl dead in his bed.

In spite of all these assertions, folk would not believe that Percy died by his own hand. Hatton bore the odium of contriving a midnight murder; for many years the event was spoken of as a political assassination; and that by men who like Sir Walter Raleigh and Sir Robert Cecil, knew every mystery of the court.

CHAPTER XXVII.

PHILIP THE CONFESSOR.

OVER the fire-place in the common room of Beauchamp tower, once tenanted by the good Lord Cobham, by 'King' Guilford, by the last White Rose, and by Monsieur Charles the moralist and spy, the eye is taken by some faint and flowing lines, looking all the weaker from contrast with so many tablets of the stern and monumental kind. These are the words in Italian letters :—

> *Quanto plus afflictionis pro Christo in hoc*
> *Sæculo, tanto plus gloriæ cum Christo in*
> *futuro.* *Arundell June 22*
> 1587.

The author of this tablet was Philip Howard, called by his Jesuit biographer Philip the Confessor.

This Philip Howard, a son of Thomas, fourth Duke of Norfolk, and Mary, sole heiress of Henry Fitz-Alan, twelfth Earl of Arundel, was born to wear the coronets of two great houses, and to enjoy the wealth of three great families. A King and Queen stood sponsors for him, and he was the heir to honours which Kings and Queens can neither give nor take away. His father was a son of Henry the Poet, who first gave musical pause and flow to our Saxon tongue. His son was the famous Marble Earl. So that Philip the Confessor, who owed his name to a Spanish King, and his title to a Jesuit Father, stands side by side in story with men whose names will be gratefully recalled so long as the memory of song and art endures.

Philip the Confessor has a dim kind of fame; first as a prisoner in the Tower; next as a martyr for his faith. The Church of Rome has done much for Philip; it vexes one to find how little he did for the Church of Rome. What was done for her glory in Philip's house, was accomplished, not by Philip, but by his wife.

Few wrong notions thrive so rankly in our books as the popular delusion that these Howards of Norfolk, Arundel, and Surrey, have been strictly loyal, through good and evil times, to the universal Church. No house in England has been so wayward in its faith.

When the new lights began to burn in Church and State, no men received them with a warmer welcome than the Howards. Thomas, third Duke of Norfolk, stood in front of the affray with Rome. He was the uncle of Anne Boleyn. A great noble and a good soldier, he pushed forward the divorce, he denounced the Pope, he crushed the Pilgrimage of Grace. The Poet, his son, was a Protestant, and more; what in these times would be called a free-thinker. The Poet's son, Duke Thomas, had the name of a reformer, and even of a persecutor; a name which the Jesuits who lived upon his son declare that he had only too well deserved. Philip, the fourth in descent since the new lights came in, was the first man of his house who went over from the English side to the side of Rome. He was Philip the Convert; hence, while the Jesuits who won him over, styled him a Confessor, the kinsmen who lost him styled him, with equal justice, an Apostate.

Since Philip's day the Howards have changed sides from father to son with a regularity to suggest the working of some natural law; the mysterious force—it may be—which compels the vane on a high tower to flow in the path of a prevailing wind. Philip converted his youngest brother, Lord William, the Ruffler, who is known as Belted Will;

but his second brother, Lord Thomas, afterwards Earl of Suffolk, lived and died in the ranks of the National Church. The Poet's second son, Lord Henry, afterwards Earl of Northampton, boxed the compass; being a Protestant in his youth, a trimmer in his middle life, a Catholic in his old age. So it has been throughout. Some of these Howards have lapsed, some have relapsed; from Philip's father, who turned Gregory Martin out of doors, down, through that Protestant Jockey of Norfolk, who was a friend of Fox, to Duke Henry, who in our own day gave up the church of his father for that of his Queen.

Philip, like the men of his house, was inclined to bear no cross unless it were his own. In early life, he was so little of a saint and confessor, that his family dare not print the charges written against his name by one of his dependent priests. We are told by this priest, that Philip left his young wife, that he fell into debt, that he wandered after strange faces, that he . . . . . then comes a suspicious blank. Philip would seem to have fallen under doubt of doing much worse things than following after damsels who were light of love. The Jesuit hints at the young Earl's vices, without telling us of what sort they were. We only know that Philip repented of them in his later and better days. When he was a prisoner in Beauchamp tower, he wrote to Father Southwell, the poet, that on going back into the world, as he then hoped, he would sell the rings and jewels which had been given to him in his wicked youth by the companions of his dissolute hours, and send the money for which he sold these tokens of evil, to the poor. 'And so far was he ever after from such faults,' says the good priest, 'that he could, and upon just occasion did, protest in another letter to the same Father, that after he became a member of the Holy Catholic Church, he never once was guilty therein.'

Yet Philip was not so much a wicked man as a weak man. Anne Dacre, the wife to whom he had been married for money when he was less than twelve years old, was a border lassie; sister and heir of George, the last Lord Dacre of the north; a woman sour in face and sly in manner, but kind to the poor, and very obedient to her church. Like all her neighbours in the north, she was a Catholic; though she was crafty enough to hide her preference from her father-in-law, the Protestant Duke. She was older than the Earl, her husband. When the Protestant Duke was put to death for his part in the Bishop of Ross's plot, she dropped the mask which she had worn so long, and filled her house with Jesuits and priests. Then, Philip, her husband, ran away.

A dull wife, with Father Southwell and a train of Jesuits in her chamber, was not to the mind of a boy who had all the gaieties of London within his reach. Anne loved the country, Philip loved the town. Anne preferred Arundel Park and Castle, with the downs and sea; Philip preferred Arundel House and gardens, with the river and the Strand. Given up to her devotions, Anne would rise with the lark to sing her matins; given up to his pleasures, Philip would lie in bed till noon, to sleep off the fumes of wine. Anne felt herself a better woman when her house was filled with priests. Philip ran away from his wife on account of these fellows, and he hated these fellows on account of his wife.

At one time, things looked likely to go wrong, indeed, between man and wife; for Philip not only left Anne without his society, but talked of denouncing their marriage, as null and void. When he first stood at the altar with Anne he was under twelve. They were married again on Philip attaining his fourteenth year; but Philip was told by some of his gay London comrades, that the second rite had no binding force. Disliking the sour woman, and hating her priests and Jesuits, he forbade her to lodge in his London house, even when he was out of town. But Anne clung to Philip, like his fate. She appealed to his higher nature and his better sense. She got his aged grandsire, the Earl of Arundel, and his rich aunt, the Lady Lumley, to interfere. These kinsfolk tried to reconcile the pair; so far at least as to persuade Philip to live with his wife under a common roof. Once they seemed to have brought him back to a sense of duty. He took his wife home, and in this interval of happy love, his son Thomas, afterwards famous as the Marble Earl, was born. But Philip could not stand the Jesuits, and rather than live a dull and decent life with them, he quarrelled with Lord Arundel and Lady Lumley; who were so deeply hurt by his cross humour, that they left away from him many a broad acre which he had thought his own.

For many years, there was a battle, as it were, between the church and the world, for this weak man's soul.

Philip, now become Earl of Arundel, in his mother's right, resolved to shine in courts; but on trial, he found how hard it was to fill men's eyes and engage their tongues in a circle adorned by courtiers like Leicester, Blount, and Raleigh. He tried to outbrave these gallants in the splendour of his tilts and tourneys. When the Queen went down to Kenning Hall, his seat in Norfolk, he invited, not only the court, but the shire, to meet her. From Kenning Hall, he carried this party of guests to Norwich; where the most reckless spendthrifts in the county stood amazed by the spectacle of his riot. Who could tell where he would stop? Who could say what dreams were in his brain? Courtiers could see that he aspired to a favourite's place. The Queen, an unmarried woman, was of his kin. Women of his line had matched with kings, and men of his family had courted queens. His father had been accepted by the Queen of Scots. Who could tell what fortune had in store?

Yet all his striving and expenditure were thrown away; for Philip had neither the wit, the genius, nor the personal beauty necessary in a contest for favour with the men who sparkled in Elizabeth's court. In his costly banquets there was little art; in his splendid joustings there was still less taste. The Queen smiled at him, but not on him. When the last pistole in his purse was gone, he began to feel how wearisome were the pleasures which he had bought; how childish the distinctions which he had won. Then, in his hour of debt and self-reproach, his wife came forward with her money and her love. She paid his debts; she touched his heart; and she healed his wounds. From that moment the ruined spendthrift was her own.

Once housed beneath her roof, with Father Southwell and Father Weston at his side, this son of a stern Protestant sire was soon reconciled to Rome.

The Queen's Council, moved by hints of his lapse from the national Church, called up the Earl and Countess of Arundel; both of whom denied that any such change had taken place. As a caution, they were parted from each other; Philip being ordered to keep his house, while Anne was lodged with Sir Thomas and Lady Shirley at Wiston, near Steyning. But in a few months, on the noise of their apostasy dying down, they were restored to each other's arms. If they had kept within the law, and avoided public scandal, they would henceforward have been left in peace; but such a course of life would not have suited the weak Earl's spiritual guides.

Philip was much in the hands of Father Grately, a priest whom Cardinal Allen had sent over to advise him how to act his difficult part. Grately was one of those poor fools who fancy that men are ruled by secret signs and private tokens. He confided to the Earl as a great mystery, that *black is white;* telling him that this secret token was to be a bond between them for ever, like the ring between a man and wife. This foolish Father Grately had a correspondent in Paris called Father Gifford, to whom he wrote a full account of what was going on. Father Gifford was a spy, who sold these secrets of the closet and the confessional for gold. By his means Secretary Walsingham was made aware of every word spoken in the privacy of the Earl's closet, while Philip supposed that his inmost thoughts were known to none save Grately and himself.

No wonder that Philip found few openings for his talents, and that Elizabeth's court was closed against him! At length the silly youth resolved to quit a country in which he found no field—to seek an asylum in the provinces of his godfather Philip the Second, and to offer himself as a leader to the discontented exiles and partizans of Rome.

If he did not carry out his scheme at once, it was because some of the Jesuits whom he met in his wife's apartments were honest men. These Fathers wanted him to serve their church; and, in order to serve their church, it was needful for him to live a decent life. Father Weston, who received his submission, told him he must live by Catholic rule as well as swear by Catholic dogma. Here was the cross. In those days Philip had no religious scruples to overcome; he had read nothing, and he knew nothing; but he was vain and frivolous, fond of dice and drink, a slave of tavern sluts. He could not give up all these things at once. But he rode down more frequently to Arundel Castle; he read the tracts of Cardinal Allen and Father Southwell; and he made such progress in spiritual knowledge that, on meeting his brother, William — Belted Will Howard — he talked that Ruffler over to the Pope!

The brothers agreed to start from England without the

Queen's license—a grave offence in men of their rank; but they could reckon on receiving a very warm welcome from King Philip of Spain, who was busy with his grand Armada, and would be glad to find two Plantagenet gentlemen, sons of the great Protestant duke, in his court and camp. Who could tell? Philip had claims to the Crown; the blood of Edward the First was in his veins; and the arms of Edward the Confessor were on his shield. Such a man might be turned to many uses by a prince so subtle and unscrupulous as Philip the Second, even before the time should come for launching his navies against the English Queen.

But the Jesuits felt that such a scheme, even though it had Cardinal Allen's sanction, would be more to the advantage of Spain than of Rome. Philip could be more useful to the Church in London than in Brussels. His great name, his high rank, and his vast estates, conferred upon him a power of encouraging and protecting missionary priests, which would be thrown away the moment he landed on a foreign soil. They tried to dissuade him; but he would not now draw back. A weak man is always afraid of seeming weak. He knew his own mind. He had weighed the business well. He had hired a boat to carry him into France. The skipper knew of his design; and not to go when his friends expected him, would be to prove that he was still a child. The Countess, who was on the side of her priest, implored him at least to take her with him when he fled: since she could neither bear a second parting from her lord, nor face the terrible anger of her Queen. Philip would not listen; he would sail for Calais; and he would sail alone.

When he got a fair wind, and put out to sea at dusk, the skipper who had bargained to take him over for so many pistoles, hung out a light; on which they were suddenly assailed with shot by a ship of war, commanded by Captain Keloway, whom Philip supposed to be a pirate. Keloway, acting the part of pirate, boarded the boat, saw the Earl, and asked him whither he was going? Philip, who never suspected that his captor was acting under orders from Walsingham, replied that he was bound for Calais. Keloway, playing the part of pirate, told him he should go free for one hundred pounds; for which sum he must give his note of hand to some confidential friend on shore. Philip sat down and wrote a letter to his sister, Lady Margaret Sackville, begging her to ask Father Grately to pay the bearer of his note one hundred pounds by this token that was betwixt them—*that black is white.* The pretended pirate took the letter, read it closely, put it in his pocket; and then, turning sharply on the writer, told him that he was no pirate, but a public officer, who had been appointed to lie in wait for him at sea, to take him in the act of breaking the law, and to bring him back by force to land.

On the 25th of April, 1585, the fugitive Earl was brought into the Tower. His brother, Belted Will, and his sister, Lady Margaret, were put under arrest, and his wife's confessor, Father Weston, was flung into the Clink.

CHAPTER XXVIII.

MASS IN THE TOWER.

The Countess Anne, so far from being overthrown by this night adventure of her husband, felt her wit fired, and her strength increased, for that conflict with the world in which she was now to engage alone.

Her first thoughts were for Father Weston, whom she missed from her side even more than she missed her wayward lord. Putting on a poor habit, so that she could walk about the City unnoted, she went down to the Stews, a vile neighbourhood in Southwark; in which stood the Clink prison, the Bear Garden, the licensed dens from which the quarter took its name, and those inn-yards in which wandering friars were wont to show the Burning of Sir John Oldcastle and the Temptation of Eve. Play-houses like the Hope and the Globe had routed these old monkish dramas from the tavern yards; but many of the dens which in olden times had been licensed by the clergy still remained under the walls of Winchester house; though the signs which had once told the story of their origin too plainly, such as the Cardinal's Hat, the Three Kings, and the Cross Keys, had been removed by the reforming clergy as too scandalous for the public eye.

The Clink jail in this district was tenanted by drabs and thieves, by pirates and monks; by the vilest scum of the river, and the filthiest sweeping of the street. Being a clerical prison, it was sometimes made a lodging for men of a better class; most of all for men arrested on suspicion of being Jesuits and priests. Hence, Father Weston, a prisoner of the Bishop of Winchester, was thrown into this loathsome den.

In her disguise, the Countess went among the stews, made friends of the Clink turnkeys, and tried to corrupt them by her gold. Her hope was to get the Father into France; and if bribes could have bought his freedom, he could certainly have got away. Thomas Cowper was then Bishop of Winchester, and Cowper's men proved loyal to their trust. They told the Countess, that Weston was not confined for money, and would never gain his liberty through money. They spoke the truth. Anne was surprised; her experience having taught her to believe in the power of gold to corrupt men's souls. When Father Blackwell, the arch-priest, was hiding in a house in Sussex, orders to search for him came down from London; and the

Father was in peril, not so much of discovery, as of hunger and thirst; since the watch kept over all the family was close enough to prevent any one from going into his secret cell. Anne rode over to the house; asked to see the captain in a private room; and, by means of a great bribe, persuaded him to connive at the arch-priest's escape. Blackwell was brought to her own house; and the captain received from her ladyship a venison pasty every Christmas day so long as he lived. At the Clink, she had to do with officers of the Church; and in spite of her disguises and allurements, Father Weston was confined in the Clink until the end of Elizabeth's reign.

Philip, brought before the Star Chamber, was charged with three offences; (1) with an attempt to leave England without the loyal license; (2) with going over from the Church of his country to that of Rome; (3) with having proposed that a foreign prince should create him Duke of Norfolk. These charges he partly evaded, partly denied. The attempt to escape into France could not be gainsaid; but he asked the judges to believe that he had no purpose in view beyond getting away from his personal foes. The apostasy from his church he denied in substance, if not in form; saying, it was true that he had confessed his sins to a priest, but that in other things he was not reconciled to Rome. The proposal, made to Cardinal Allen, that he should be raised to the rank of Duke, he denied in terms.

The court, believing the evidence against him on all three points, and on two out of the three there could be no room for doubt, condemned him to imprisonment during pleasure, and to a fine of ten thousand pounds.

The Countess was left at large, though she was occasionally brought before the judges and questioned as to her household. Backed by her Jesuits, she was a match in the cunning and knavery of police for Walsingham himself. As the Earl was not a felon, his estates were spared; and while Anne had plenty of money in her purse, she knew a hundred ways in which justice could be baffled and her enemies put to shame.

For more than a year the Earl's confinement in the middle room of Beauchamp tower was rather close. A gentleman was appointed as his keeper, and when he walked in the garden for exercise, either this keeper or the Lieutenant was bound to walk at his side. After awhile he was allowed to have servants of his own; but these fellows were of little use, since they sickened of the Tower, and wanted more indulgence than their lord. Roger, the Lieutenant's man, was the chief person in his room.

The steady old Catholics were not gained over by the Earl, and some of them expressed for him all the contempt which his weakness provoked. One Catholic priest said Arundel had no religion at all; another said he was weak enough to hear mass of a morning and sermon of an afternoon. Many of the priests declared that he pretended conversion to their church out of policy. But for the Countess Anne they held another speech. She was a Dacre of the North; and those Dacres of the North had been always staunch and true.

Anne made many brave efforts to see her husband in the Tower. If the Council would have let her, she would have taken up her quarters in his room, and made that room the base for fresh attacks upon her Queen. It could not be. The time was too restless, Anne too clever, for such indulgence to be offered. But the Countess understood that it was the plotter, not the wife, who was denied admission to the Tower. Other ladies were let in, while she was sent away.

Then a wild thought came into her head—a woman's thought, full of daring and of peril, which pleased her fancy, and of which she did not pause to count the cost. If she could not carry to her lord the comforts of her own presence, she could provide him with the consolations of his own religion. Yea, if such thing could be contrived by woman's wit, and paid for by the Dacre purse, there should be mass in his room; yea, there should be mass under the Queen's nose, in the midst of her chains and bolts, her guns and pikes, her generals and councillors; yea, in that year of the Armada, when the Spanish infantry were jumping on shore in Kent and Essex, there should be mass in the Queen's palace, mass for their success in Her Majesty's Tower!

Anne never paused to ask what influence such a fact might have upon her lord. She knew that he would do her will. She may have hoped to make his fortune and to save his soul. For she reckoned, as all her Jesuits reckoned, that the Spaniards who were arriving would win the fight; that London would fall as Antwerp had fallen; and that England would become the Flanders of her race.

In the Belfry, which communicates with Beauchamp tower, by the gallery known as the Prisoners' walk, lay in those days an old priest named William Bennet; a man who had changed his religion more than once; and who was now, in hope of the Spanish invasion, a very warm Catholic. Lady Arundel went to Mistress Hopton, daughter of Sir Owen the Lieutenant, and with a bribe of thirty pounds induced that young lady to leave open the gate in Prisoners' walk so as to allow of Father Bennet passing into the Earl's room unseen. The first point was gained—Philip had obtained the services of a priest. A rude altar was now raised, a chalice obtained, a garment for the priest sent in, with all the things required in celebrating mass. Philip invited Sir Thomas Gerard of Lancashire, and William Shelley of Sussex, Catholic prisoners then in the Tower, to his chamber, which was now in their eyes a chapel. To the old tablet over the fire-place, he added in the same flowing Italian letter:

Gloria et honore eum coronasti domine
in memoria æterna erit justus.

When the two Catholic gentlemen were come in, and the doors closed, Father Bennet began a mass for the success of Spain; Philip doing duty as an acolyte, and the other gentlemen kneeling and taking part.

Nor was this act the worst of which Philip was guilty in the Tower. While the Spanish ships were in the Channel, he instituted a prayer for their success, which was to continue day and night without ceasing, among all the Catholic prisoners in the Tower, and among all their friends outside, until the Spaniards had shot down London bridge. At this time Philip was in high spirits. He fancied he would soon be King, and he promised Father Bennet that his first act of royal grace should be to make him Dean of St. Paul's.

The year of the grand Armada passed away. Before it was yet gone, Hatton had been down to the Tower inquiring into the truth. That men of English race might differ in opinion as to the real presence in the bread and wine, was credible. That men of English race should offer up prayers for an enemy on our shores, was incredible. Yet the evidence which Hatton found of that monstrous deed was overwhelming. Father Bennet turned on his employer. Sir Thomas Gerard betrayed his friend. William Shelley, after some suffering, told his secret. It was now a question of high treason; of the basest kind of high treason; and the poor Catholic gentlemen who had sins of their own enough, were only too prompt in throwing all blame upon the Earl. If the Spaniards had won their prize, the men who had said mass for them in Her Majesty's Tower would have been heroes in the Spaniard's court. The Spaniards had not won their prize; and these gentlemen could only save their lives by keen alacrity in accusing each other of their common crime.

Philip was tried in the ensuing spring for high treason. Bennet and Gerard were the chief witnesses against him, and the lords had no choice but to condemn him. Anne was not arrested. It is possible that her part in the business was unknown; we only know it from the revelations of her Jesuit biographer; in whose eyes her corruption of the Lieutenant's daughter by a purse of thirty pounds was a meritorious act. She was left at large; though she suffered, of course, from the loss of her husband's property.

The Queen could not make up her mind to take Philip's life. On the trial, Burghley gave him a last chance of acquittal, by asking whether he held that the Pope could depose the Queen? He would not answer. Would he defend the Queen against a foreign prince? Yes. Would he defend her, asked Hunsdon, against the Pope? To this question he would give no answer, yea or nay. Then the Earl of Derby, as Lord High Steward, pronounced on him the sentence of death.

The day after his sentence, he wrote two letters in the Beauchamp tower; one to the Lord Chancellor, the other to Father Southwell. In the first, he made humble suit to the Queen, that Her Majesty would graciously forgive him the many offences which he had committed against her, and for which he expressed his hearty sorrow. In the second, he explained to the Jesuit Father, that his letter to the Queen was written in an equivocal sense. It was plain that his letter to the Lord Chancellor would be read as expressing a hearty sorrow for his crimes; but he wished Southwell to know that this was not the true meaning of what he wrote. He wanted his spiritual guide to understand that he was *not* sorry for his public offences against his country; but that he was sorry for any trifling annoyance which he might have caused Her Majesty during his many years of service in her court! This was the moral of his token, *that black is white.*

What could be done with a man so feeble and so subtle? Leave him alone, thought the Queen. Enough of the Howard blood had fallen; the blood of stronger and better men than Philip. Duke Thomas, his sire, had died beneath the axe. Earl Henry, his grandsire, had died beneath the axe. Philip's crimes were blacker and baser than their offences; but these men had been dangerous and he was not dangerous. Thus the Queen's decision was that he should not die.

Then began the better part of Philip's life, the only part, indeed, on which a man of any creed can now look back with pity. Left alone in Beauchamp tower, he laid down a plan of living to God, according to his church, which he carried out in a way which takes the heart even while it provokes a smile. The two points of his duty were—how to pray and how to fast.

As to the first, he divided his day into three parts; morning, afternoon, and evening. In the morning he gave up two hours to prayer; in the afternoon, he gave up one hour and a half; and in the evening, he gave a quarter of an hour to severe examination of his conscience. But, this arrangement did not satisfy him long; and, being troubled in his mind about the worldliness of his life, he added to his devotions a recital of the priestly office.

As to the second, he began, immediately after his condemnation, to fast three days in the week; Monday, Wednesday, and Friday; on which days he would touch neither fish nor flesh. When his health gave way under this stern rule, he altered it, so far as to eat flesh once on Monday, and fish once on Wednesday. He gave up wine; though he took a little metheglin for his stomach's sake. On the day of his sentence he felt so wasted that he was induced to have a little supper in his room. On certain feasts of his church, as on the vigil of the Feast of Corpus Christi, of Ascension Day, and of the Virgin, he would touch neither food nor drink. Yet this strict rule was carried out in such sly and serpentine ways, that the new Lieutenant, Sir Michael Blount, and the keepers appointed by the Queen, never heard of his fasts and prayers.

Philip engaged a man of enormous appetite to wait upon him. When the viands were brought into his room and laid upon the table, his servants were sent out, and the door was shut fast; then, the man with enormous appetite fell upon the dishes and tankards; ate up the meats, tossed off the wines; clearing the trenchers of their contents, just as when Arundel dined on ordinary days.

Philip was proud of the tablet which he had written over the fireplace, and he not only stood before it for hours at a time, repeating the pious phrase:

Quanto plus afflictionis pro Christo in hoc sæculo,
Tanto plus gloriæ cum Christo in futuro,

but pointed the words out to his servants and visitors for their remembrance when he should be no more. One of his chief sorrows as a prisoner was the news which came to him in Beauchamp tower, that his wife's confessor and his own correspondent, Father Southwell, was arrested, tried, condemned, and hung.

Philip lingered on, in his ascetic way, for ten years, and died at length of a roasted teal. Long fasting had so slackened his powers, that the roast teal brought on a cast, which ended in dysentery. Of course, some voices cried out poison, and his old servant Nicholas Rainberde, was accused of having bribed his cook to put poison in the dish. Rainberde had some quarrel with his lord about money. But the rumour of foul play soon died the death of all noxious things. When Philip was dying, Sir Michael Blount, the Lieutenant, came to his bedside and asked his forgiveness for any offence which he might have given him in discharging his duties. 'Do you ask forgiveness?' said Philip. 'Why, then I forgive you in the same sort as I desire myself to be forgiven at the hands of God.' The two men grasped each other's hands. But then the Earl, weak and wayward to the last, rose on his pillow and looking Blount in the face, cried, 'You have showed me and my men very hard measures.' 'Wherein, my lord?' asked the surprised Sir Michael. 'Nay,' said the Earl, 'I will not make a recapitulation of anything . . . . Remember, good Mr. Lieutenant, that God, who with his finger turneth the unstable wheel of this variable world, can in the revolution of a few days bring *you* to be a prisoner also, and to be kept in the same place where now you keep others.'

The Jesuits say it was a prophetic voice. Certainly, the Earl had not been dead two months before Sir Michael Blount had lost his place, and was himself a prisoner in Beauchamp tower.

CHAPTER XXIX.

SIR WALTER RALEIGH.

The most eminent and interesting prisoner ever lodged in the Tower is Raleigh; eminent by his personal genius, interesting from his political fortune. Raleigh has in higher degree than any other captive who fills the Tower with story, the distinction that he was not the prisoner of his country, but the prisoner of Spain.

Many years ago I noted in the State Papers evidence, then unknown, that a very great part of the second and long imprisonment of the founder of Virginia was spent in the Bloody tower and the adjoining Garden house; writing at this grated window; working in the little garden on which it opened; pacing the terrace on this wall, which was afterwards famous as Raleigh's Walk. Hither came to him the wits and poets, the scholars and inventors of his time; Jonson and Burrell, Hariot and Pett; to crack light jokes; to discuss rabbinical lore; to sound the depths of philosophy; to map out Virginia; to study the ship-builder's art. In the Garden house he distilled essences and spirits; compounded his great cordial; discovered a method (afterwards lost) of turning salt water into sweet; received the visits of Prince Henry; wrote his political tracts; invented the modern war-ship; wrote his History of the World.

Many other vaults and cells in the Tower assume the glory of having been Raleigh's home; the hole in Little Ease, the recess in the crypt, Martin tower, Beauchamp tower; but these assumptions find no warrant in actual fact. Raleigh lay in the Tower four several times, and in his third and fourth imprisonments his room was changed; but we know his exact resting-place in each of these trials. During his first restraint he was lodged in the Brick tower, the residence of his cousin, Sir George (afterwards Lord) Carew, Master of the Ordnance. During his second restraint he was lodged in the Bloody tower. During his third restraint he was lodged in the same; until, on account of failing health, he was suffered to change that cell for the Garden house in which Latimer had lain. In his fourth restraint, after the Guiana voyage, he was lodged in the Wardrobe tower, until the last change of all occur red, when he was transferred to the topmost room of his first prison, the Brick tower.

He was never lodged in the dark hole of the crypt, now shown and figured as Raleigh's cell.

In a pleasant room of Durham house, in the Strand,—a room overhanging a lovely garden, with the river, the old bridge, the towers of Lambeth Palace, and the flags of Paris Garden and the Globe in view,—three men may have often met and smoked a pipe in the days of Good Queen Bess, who are dear to all readers of English blood; because, in the first place, they were the highest types of our race in genius and in daring; in the second place, because the work of their hands has shaped the whole after-life of their countrymen in every sphere of enterprise and thought.

That splendid Durham house, in which the nine days' queen had been married to Guilford Dudley, and which had afterwards been the town house of Elizabeth, belonged to Sir Walter Raleigh, by whom it was held on lease from the Queen. Raleigh, a friend of William Shakspeare and the players, was also a friend of Francis Bacon and the philosophers. Raleigh is said to have founded the Mermaid Club; and it is certain that he numbered friends among the poets and players. The proofs of his having known Shakspeare, though indirect, are strong. Of his long intercourse with Bacon every one is aware.

Thus, it requires no effort of the fancy to picture these three men as lounging in a window of Durham house, puffing the new Indian weed from silver bowls, discussing the highest themes in poetry and science, while gazing on the flower-beds and the river, the darting barges of dame and cavalier, and the distant pavilions of Paris Garden and the Globe.

With the exception of his two friends, Raleigh has had more books written about him than any other man of English race. Every new generation begins with unslackening curiosity about this proud and brilliant man,—curiosity as to what he was, what he said, and what he wrought. Men who are yet young have seen a dozen new lives of Raleigh; and men who are now old may live to see many more.

This public interest in Raleigh seems, at first thought, strange. The man was not lovable; he had some bad qualities; his career was apparently a failure. Yet Raleigh is one of the undoubted heroes of English story; one of the men about whom authors love to write and the public delight to read.

The reasons for what seems at first sight a contradiction are not far to seek.

In the first place, every one feels that Raleigh, when all has been said against him, was a *man;* a proud man, if you like; nay, a cruel and selfish man, if you insist; yet a vital force in the city, in the court, in the camp; not a form, a phrase, a convention, as the masses of men are and must be in every age and in every place. You may like an original force in your midst, or you may dislike it; most men distrust a power which disturbs them with a sense of the untried and the unknown; but you cannot help being drawn towards such a force for either love or hate. Raleigh was a man; and what a man! Even among a race of giants to what a size he grew! Other men, when we come to them, may be great in parts; this man was great in all parts. From the highest masters in special arts he had nothing to learn. Spenser could not teach him song. Hatton was danced by him out of court and fortune. Burghley feared his subtlety and craft. Mayerne took lessons from him in physic. Jonson consulted him on dramatic art. Effingham praised him as a sailor. Bacon thought it an honour to contend with him for the prize of eloquence. Hawkins, Frobisher, all the adventurous seamen of his generation, looked upon him as their master. Bilson retired from a tussle with him on theology, admitting his defeat. Pett learned from Raleigh how to build ships. No man of his generation offered to compete with him as a writer of English prose. Even in the trifle of personal beauty few were his equals. Poet, student, soldier, sailor, courtier, orator, historian, statesman—in each and every sphere he seemed to have a special power and a separate life.

In the second place, Raleigh is still a power among us; a power in the Old World and in the New World; hardly less visible in England than in America, where the beautiful capital of a chivalrous nation bears his name. Raleigh's public life was spent in raising England to her true rank; and the mode by which he sought to raise her was by making her the mother of Free States.

In Raleigh's time the leading influence on this planet lay in Spain; an influence which was hostile to England in every way; hostile to her religion, hostile to her commerce, hostile to her liberty, hostile to her law. Spain continued to assume that the English were a God-abandoned people, whom it was her sacred duty to chastise and save. She sent her spies and bravos into London. She landed her troops in Connaught. By her gold and by her craft she raised up enemies against our peace beyond the Scottish border and in the Low Country camps. Even when her policy was that of peace, she drove our ships from the ocean and cast our sailors into prison. She closed the Levant against our merchants, and forbade all intercourse of England with America. Every foe of this country found in her a friend. She sharpened the dirks of Babington and his crew. She stirred up Rome against us. When she could not fight, she never ceased to plot. If the Irish kernes rebelled, she flung her troops into Cork; regular troops, who fought under her banner; and only disavowed them when they failed. In brief, at all times, in all places, our fathers had to count with Spain as their most deadly foe.

Against that country Raleigh set his teeth. It was Spain which he braved in Guiana; which he humiliated at Cadiz; which he outwitted in Virginia. Towards Spain the most splendid Englishman ever born nursed the hostile passion which Hannibal fed against Rome. In the end, a great country wears out a great man; and, after fighting Spain for forty years, fighting her with the sword and with the pen, Raleigh was murdered, at the command of Philip the Third, in Palace Yard.

Raleigh's life divides itself into three main periods: the first period ending with his seduction of Bessie Throgmorton, the Queen's Maid of Honour; the second period with his arrest by Cecil, on a charge of conspiring to raise Arabella Stuart to the throne; the third period with his execution in Palace Yard, on the demand of his great enemy, Philip the Third. Sunshine floods the first; tempests beat the second; gloom enwraps the third.

Raleigh's first detention in the Tower, which can scarcely be called an imprisonment, was caused by his affair with Bessie Throgmorton, one of the stars of Queen Elizabeth's court. Bessie was lovely, witty, and an orphan. All the gay lordlings of the court admired her. Tall, slender, fair, with light blue eyes and golden hair, she was a perfect contrast to Raleigh, whose dark and saturnine beauty half repelled while it strangely allured the beholder's eye. Bessie listened to his words, as shepherdesses listen to their swains in those pastoral tales which were only too much in vogue.

As at noon Dulcina rested
In her sweet and shady bower,
Came a shepherd . . .

the like of whom has seldom tempted woman to her sorrow. He was no lout with bill and crook; but a shining youth, bright with the sun and tawny with the sea. Spenser has pictured him in glowing verse. 'The Shepherd of the Ocean' he was dight; but the softer arts were all to him like the sciences of the sea. He knew them all; and most, as Spenser writes, he knew the seducing phrase of love.

Full sweetly tempered is that muse of his,
That can empierce a prince's mighty heart.

Dulcina listened to his lays, and whispering tongues soon bore the news of her deception to the Queen.

Elizabeth was deeply hurt; not, as the triflers say, because Raleigh deserted her side for that of a younger beauty; but because he sullied her court and wronged his own manhood by scandalous amour. To Bessie, her orphan maid of honour, the Queen was like a mother; and friends at court sent word to Raleigh, who was then at Chatham, making ready for a voyage, that he would have to stay at home and wed a wife. The lover laughed over words which he received as an idle threat. 'Marry,' he cried, 'there is none on the face of the earth that I will be fastened unto.' But the Queen was not a woman to forgive him such a deed; and when he slipt away to sea in the *Garland*, hoping to fall in with the Spanish silver fleet, and come home crowned with glory and rich with spoil, she sent Sir Martin Frobisher in her swift pinnace, the *Disdain*, to fetch him back.

Given in charge to his cousin, Sir George Carew, Master of the Ordnance, he lived in the spacious Brick tower, Carew's official residence, until he married the maid of honour, when he left his prison with the young and lovely woman, who was at once his brightest glory and his darkest shame. Much of the grace of life departed from Raleigh when Bessie was deceived. Repentance came; but came too late. The Queen appeared to forgive him; but the outrage lived in her heart; and Raleigh never became for her again the hero of his spotless prime.

On the coming in of James the First, Raleigh returned to his imprisonment in a new cause; to suffer in which was worthy of even his fame and genius. He came back to the Tower a sacrifice for his native land.

The new king had a policy of his own, of which amity with Spain was the corner-stone.

James had the strange disease, so rare in Scottish men, of physical cowardice. He was not tender of heart; he was, in fact, so fond of seeing pain that he more than once came down to the Tower, that he might feast his eyes on broken joints and quivering flesh; yet his life was spent in one long spasm of personal fear. He fainted at the sight of a drawn sword; he trembled at the roar of saluting guns; the name of a renowned warrior filled him with superstitious dread. On this base weakness, the adversaries of his country worked. They filled his mind with pictures of secret poisoners and assassins; so that his dreams became hot with visions of Jesuits and conspirators; and his soul was cowed by phantoms, taking the shape of agile and unscrupulous men, who from the vantage-ground of a distant court could either drop arsenic into his wine, or sharpen against him a bravo's knife.

James found by private question, that he could have peace with Philip the Third on one condition: ruin of the man who had sworn undying enmity to Spain, and to all that Spain then represented in the world. As a first step towards peace, he was told that Raleigh must be thrown into the Tower.

In his second restraint, Raleigh was not lodged in a kinsman's house, but in the more courtly and ominous Bloody tower; under the immediate eyes of Sir John Peyton, the Lieutenant; a man whose zeal in the new King's service was quickened by hints that in case of Raleigh's ruin he might receive, as his share of the spoil, the governorship of Jersey, one of the many high offices which his prisoner held. How Peyton was to earn this guerdon we can only guess; but more than one great councillor was known to have said that the King's coming in would be Raleigh's *doom.*

The confinement was close and the treatment mean. Cecil told the world that Raleigh's lodgings in the Tower were as pleasant as the rooms in Durham house; but the Lieutenant's weekly bills tell a different tale. He had only two small chambers; only two servants were allowed him; and the charge for diet, coals and candles, for his household, was four pounds a-week.

The pretext for his seizure was a parley which he had held with Lord Cobham on affairs of state. Cobham was a disappointed man. Most of his kinsfolk were in office. His brother-in-law, Sir Robert Cecil, was the first Secretary of State; his father-in-law, Effingham, Lord Admiral; his wife's cousin, Lord Henry Howard, a Privy Councillor; yet his own great talents were thrust aside. An idea struck him, that he could bring himself into notice by espousing the claim of Arabella Stuart to the throne; in favour of which claim he felt sure that he could count on Spain. This project he broached to Raleigh, who laughed in his face as a dreamer; and that light laugh sent Raleigh to the Tower—as an accomplice in the Arabella Plot!

CHAPTER XXX.

THE ARABELLA PLOT.

During the first three months of James's reign a very sharp struggle for power took place; the men in office wishing to keep in, the men out of office trying to get in. Cecil, Howard, Effingham, were in; Raleigh, Cobham, Northumberland, were out. Those who were in were the men of peace; those who were out were the men of war. Each party accused the other of foul play, of setting up pretenders, of intriguing with foreign courts. The men in power had the great advantage over their rivals of material strength; of having in their control the fleet, the guards, the bench, the Tower, and the block.

A dozen mad schemes were known to be on foot; any one of which might be called a plot, should Sir Robert Cecil see cause to arrest a friend. Cobham was prattling of Arabella. Percy was sulking at Sion. Grey wanted favours for the Puritans. Watson and Clarke, two seminary priests, were eager to serve the Pope. Copley, one of Cecil's spies, who lived in the best Catholic society, kept his master informed of all these movements; so that when Cecil struck his blow, the Tower was pretty nigh filled with victims; among whom he counted Sir Walter Raleigh, Lord Cobham, Lord Grey of Wilton, Sir Griffin Markham, George Brooke, a younger brother of Lord Cobham, Anthony Copley the spy, and the two secular priests, William Watson and William Clarke.

Lord Cobham had lodgings in the Lieutenant's house; but the contriver of what Cecil called the Arabella Plot, was kept in close confinement, with only a single servant to wait upon him day and night.

Few things in the story of our State prison strike the imagination like the change which a few days of sharp privation wrought in the character of this rich and powerful peer. When out of peril, Cobham appeared to be frank and fair. Faults he had in plenty; but his vices were those of a warm and generous nature; pride in his house, heat in his blood, an insatiable greed of gold, an unconquerable lust of power. Yet a few weeks of sharp privation broke his spirit. In the court he had been a bold and saucy baron; in the Tower he became a mean and abject serf. He knew that the judges and councillors who came down to question him could not torture him on account of his nobility; but he also knew that these judges and councillors could take away his life; and life was a thing which this degenerate bearer of the name of Cobham prized above either an easy conscience or a stainless name.

To the great misfortune of Raleigh, this rich court friend was connected by marriage with the families of Howard and of Cecil; both of whom might hope to profit by his death. His wife was sent to tell him that his only hope of saving his neck, was to bring about Raleigh's ruin; and when Cecil, the chief of his inquisitors, told him the odious lie that Raleigh had accused him of high treason in the matter of Arabella, he pronounced the very words which Cecil wanted from his lips. If he were guilty of high treason, he said, Raleigh was guilty too, since he had been a partaker in all his plans. Cecil knew that the second lie was like the first; but knowing the value of lies to a clever and unscrupulous lawyer, he sent Cobham's falsehood to the Attorney-General, Sir Edward Coke.

Raleigh found means to communicate with Cobham in the Lieutenant's house. In fact he made a friend of Peyton's son, also called Sir John, by whom messages were carried between the two prisoners. Cobham, looking out of his room, saw young Peyton standing in the garden talking to Raleigh at a window, and when the young man came to see him, two or three hours later, he cried out: 'I saw you with Sir Walter Raleigh. God forgive him! He hath accused me; but I cannot accuse him.' Peyton replied, 'That is what he says of you. You have accused him; but he cannot accuse you.'

Next day (as it would seem) Cecil came down to the Tower, with a view to complete his case for Coke by a final examination of Cobham. To his amazement, Cobham retracted every word which he had said. Raleigh had nothing to do with his plots; had never adopted Arabella's claims; had never spoken of Spanish help. Under such a change, the Council, as Count de Beaumont wrote to Henri, found it very difficult to proceed in the charge.

Then came out a mysterious rumour that the great offender had laid hands upon himself. For some days it had been whispered in court and city that Raleigh was morose and proud; a prey to melancholy thoughts and restive dreams; as though he were aching of some inward sore. At length, the rumour ran that Raleigh, sitting at Peyton's table, as his custom was, had snatched up a knife, bared his breast, and plunged the steel into his flesh. He was not dead. The point had struck on a bone and glanced aside from the vital part; on which Raleigh had thrown away the weapon, crying, 'There, an end.'

For reasons which may be guessed, the court desired this bruit to spread. Cecil spoke of it, and wrote of it, to several persons. He told the tale to Signor Molino, ambassador from the Doge of Venice; he wrote it to Sir Thomas Parry, his agent at the court of Henri the Great. Of course he sent the news to James, who was in the country. James was highly pleased, for an attempt at suicide seemed to him proof of Sir Walter's guilt. James wrote back to Cecil, 'Let him be well probed; have a good preacher with you; and make him see that it is his soul he should wound and not his body.'

It is impossible to believe this story true. Raleigh never spoke of an attempt on his own life. Cecil dropped the tale when it had served his turn. Coke, though straining every act and word of the accused into the vile suggestion that he cared for neither God nor devil, passed over this damning proof. Had the tale been true, would not Coke have told it in open court?

Again, if such a man as Raleigh had wished to kill himself, how could he have failed? A man has choice of a thousand deaths, and Raleigh was familiar with them all. He had knives in his cell. He had about him spirits and poisons of many sorts. He could have opened a vein; he could have thrown himself from the wall. Raleigh knew that nothing is easier than for a willing mind to part with life. When, in his later troubles, Wilson spoke of seizing his jars and simples on the ground that he might some day poison himself and escape from justice, Raleigh answered with contempt, 'Why, man, if I wished to die, could I not dash my head against that wall?'

A few years ago, a letter was printed for the first time, pretending to be written by Raleigh to his wife, which seemed to support Cecil's tale. That letter is not only a forgery, but a very impudent forgery. Its purpose was, not to sustain the lie about Raleigh's project of suicide, but to taint his name as an unfaithful husband to his wife. Of course that letter was not read on the trial; of course it is only a copy; and equally of course the original is not known. The copy was found among a lawyer's papers; a lawyer who was employed against Raleigh in his later days; and the paper was probably one of the countless forgeries which his enemies had the baseness to prepare, but not the hardihood to produce.

Many persons suspected that the rumour of suicide was sent abroad as a test of public feeling. James was afraid of Raleigh's name. 'I ha' heard rawly of thee, mon,' was his first greeting of the hero of Cadiz and Guiana. Indeed, that name was a power in the land before which a bolder prince than James might have bent his brows. During Raleigh's first restraint in the Brick tower, Elizabeth had been moved by reports of his amazing credit with her fleet. As a seaman, Raleigh stood alone. Essex owned in him a master; and Effingham, though bearing the rank of Lord High Admiral of England, had been seen to pay him the extraordinary homage of wiping the dust from his shoes. If the king's advisers meant to 'cut the throat' of such a man, it may have been thought wise to learn how a report of his sudden death in the Tower would be received in the city, in the fleet, and in foreign courts.

The result was probably such as to dissuade them from using violent means. We hear no more of Raleigh being probed. Cecil came to see him, without bringing the godly preacher who was to search into his soul. In three or four days, the prisoner was reported well. Then Sir John Peyton was dismissed from his great office, and a new and less scrupulous Lieutenant, Sir George Harvey, was installed in his house.

The Peytons being sent away, as men unequal to their trust, a duel began between Cecil and Raleigh for the possession of Cobham's soul. The prize was not much; not worth either the inquisitor's craft or the statesman's skill; but fate had given into the hands of that weak and angry peer the power of either saving or destroying by a word the greatest hero in his native land.

Raleigh and Cecil were not ill matched; for if one had incomparably the finer genius, the other had incomparably the deeper craft. But Cecil was free while his antagonist lay bound. Cecil was a minister who could send Cobham to the block; Raleigh was a fallen man, who could do him neither good nor harm. Yet Raleigh fought it out. If he could get at Cobham, he might work upon his deeper and better feelings. How was he to get at Cobham? The new Lieutenant was Cecil's creature; a man of low, serpentine ways; not radically wicked, yet fit for work of which a downright villain would have been ashamed. When Raleigh saw that he could do nothing with Sir George, he made a serviceable friend of Sir George's son; a brave lad, through whom he kept up an irregular correspondence with Cobham, who had been lately moved from the Lieutenant's house to the more distant and lonely Wardrobe tower.

A few weeks of harsh confinement in the Tower had so far unstrung Cobham's moral fibre, that he answered each of his questioners with a different tale; one day charging Raleigh with a guilty knowledge of his designs; next day drawing back that charge as a monstrous lie; a third day whining over a weakness which he could not help; a fourth day going back to his original accusation, adding to it, blackening it; then, after a brief interval, on a fresh appeal to his moral sense, retracting every word that he had spoken when the fit of fear was on his soul. It was a sight to see. In the presence of men who held his life in their hands, this English Claudio, dazed by mortal terror, answered all questions as they bade him by their looks and tones. Still, he could not stick to these lies when they were sworn. On Raleigh's remonstrance, he withdrew his accusations, calling God to witness that now, and now only, he spoke the truth. Young

Harvey brought this answer from the Wardrobe to the Bloody tower.

Raleigh knew that his young and devoted helper ran much risk in carrying messages to the Wardrobe tower; and when the time of his trial drew near, he employed his own servant, William Cottrel, to take an apple, into which he had put a note, and, watching his happy chance when no one saw him, to throw it into Cobham's room. This note contained a passionate prayer to Cobham that, for love of God, and the sake of his wife and children, he would tell the truth in writing, so that his last confession could be read in court. The Wardrobe tower, to which Cobham had been sent, was in a lonely quarter, looking on the Queen's garden. Cottrel threw in his apple and received an answer to his master's message. That answer contained these words in Cobham's hand:—

'To clear my conscience, satisfy the world, and free myself from the cry of your blood, I protest, upon my soul, and before God and his angels, I never had conference with you in any treason; nor was ever moved by you to the thing I heretofore accused you of. . . . . And so God deal with me and have mercy on my soul, as this is true.'

These words were penned four days before the prisoners left the Tower for Winchester. One week later, Cobham was in that city among his inquisitors, who persuaded him to declare that these last words sent to Raleigh had been got from him by artifice, and that they were not true!

Yet Cobham had made a statement to Sir George Harvey of the same kind, and of his own free-will. He had told Sir George that Raleigh knew nothing about his plot. This free and independent declaration of Raleigh's innocence Sir George Harvey kept back until the trial was over and the verdict given, when he told it in confidence to Cecil.

A rare Lieutenant of the Tower!

CHAPTER XXXI.

RALEIGH'S WALK.

After those shameful scenes at Winchester, which Chief Justice Gaudy, one of the presiding judges, described on his dying bed as having degraded for ever the character of English justice, Raleigh was brought back to the Tower, and lodged in his previous room; the upper chamber of the Bloody tower; the hinder passage of which led out by a door to the terrace, now known as Raleigh's Walk. From this walk—his favourite exercise for years—he could look down, on one side over the wharf and river, on the other side over the Lieutenant's garden and the green.

No one thought as yet of his living in that room, of his pacing that walk, for fourteen years. The trial at Winchester exalted his credit for eloquence and patriotism; he was the idol and the hero of young and old. Nobody believed in the Arabella Plot; the princess herself had never heard of it; and the hint that Raleigh, the hero of Cadiz, the founder of Free States, had been in league with Philip the Third against his country, was met by universal scorn. The noblest men and the holiest women were on Raleigh's side. Queen Anne admired him. Mary Sydney wrought for him; charging her son, Lord Pembroke, as he valued her blessing, to use his utmost power, and that of all his friends, in Raleigh's favour. Arabella did what she could. Cecil and Harvey kept their secret; yet no one believed that the great captain, who was engaged in planting a Free State in the New World, could be penned for many weeks in the Tower, to please the mortal enemies of their native land.

The allowance for diet, fire, and candle, was increased from four pounds a-week to five. Two servants besides William Cottrel had warrants to share his cell. Thomas Hariot, and other friends, were suffered to see him; and Lady Raleigh and her boy, little Wat, were often at his side.

Early in this new imprisonment, hope came gaily into his cell. The King was coming to the Tower on an act of grace; coming in his state barge down the Thames, accompanied by the Queen and Prince, and followed by all his court; coming to make golden holidays; to throw open the doors of every vault; to set the prisoners free; and to crown his act of grace by a mighty feast and show. This tale was partly true; James sailed down the river; but the day before he landed at the Queen's stair his great prisoner was carried to the Fleet, so that the king and a rout of lords and ladies might flutter through his empty cell.

Raleigh remained two weeks and a half in the Fleet Prison, attended by his servants, with the same allowance for food, fire, and candle, as in the Tower. At the end of seventeen days, the court fooleries being then over, the prisoners were brought back and lodged once more in their empty cells.

It was long before either Raleigh or Lady Raleigh could be brought to see that the men in power were bent on holding him fast for life. Raleigh could not know that he was held in bonds for Spain; he could not tell the sums for which Cecil and Howard had sold him to Philip the Third. But neither Raleigh nor his wife was patient under wrong. Lady Raleigh came to live at the Tower, with little Wat; and in the chamber in which King Edward had been killed, her second son, baby Carew, was born. But she could not sit by her husband's side, a silent witness of his pain. She was often at Sherborne Castle, their magnificent home in Dorset; oftener still in the galleries of Whitehall, on the terraces of Windsor, among the fish-ponds at Theobalds; wearying the King with her petitions; troubling the court with a remembrance of her wrongs. No captive ever found a bolder, a more winning advocate than Lady Raleigh. Her efforts were all in vain; yet years passed by ere Raleigh could be brought to see that men who had served in the same field, sat on the same board with himself, under the great Queen, could sink into the depths of infamy into which Howard and Cecil had fallen as the pensioners of Spain.

Of course their high pretence was fear of Philip. If England wanted peace at any cost, why haggle in the chambers of Madrid? But they had lower motives. Rich in money and in friends, Raleigh might find a thousand ways of making his anger felt; and they had done him wrongs which they could never expect a proud man to forgive. Exile would not serve with him, as with his fellow-captive Markham, whom they sent abroad, with leave to sell his sword in a foreign camp. Raleigh was too great a captain to send away in search of bread. If he went abroad, he might find not only bread but power; for princely offers were being already made to him by foreign states. Henri of France strove hard to obtain his sword. The Dutch would have sent him to the Indies. Christiern of Denmark wanted him as admiral of his fleets. In Italy his services were sought. Had Raleigh been thrown into a boat, like an old Celtic criminal, and turned adrift at sea with a jar of water and a pole, he would probably have been found in three or four years directing the councils and leading the forces of some powerful king.

Not daring to deal with him as they would have dealt with ordinary men, they locked him fast in the Tower, and plundered his estates. One of the spoilers, sad to say, was the great sailor Effingham, who had once thought it no dishonour to be seen wiping the dust from Raleigh's shoes with his own silken cloak. Though Effingham was rich and old, he begged for Raleigh's wine-patent; the chief source of his old friend's income, the reward for many years of service; and he got it. 'His lordship hath six thousand pounds,' wrote Lady Raleigh, 'and three thousand pounds a-year, by my husband's fall.' Effingham claimed still more, and the weak King, whose penniless cousin he had married, gave him what he asked. 'If his conscience warrant him,' wrote Lady Raleigh, in despair, 'we must yield to God's will and the King's. . . . The bread and food taken from me and my children will never augment my lord's table, though it famish us.'

In the stress of his poverty, Raleigh had to part from some of those companions who lived at his board and slept under his roof. One of the nearest of these old friends was Thomas Hariot, the famous voyager and algebraist, from whose 'Brief View of Virginia,' Raleigh learned much of his geography, and from whose 'Artis Analytica Praxis,' Des Cartes was accused of having stolen most of his mathematics. Raleigh had sent Hariot out to Virginia in 1584, and for the next twenty years had kept him in his household. When his fortunes were broken, his manors seized, and his means cut off, he gave this faithful servant of science a letter to Northumberland, who carried him down to Petworth, helped him in his studies, and settled on him a pension of 120*l.* a-year for life.

Though Raleigh was now lodged in the Tower, with three poor servants, living on five pounds a-week for food and fire, the men in office considered him far too strong.

His fame was rising, instead of falling. Great ladies from the court cast wistful glances at his room. Men from the streets and ships came crowding to the wharf whence they could see him walking on the wall.

Raleigh was a sight to see; not only for his fame and name, but for his picturesque and dazzling figure. Fifty-one years old; tall, tawny, splendid; with the bronze of tropical suns on his leonine cheek; a bushy beard, a round moustache, and a ripple of curling hair, which his man Peter took an hour to dress. Apparelled as became such a figure, in scarf and band of the richest colour and costliest stuff, in cap and plume worth a ransom, in jacket powdered with gems; his whole attire, from cap to shoe-strings blazing with rubies, emeralds, and pearls; he was allowed to be one of the handsomest men alive.

The council got alarmed at the crowds who came down to see him. Harvey was thought too careless; and a stricter gaoler was appointed to take his place. Sir William Waad ('that villain, Waad,' as Raleigh had only too much cause to style him), began his service as Lieutenant by proposing to abridge the very few liberties which Raleigh then enjoyed.

CHAPTER XXXII.

THE VILLAIN WAAD.

A WAKEFUL spy and unscrupulous tool, one of the secret agents who had been employed by Cecil in watching Percy and Catesby, the Gunpowder Plotters, Waad was sent to the Tower in the hope that his evil genius might invent some method of connecting Raleigh with that plot.

Raleigh had, in truth, as much to do with the Gunpowder

Plot as with the Arabella Plot, and it seemed likely enough that he would be tried again, if not sentenced again, on some new charge. Only the fear of an acquittal stopped the game.

In the little garden lying under Raleigh's Walk stood that Garden house in which Latimer had lived; a small house of lath and plaster, which was now used by the warden as a hen-roost. Raleigh had obtained from Sir George Harvey the use of this Garden house as a still-room for his experiments. He was bent on following Nature into her secret haunts. He wished to solve the great problem of converting salt water into fresh. He dreamt of cordials for preserving health, and even hoped to find an elixir of life. Some things he had already done in the way of cordials, the fame of which had taken wings.

One day the Countess de Beaumont, who had come down to the Tower with a bevy of ladies in her train, bowed to him as he was walking in his garden, and asked him if he would give her a little of his famous balsam of Guiana. He gallantly promised to prepare and send it. Waad, who could not bear to see great ladies bowing to his prisoner, wrote to Cecil, 'Sir Walter Raleigh hath converted a little hen-house in the garden into a still, where he doth spend his time all day in his distillations. If a brick wall were built it would be more safe and convenient.' Nor was this interference with his chemical labours all that he had to bear from Waad. A few months later, the Lieutenant found a fresh cause of offence in the popular homage paid to the man whom he had been set to watch. 'Raleigh,' he wrote to Cecil, 'doth show himself upon the wall in his garden to the view of the people, who gaze upon him; which made me bold to restrain him again.'

Slowly, very slowly, the man of action paled into the man of thought. Under Harvey's rule, nothing more had been heard of his pride and melancholy. He rose at dawn, curled his dark hair and beard, made an early meal, wrote all the morning, walked in his garden, played a game of bowls with Sir George, and quaffed a horn of good English beer. Dining at the Lieutenant's table, he chatted with the guests about Virginia and the Spanish main. As time went by, and no pardon came, he bent his mind to more serious work. A thousand things which had crossed him in his busier days, came back in his cell and occupied his thoughts. One of these subjects was the sufferings endured by men at sea from want of water fit for drink. Having caught the idea of a new method of purging the brine from water, he fell to work. Lighting his fires, and boiling his sea-water, he struck upon a way of expelling salt; a precious discovery, which he tested in his latest voyage, and found to act; but the secret of which was unhappily lost, with much that was still more precious, in Palace Yard. Two hundred years elapsed before men of science got the clue again, when Irving recovered the lost secret; but no doubt can exist as to Raleigh's claim. Wilson wrote down the words from Raleigh's lips:—'He fell to tell me of his inventing the means to make salt water fresh or sweet, by furnaces of copper in the forecastle, and distilling of the salt water as it were by a bucket, putting in a pipe, and within a quarter of an hour it will run by a spigot, and the water as sweet as milk.'

These studies, so precious to mankind, were interrupted by 'that villain Waad,' in the interest of his master Cecil, who was only too ready to propitiate his bountiful patrons in Madrid. Cecil was building Hatfield house; and that princely house was being built and furnished with Spanish gold. If any excuse could be found for taking Raleigh's life, the student would be offered without scruple as a sacrifice to Philip the Third. If a pretext could not be found, it might be made.

When the Countess de Beaumont spoke to Raleigh in his garden, she had a gentleman in her train whom Raleigh knew by sight; Captain Whitelocke, a retainer of his old friend Northumberland. Whitelocke came down to the Tower for that balsam of Guiana which was to be made for the French countess. This was all that either Waad or Cecil knew; it was very little; yet it was nearly as good evidence as Coke had been able to adduce at Winchester, in proof of his complicity in the Arabella Plot. Northumberland was a kinsman of Percy, one of the plotters; Whitelocke was a servant of Northumberland; Raleigh was an acquaintance of Whitelocke. On these grounds, Raleigh's name was entered on a suspected list; and commissioners were sent to examine him in the Bloody tower. Waad was one of these commissioners; and being the Lieutenant also, he had rare opportunities of making his obstinate and contemptuous prisoner feel his claws. Nothing could be wrung from Raleigh. Waad recommended the King to handle him more roundly, so as to break his pride; and on the villain's suggestion, Raleigh was put under close restraint. He was turned out of his still-room, he was denied the use of his walk, and he was locked up in his cell at an early hour of the afternoon.

Lady Raleigh and her two boys were sent away from the Tower; and, in order to be near her husband, the poor lady was compelled to take lodgings on the hill outside, near Barking Church.

Under these new privations Raleigh's health gave way. Sleeping in a stone room, with little air, with no fire, the man of active life, whose feet had been on the quarter-deck, whose days on land had been spent in the saddle, broke down into a pitiable wreck of his former self. The winter being cold, his flesh became chilled and numb. One hand fell feebly to his side; the sinews of his arm shrank up. 'Every second or third night,' he wrote to Cecil, 'I am in danger of either sudden death or of the loss of my limbs and senses, being sometimes two hours without feeling or motion of my hand and whole arm.' Then he added, with some bitterness of heart, 'I complain not; I know it is vain.'

Peter Turner, a physician, who was allowed to see him, gave so bad an account of his condition that the very courtiers who were paid by Spain for keeping him, as it were, in chains, were startled into pity. His left side was described by the good doctor as quite numb; the fingers of his left hand were curled; his tongue was so hardened that he could not speak. The lodging in which he lay, said the physician, was too cold for any man to sleep in; and he recommended that Waad should be ordered to remove him into a warmer room. Turner suggested that he should be lodged in that little Garden-house in which Latimer had lain, and in which his own experiments had been made.

The men in office may have been moved by pity for an old friend; they may have seen their advantage in offering to indulge a dying hero. They had many troubles on their hands just then, and may have thought the prisoner in the Bloody tower a useful factor in their game. The King of Spain was causing them some trouble, and the name of Arabella Stuart was again in every man's mouth; for this royal lady had chosen to marry without the King's consent, and her youthful husband, himself a pretender to James' crown, was a fugitive in Philip's Flemish court.

For some of these reasons, the men in power relented so far towards the prisoner, that on Turner's formal request for a change being made, the Council gave orders to Waad for his removal from the Bloody tower into the little Garden-house in which he kept his books and drugs.

CHAPTER XXXIII.

THE GARDEN-HOUSE.

The lodge into which Raleigh was moved, on the suggestion of his physician, leaned against the Tower wall. It was warm and dry; covered from the Thames blast, and peeping out among trees and flowers. In this Garden-house Raleigh was to spend the noblest years of his life.

His first love was science. In the hope of finding a specific cure for every evil to which flesh, as flesh, is heir, Raleigh sat in his still room, before his furnace and retort, day after day, year after year, questioning Nature with a keen eye, and tracking her secrets with a cunning hand. While he was bent on these great trials, he hit upon that powerful potion, which became widely known and universally admired, as Raleigh's Great Cordial.

Learned essays have been written to expound the virtues of this mixture; a blending of pearl, musk, hartshorn, bezoar stone, mint, borrage, gentian, mace, red rose, aloes, sugar, sassafras, spirits of wine, with twenty other things; a charm against disease which was high in favour, not alone with city madams and country squires, but with the noblest persons in the land, notably with Queen Anne, with her son Charles the First, and her grandson Charles the Second. The ablest chemists tried to improve it; the wisest physicians sought to explain it. Digby proposed to increase its power by adding viper's heart and flesh. Frasier studied the science of its combination. Lefebre, the French physician, wrote a treatise, by the king's command, on its sovereign virtues. Queen Anne believed that it saved her life. Charles the Second would take no other medicine; and even now the Great Cordial finds a place in our accepted medical schools.

Drawing from his little fire in the still-room, these spirits and essences of nature, Raleigh came to be regarded by simple folk as a great doctor. His room was filled with vases, jars, and phials; which that paid spy and profane rascal, Sir Thomas Wilson, afterwards described as containing 'all the spirits in the world, except the Spirit of God.' Men of science came to learn from him. The Wizard Earl stood by his side in the still-room. Hariot and Allen watched his experiments with a curious eye. Mayerne admitted his supreme knowledge of drugs, and went very near to allowing his superior skill in judging of disease. Folk sent to consult him in their sickness; and if he had been free to go about, he might have gained a very large practice as a medical man.

Hapless Lady Raleigh could not turn her heart to books and cordials. Raving on year by year, she could not be comforted and would not be silenced. In her ardent wrestling with her fate, she complained of him, the recluse in the Tower; saying, in her blind love, that even he would make no effort to get free. Absorbed with his books and phials, she fancied him wishing to be left alone to his own undoing. One day, as he sat before his desk writing, she burst into his room, just as she used to lie in wait for the King, holding little Wat by the hand, pressing her baby to her heart; and standing thus before her husband, she asked him how he could be so cruel to his wife and babes, as to sit there, wasting his life, in poring over books and maps? Poor captive! This was the hardest trial he was called to bear. He could not blame her, and he could not help her.

Days, months, years went by. One by one his honours, offices, and estates were taken away by James. Durham house was one of the first to go. Sherborne Castle was still left to him; but Sir Robert Carr, a new and grasping favourite, having heard that the house was good, that the site was beautiful, that the soil was rich, begged it from the King. When Lady Raleigh threw herself at James's feet, beseeching him not to take the bread from her children's mouths, the King coarsely answered, 'Madame, I maun ha' it; I maun ha' it for Carr.' Lady Raleigh, hot with holy wrath, threw up her hands, and called on Heaven to launch its bolts on the man who robbed her fatherless children of their bread!

Those bolts were not long in coming.

Raleigh's lodge under the Tower wall became a court, to which a crowd of men who stood highest among the learned and the great repaired for profit and delight. Raleigh was still a centre. Bacon sought in him a patron of the new learning. Percy dined with him in the Lieutenant's house. Hariot brought him books and maps. Pett came over with his models; Jonson with his epigrams and underwoods. The *magi*—Hariot Hues, and Warner, made a part of Raleigh's court. Selden was often here; Mayerne sometimes, Bilson now and then. Nor were these all. Queen Anne sent messages to the prisoner. Prince Henry rode down from Whitehall to hear him talk. The young prince, who was eager about his sister's marriage, learned from Raleigh to distrust the policy of a Savoy match; and from the same high source, he caught his leaning towards the court of France. Princess Elizabeth looked on her brother's friend as her own best guide. For the young prince Raleigh wrote his 'Discourse touching a marriage between Prince Henry of England and a daughter of Savoy;' for the young princess his 'Discourse touching a match between the Lady Elizabeth and the Prince of Piedmont.' In both these treatises he gave new and deadly offence to his foes in Madrid. The Spanish faction at Whitehall were furious; for the Prince and Princess made no secret of their own adhesion to Raleigh's views. It seemed to those pensioners of Philip that Raleigh was establishing a second government in the Tower, from which he presumed to dictate his policy to the King. And they were right. Raleigh's writings struck the note of opposition, everywhere slumbering in men's hearts, against a match with either Spain or an ally of Spain. Elizabeth married a German Prince; setting the example, so largely followed in all coming years, of seeking alliances for our reigning house, not among strange races, but among our own Teutonic kin.

But the talk of the old sailor and the young prince ran much on the sea, on ships, and on naval war, for which the lad was already quickening with heroic fire. Raleigh promised to reduce his thoughts on these high things to order, in a regular treatise on 'The Art of War by Sea.' Riding away from the Tower after one of the mornings thus spent, the Prince cried aloud to his attendants, 'No man but my father would keep such a bird in a cage.'

When the Prince fell sick, Queen Anne insisted that he should take Raleigh's cordial; a medicine which had saved her own life, she said, when every other remedy had failed. It came too late; the hope of England died; and the projected treatise on naval war was laid aside.

In this Garden-house Raleigh finished, if he did not begin, the first part of his magnificent 'History of the World;' a work without an original; though it has had a thousand successors. The tale there told in part was to have been a great prose epic; its theme, the life of man on our mother earth. In the eleventh year of his confinement, Raleigh produced one volume of his labours; all that he lived to write; and it is no new thing to say that this volume of universal history is one of the grandest fragments on our library shelf.

Opinions vary as to Raleigh's share in the production of his work. Ben Jonson told his friend Drummond, that the history was composed by a circle of wits; but this account can hardly have been true. Ben wrote the poetic prefix, though he did not dare to sign it. There, I think the foreign work begins and ends. The style is uniform throughout; a style too pure for any other pen to claim. No doubt the historian sought such help as every historian seeks and finds. Burrell aided him with Hebrew; Hariot gave him hints on science; others may have helped him in questions beyond his ken. But the book, as book, is certainly Raleigh's own.

From the Garden-house he sent forth other writings; some of great value, others trifles of the day. Among these works may be named 'A Discourse on the invention of Ships,' and 'Observations on the Sea Service.'

But his main solace after all was the heroic work in which he had embarked his fame and fortunes from his earliest times; that of founding Free States; fighting the Spaniards with a weapon that would renew itself for ever. From the Bloody tower he directed operations in Guiana and in Virginia; never ceasing to drop his purse into that scale into which he could no longer dash his sword.

On the episode of Raleigh's release from prison, his western voyage, his unhappy return, and his fresh arrest, there is little need to dwell. These events make the history of England for one troubled and shameful year. When he came back a prisoner, he found his apartments in the Bloody tower and the Garden lodge occupied by his spoilers, Carr and his new wife, now Earl and Countess of Somerset.

CHAPTER XXXIV.

THE BRICK TOWER.

THE Brick tower stands on the northern wall, a little to the west of Martin tower, with which it communicates by a secret passage. This tower overlooks the lines from Brass Mount to Legge Mount, and sweeps the opposite slope and ditch. The men who held the tower were gunners; and the captain of these troops was the real master of the Thames and of the approaches to London. Hence the Master of the Ordnance was generally a man of rank, and always a man of trust. In the reign of Elizabeth that office was filled by Charles, Earl of Devonshire; to whom succeeded George, Lord Carew; Raleigh's cousin, who held his post during the whole of James's reign.

The rooms being good, and the master seldom in residence, this house was placed at the disposal of any person of rank to whom the Government wished to show favour. Thus, when Raleigh was committed for his amour with the maid of honour, he was lodged in the master's house. Raleigh had the liberty of the Tower within the walls; he kept a great table, had a crowd of servants, and received the visits of many friends. The small upper room was filled by his domestics, and the brilliant seamen, looking on his recall from sea as a royal jest, could hardly have dreamed that in his wan and premature age that upper room, into which he would not willingly have thrust a dog, would become his own miserable home.

Northumberland, who had hired the Brick tower from Lord Carew, for his son Algernon's use, kept his tenancy until he was thrust out of his lodgings by Sir Thomas Wilson, with a view, as it would seem, to some such crime as that by which his grandfather had been done to death in the Bloody tower.

When Raleigh was brought back to the Tower, after his disastrous voyage, his old rooms in the Bloody tower and the Garden-house being occupied by Lord and Lady Somerset, he was lodged for a few days with the Lieutenant, Sir Allan Apsley—a man who admired and loved him—until the spacious Wardrobe tower could be furnished and arranged for his use. In that pleasant chamber, looking on the Queen's garden and across the Thames, into which Cottrel had thrown the apple, he took up his abode, with his books, his globes, his phials, and his plants. Beginning his life anew, he set about the great experiments on which he had already spent his time to such noble ends. His rooms were large; and he had the free use of a garden. In the Wardrobe, he kept his health, until Wilson came down from court on what was seen from the first to be a bloody purpose.

James was in a strait. The Spanish agents who were promising him an Infanta for his son, were yelling in his ear for Raleigh's blood. The King, though willing enough to yield, was not daring enough to face the consequences of murdering Raleigh by legal means. In fact, while he did not scruple to do wrong, he shrank from the infamy which he felt would fall upon his name. If Raleigh would only kill himself, all would be well. Even if he could be taken off privately, so as to leave the case in doubt, it might be better than a public murder. Secretary Naunton, who knew the King's secret wishes, found Wilson in his pay, and thought him the man to repeat Bailiff's work. Naunton brought Wilson into James's presence, and from that secret interview with the King, the wretch came down to the Tower and surveyed his ground. The moment he was seen, a whisper ran about the Tower that he had come to murder Raleigh; on which the honest Lieutenant, Sir Allan Apsley, stood upon his guard. Apsley not only admired his prisoner, but wished to avoid his foregoer's fate.

Wilson had brought down to Sir Allan a most unusual warrant. This order from the Council authorized Wilson to take charge of Raleigh; to remain constantly in his company; to keep him a close prisoner; to prevent any one from speaking with him, or even coming near him, except in case of necessity, and only then in his own presence. Apsley, though he must have been surprised, was not cowed. A Lieutenant of the Tower, he was responsible to the law for what took place within the gates; and though he admitted Wilson into the Wardrobe by day, he turned him out at night, and resolutely objected to give up his keys. Wilson complained to Naunton that he could do nothing in that place and in that way. The Wardrobe tower, he said, was a big house, with two windows, from either of which letters might be thrown into the Queen's garden, and through which nearly everything passing in Raleigh's chamber might be seen. He wanted a place, he said, less open to observation; one in which his prisoner would have to sleep in a room either above or within his own. Such a place, he said, after searching the Tower from end to end, he had found in the house then occupied by Lord Percy. These rooms he must have. But the Earl of Northumberland, having hired these lodgings for his son, refused to give them up, just as Sir Allan Apsley refused to give up his keys. Wilson went back to his employers. Not give up the keys? Not give up the Brick tower? A peremptory order came from court, which showed Sir Allan who was now to be master in the tower. Apsley was ordered to give up Raleigh into Wilson's charge: to allow him the

Brick tower as a lodging; to deliver up the keys; to send away Raleigh's servant, and replace him by one of Wilson's men. Sir Allan was forbidden to let any doctor see his prisoner, except in Wilson's presence and by his consent.

Naunton wrote to Wilson that the King was pleased with what was done; that he waited the ripening of his prescription; that he hoped Wilson would get the better hand of the hypocrite; and that he felt much comfort in the knowledge that he should not be troubled with Raleigh long.

If Secretary Naunton's words do not imply the intention to murder Raleigh, language has no meaning.

With the cunning of his black purpose, Wilson lodged his captive in the topmost room of the Brick tower, while he appropriated Lord Carew's comfortable chambers to himself and his men. 'I have been employed,' he wrote to the King's secretary, 'in removing this man to safer and higher lodging, which, though it seems nearer heaven, yet is there no means of escape from thence for him to any place but hell.' In the Wardrobe, Raleigh had kept up his chemical experiments, the value of which he had tested in his late voyage, when he put his copper furnace on board his ship, and gave out to each of his crew of two hundred and forty men, several quarts of fresh water every day. Wilson took away his drugs and phials, under the absurd pretence that he might poison himself. 'Why,' said Raleigh, with contempt, 'if I want to kill myself, I can dash my head against that wall.' The ignorant apothecaries who seized his jars and spirits, said they could not answer for the effect of swallowing his stuff unless they knew what it was made of; and through the violence of these mountebanks the great secret of distilling salt water into sweet was lost to mankind.

Yet the mysterious hint which had given the King such

comfort bore no fruit. If Wilson meant murder, he found no opportunity to carry out his plan. Indeed, to assassinate such a master of fence as Raleigh would have been no easy work, and a mean and brutal coward like Wilson was hardly the man to try. Raleigh would have spurned him like a dog or felled him like a slave. Nor could Wilson draw his prisoner to the point of suicide. Day after day he put a knife, as it were, into his captive's hand, by talking of men who had killed themselves to escape a shameful death. Raleigh would not take his hints. Once, when he praised the old Roman senators, Wilson hoped that something would ensue; but his prisoner gave no sign of following the

High Roman fashion,

and when Wilson renewed the subject another day, Raleigh spoke very gravely against self-murder, saying that for himself he would die in the light of day and in the face of his countrymen.

The Spaniards could not wait. They clamoured for his death; the King of Spain declaring, under his own hand and seal, that Raleigh must be instantly put to death. To the last moment there was doubt and strife at court. The Queen was for saving Raleigh; and the Queen was supported in her efforts by all those persons who leaned towards the policy of a French alliance for the Prince of Wales. Spain tempted the King with a larger dowry than France. Queen Anne said she did not care for money; and would prefer a French princess for her son, to an Infanta with all her gold. But gold tempted James, and the profligate minion of James. Finally, the order for his execution—the end for which he had waited long—was signed.

Wilson, who had failed in his infamous mission, was sent away; the Brick tower was restored to the honourable custody of Sir Allan; and the last ten days of Raleigh's life on earth were spent in peace. The bitterness of strife was passed; he knew that he must now die; and with the certainty of his fate came back to him, not only his high spirit, his ready wit, and his gay demeanour, but in some degree his physical health.

The warrant for his death reached the Tower at eight o'clock on a dark October morning. Raleigh was in bed; but on hearing the Lieutenant's voice, he sprang lightly to his feet, threw on his hose and doublet, and left his room. At the door he met Peter, his barber, coming in. 'Sir,' said Peter, 'we have not curled your head this morning.' Raleigh smiled; 'Let them comb it that shall have it.' Peter followed him to the gate, while Raleigh kept on joking in his usual vein. 'Peter,' he asked, 'canst thou give me any plaster to set on a man's head when it is off?'

Next day it was off in Palace Yard; the proudest head that ever rolled into English dust.

That day was thought to be a very sad day for Englishmen. The partizans of Spain went mad with joy.

Yet the victory was not to Spain. A higher power than man's directs the course of a nation's life; the death of a hero is not failure; for the martyr's blood is stronger than a thousand swords. The day of Raleigh's death was the day of a new English birth. Eliot was not the only youth of ardent soul who stood by the scaffold in Palace Yard, to note the matchless spirit in which the martyr met his fate, and walked away from that solemnity—a new man. Thousands of men in every part of England who had led a careless life became from that very hour the sleepless enemies of Spain. The purposes of Raleigh were accomplished, in the very way which his genius had contrived. Spain held the dominion of the sea, and England took it from her. Spain excluded England from the New World, and the genius of that New World is English.

The large contest in the new political system of the

world, then young, but clearly enough defined, had come to turn upon this question—Shall America be mainly Spanish and theocratic, or English and free? Raleigh said it should be English and free. He gave his blood, his fortune, and his genius, to the great thought in his heart; and in spite of that scene in Palace Yard, which struck men as the victory of Spain, America is at this moment English and free.

INDEX.

THE END.

Made in the USA
Monee, IL
20 October 2026

66035300R00154